About This Book

The populations of many Third World megacities have far out-
stripped any apparent economic basis for their size and survival. The
7 million Congolese living in Kinshasa have a rich reputation for
the courageous and innovative ways in which ordinary people have
created new social institutions, practices, networks and ways of living.
These have enabled them to survive in an urban environment where
public provision has been overwhelmed by scale, underfunding and
a malfunctioning political system with little or no commitment to
delivering anything to its citizen subjects.

In this volume Congolese and Western social scientists cover most
aspects of urban life in Kinshasa – how ordinary people, in the
absence of formal sector jobs, hustle for a modest living; the famous
'bargaining' system ordinary Kinois have developed, and how they
access food, water, health care and education. The NGOization of
service provision is analysed, as is the quite rare incidence of urban
riots. Equally interesting are the studies of popular discourses, including
street rumour, witchcraft, and attitudes to 'big men' like musicians
and preachers. The studies are full of the most startling facts and
the wonderfully evocative phrases coined by ordinary Kinois as they
confront the huge obstacle course that is urban life.

This is urban sociology at its best – richly empirical, unjargonized,
descriptive of the lives of ordinary people and weaving into its
analysis how they see and experience life. Concrete, readable, intensely
interesting and always illuminating, this book is a model of how to
do urban sociology in the developing world today.

Reinventing Order in the Congo

How People Repond to State Failure in Kinshasa

Edited by Theodore Trefon

ZED BOOKS
London & New York

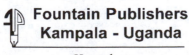

Kampala

Revinventing Order in the Congo was first published in 2004
by Zed Books Ltd, 7 Cynthia Street, London N1 9JF, UK,
and Room 400, 175 Fifth Avenue, New York, NY 10010, USA

www.zedbooks.co.uk

Published in Uganda by Fountain Publishers, Fountain House,
55 Nkrumah Road, PO Box 488, Kampala, Uganda
www.fountainpublishers.co.ug

Publication of this book has been made possible thanks to funding by the
Vrije Universiteit Brussels and by the Université Libre de Bruxelles

The right of Theodore Trefon to be identified as the author
of this work has been asserted by him in accordance with the
Copyright, Designs and Patents Act, 1988

Designed and typeset in Monotype Bembo by Illuminati, Grosmont
Cover designed by Andrew Corbett
Printed and bound in the EU by Biddles Ltd, King's Lynn, Norfolk

Distributed in the USA exclusively by Palgrave Macmillan,
a division of St Martin's Press, LLC, 175 Fifth Avenue, New York, NY 10010

A catalogue record for this book is available from the British Library
Library of Congress Cataloging-in-Publication Data available

ISBN 1 84277 490 5 (Hb)
ISBN 1 84277 491 3 (Pb)
UGANDA ISBN 9970 02 485 x (Pb)

Contents

Figures and Tables

Acknowledgements

Many people and institutions in the Democratic Republic of Congo and Belgium have made this book possible. The ordinary people of Kinshasa deserve the first round of thanks. Were it not for their creativity and kindness, this book would not make any sense. The Flemish Vrije Universiteit Brussels (VUB), in the framework of a four-year research project, provided the financial wherewithal in the form of salary, travel allowance and expenses. The Université Libre de Bruxelles (the VUB's French-speaking counterpart) offered a comfortable office and administrative facilities. Both of these institutions contributed to the book's direct publishing costs.

My VUB colleagues Saskia Van Hoyweghen and Stefaan Smis provided stimulating theoretical discussions on the changing nature of the state in Africa that have helped me conceptualize the political implications of Kinshasa's rapidly changing urban dynamics. In the early phases of the book project, René Devisch (Catholic University of Louvain) and Didier de Lannoy (formerly of the Laboratoire de l'analyse sociale de Kinshasa) offered suggestions on content and potential contributors. Stephan Ellis (African Studies Centre, Leiden) gave me very practical advice on how to present an edited volume in a harmonious and readable style to avoid the trap of ending up with a loosely connected collection of essays. In Kinshasa, Professor Shango Mutambwe (ERAIFT/University of Kinshasa) served as a host and guide *par excellence*: the knowledge of Kinshasa and Kinois he shared with me has been invaluable, both in terms of intellectual scrutiny and personal enrichment.

As draft chapters started to take form, friends and colleagues gave critical empirical advice; as many individuals read most chapters, it is not possible to name them all here. Particular thanks, however, are offered to Charles Cutter of San Diego State University for his moral support and very careful proofreading of the later versions of the chapters. Professor Edouard Bustin of Boston University, who first got me interested in the politics of Congo some twenty ago, is very kindly thanked for his ongoing interest in my work. Pierre de Maret, Director of the Centre of Cultural Anthropology (ULB), has also been a friend and supporter of this book project. Enrico Pironio and Filippo Saracco of the European Commission, Jim Graham and John Flynn of USAID, and Samy Mankoto of UNESCO have provided indirect advantages in helping this book come to fruition. My ultimate thanks go to the contributors to this volume for their commitment, expertise and patience. I hope that when my family in Brussels and Boston read through this volume, they will understand why I spend so much time in Kinshasa.

Figure 1 Democratic Republic of Congo state map

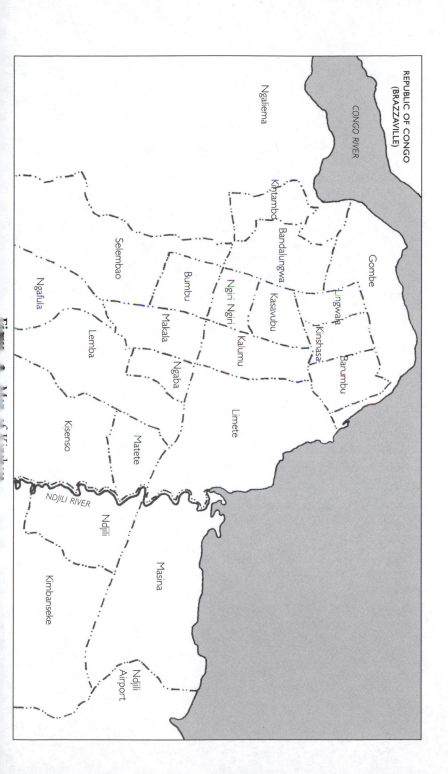

REPUBLIC OF CONGO
(BRAZZAVILLE)

CONGO RIVER

Ngaliema

Kintambo

Bandalungwa

Gombe

Selembo

Bumbu

Ngiri Ngiri

Kasavubu

Lingwala

Kinshasa

Ngafula

Makala

Kalumu

Barumbu

Lemba

Ngaba

Limete

Kisenso

Matete

Ndjili

NDJILI RIVER

Kimbanseke

Masina

Ndjili
Airport

Dedicated to
the ordinary people of Kinshasa

I

Introduction:
Reinventing Order

Theodore Trefon

Kinois and the state

Kinshasa is often portrayed as a forsaken black hole characterized by calamity, chaos, confusion, and a bizarre form of social cannibalism where society is its own prey. The ostensible sense of anarchy is based on daily hardship and sacrifice. The capital of the Democratic Republic of Congo (formerly Zaire) has practically no formal economy and an ecologically devastated hinterland. The remnants of its administration provide little in terms of social services or infrastructure. Atrociously victimized, the population refers to basic public services as 'memories'. People are poor, sick, hungry, unschooled, underinformed and disillusioned by decades of political oppression, economic crisis and war. The toll of marginalization, exclusion and social stratification has been heavy. Outbreaks of violence have reached frightening proportions.

This 'heart of darkness' mode of representation, nonetheless, needs some serious critical scrutiny, which is one of the primary objectives of this book. Despite outrageous problems, Kinshasa (formerly Leopoldville) is also a fascinating and fantastic social space. It is a city of nightlife, music, fashion and free women (*ndumba*). It is a vast stage (*une ville-spectacle*) characterized by hedonism, narcissism, celebration and myth building (Yoka 1999: 15–23). It is a city of paradox, contrast and contradiction where new and remarkable patterns of stability, organization and quest for well-being have emerged.

These patterns have arisen in spite of, and due to, deep-rooted and multiform crisis. Function and dysfunction intersect and overlap. There is order in the disorder. This applies to all social and political levels, ranging from neighbourhood, professional or ethnic associations and networks to the level where political decisions are made. It pertains to simple prosaic activities such as securing a seat in a collective taxi, and to complex multi-actor priorities, like water purification and distribution, or vaccination campaigns.

Kinois, which is what the people of Kinshasa call themselves, are reinventing order. The concept refers to the dynamic new forms of social organization that are constantly taking shape to compensate for the overwhelming failures of the post-colonial nation-state. It is a rapidly shifting process that enables people simply to carry on with life and get things done. It entails juxtaposing opportunities and interests, capitalizing on old alliances and creating new networks. It means multiplying possibilities in the hope of achieving a result. Reinventing order is also a hybrid phenomenon because it is based on the combination of global and local approaches and on the intermingling of traditional cultural systems and practices with new forms and perceptions of modernity. The order that is being reinvented by Kinois is a people's initiative having nothing to do with Weberian political order with its functioning bureaucracy, democratically elected representatives, tax collectors, law enforcement agents and impartial judicial system.

The process of reinventing of order by Kinois became particularly apparent in the early 1990s. It goes well beyond the *débrouille* (survival) economy that took form in the mid-1980s in response to the multiform crisis then emerging. The political and economic context of Congo in general and Kinshasa in particular has changed dramatically over the past decade, resulting in a dynamic reconfiguration of social norms. Although the reinvention of order is the common denominator that runs through the different chapters of this book, the process has been far from being harmonious or uniform. It has been characterized by tension, conflict, violence and betrayal, as much as by innovative forms of solidarity, networks, commercial accommodation and interdependencies. These contradictory forces have resulted in the change that we are now witnessing in Kinshasa, changes that are tracked in the following chapters.

The reinvention of order has specific resonance in Kinshasa, but it also provides a window through which dynamics in other urban centres in the Congo (such as Lubumbashi or Kisangani) and other African cities can be understood. Although the book analyses the rapidly changing patterns of social and political reorganization in Kinshasa, it is assumed that as other African cities become increasingly ungoverned and ungovernable, the Kinshasa situation can help us understand urban dynamics elsewhere in Africa. Urban populations all over the continent design mechanisms to adapt to political and economic constraints. The situation in Kinshasa, however, is exceptional because of the degree and longevity of crisis.

In sardonic self-mockery, Kinois bemoan, 'When you are rock bottom, you can still dig deeper.' The Kinshasa situation is also exceptional because of the legendary cleverness and inventiveness of peoples' practices and mental constructions. Although these systems contribute to very basic survival at the individual and family levels, they cannot contribute to broader sustainable economic and political development of the type elaborated and advocated by Western development theorists. Many attitudes and behaviours omnipresent in Kinshasa go beyond Western logic, which helps explain the perpetuation of misguided 'heart of darkness' clichés.

Crisis in post-Mobutu Congo and its implications for the residents of Kinshasa are intimately linked to the failure of the post-colonial nation-state system that was hastily fabricated by Belgian interest groups. This failure, in turn, is best understood by looking at the broader failure of the nation-state model throughout Africa. The model is challenged from *above* (generally poor leadership), *below* (disconnected from peoples' expectations) and *outside* (Cold War policies and new wars) (Migdal 1988; Zartman 1995; Young 1999). Nonetheless, the interplay between order and disorder and the institutionalized overlapping between function and dysfunction (Chabal and Daloz 1999) prove the urgency to redefine the dominant political-science view whereby African states are collapsed, corrupt, criminal, weak, failed, patrimonial or predatory (Dunn 2001).

As in other typically failed states such as Liberia, Sierra Leone and Somalia, the complexities of statehood in the Congo are legendary. This immense country, however, has not imploded along the lines of these other countries. The state remains omnipresent on the social, economic and political landscape. Bayart's argument that non-state actors penetrate the state is clearly pertinent to Congo because there are no neat demarcations between state and society (1992). State (and state-like) actors continue to dominate social relations and influence how strategies on the ground are elaborated and implemented. As highlighted by René Lemarchand, state 'failure is a relative concept' (2001: 16). State agents and agencies play important roles in the NGOization of the country (Giovannoni, Trefon, Kasongo and Mwema, Chapter 7), in relations with bilateral and international donors and in the informalization of the economic sector. This view of the Congo–Zaire state reveals how rapidly the state–society cleavage during the apex of Mobutu's reign has evolved (Callaghy 1984).

Sacrifice is omnipresent in contemporary Kinshasa. The term here pertains to the hard reality of doing without. People do without food, they do without fuelwood, they do without primary health services and they do without safe drinking water. They also do without political participation, security, leisure or the ability to organize their time as they would like. Parents are not only forced to decide which children will be able to go to school in a given year, they also have to decide who shall eat one day and who shall eat the next. In Lingala,[1] the noun used to express sacrifice, *tokokufa*, literally means 'we are dying'.

Caring for the sick and burying the dead are a major challenge in Kinshasa (Grootaers 1998a). Average life expectancy for Congolese in general is under 50. When we look at economic and social indicators, Kinshasa should be a vast dying ground. 'Its inhabitants', writes De Boeck, 'are more dead than alive' (2001a: 63). People who have not died of AIDS should be dead from starvation. Those who have not died of hunger should be dead from either water-related diseases or exhaustion because, instead of taking a bus or taxi, people walk to wherever they have to go. The vast majority of households in Kinshasa have less than $50 per month, which is barely enough to cover the food bill. Many families have less. In the early 1990s, opposition groups chose the strategy of *journée ville morte* (dead city days) to fight Mobutu (de Villers and Omasombo, Chapter 9). The objective of *ville morte* is to bring a city to a halt by asking people simply to stay home. The symbolism of *ville morte* is appropriate because the concept of death describes the spirit of the city's inhabitants. There are also the countless political dead. Mobutu dispatched *hiboux* (executioners, literally 'owls') to commit nocturnal executions of political opponents.

Until the fall of the Berlin Wall, the West unconditionally backed Mobutu. His regime was characterized by violence, nepotism, personality cult, human rights abuses and the absence of freedom of expression. By the early 1990s, however, Mobutu had outlived his political usefulness to the West. The erstwhile trusted ally had become a political liability and embarrassment (Wrong 2000). In April 1990 he announced a period of democratic transition and the end of his Second Republic (1965–90) but continued to control the political landscape until the mid-1990s. Eventually, however, his regime's patrimonial and predatory networks reached their limits. Its self-destructive system consumed itself, leaving only remnants of a state. This situation was exacerbated by the failing health of the dictator due to the prostate cancer that ended his life shortly after Laurent Désiré Kabila's capture of power in May 1997.

The transition from authoritarian rule and the multiple implications of conflict has been a period of intense social stress. Although one would think that social institutions fall apart in this context, in Kinshasa they appear to be diversifying and even strengthening. This has taken place through the development of civil society institutions, shifts in class and gender formations, and the evolving roles of ethnicity and solidarity. Paradoxically, thirty-two years of dictatorship and crisis, and subsequently an unfinished transition period dominated by war, pillage and rebellion, has helped the Kinois invent new political, economic, cultural and social realities. While much of this volume focuses on people-based responses to political constraints, examples of Congo's relations with the international community are also addressed. The data and analysis presented in all chapters pertain to the post-1990 transition period, although the chapters by de Villers and Omasombo (Chapter 9) and Persyn and Ladrière (Chapter 5) both address historical issues.

Research space

Kinshasa has been studied from numerous angles. Its spatial organization, expansion and infrastructure were painstakingly documented by two French geographers/urbanists in the late 1970s and early 1980s (Pain 1984; de Maximy 1984). Bruneau (1995) has analysed the city's demographic trends; work followed up by Congolese researchers at the University of Kinshasa's demography department (DDK 1998). Janet MacGaffey influenced a generation of scholars through her reinterpretation of the popular economy, emphasizing the 'fending for yourself' phenomenon (1986, 1991a, 1997; MacGaffey and Bazenguissa-Ganga 2000). De Herdt and Marysse (1996, 1999) and De Herdt (Chapter 8 in this volume), continuing the household surveys initiated by Houyoux in the 1970s (1973), have also carried out very useful surveys in Kinshasa on individual and family-level survival strategies. Shapiro and Tollens (1992), Goossens et al. (1994), Mukadi and Tollens (2001) and Tollens (Chapter 4 in this volume) have monitored the pressing issue of food security.

Since 1961, the monthly journal published in Kinshasa *Congo–Afrique*, thanks largely to the commitment of Jesuit father Léon de Saint Moulin, has documented a wide range of social, economic, political, cultural and administrative issues for all of Congo: Kinshasa is regularly the focus of contributions. Belgium's Institut Africain (formerly CEDAF) has also produced an impressive collection of volumes on Congo in which Kinois issues of popular economy, religion, culture, media and transportation are remarkably well documented. Included in this series is probably the sharpest commentary on contemporary Kinshasa sociology, produced by Yoka (1995, 1999). Yoka's narratives offer a real Kinois' view of people's attitudes and practices in response to crisis and their perceptions of what it means to be Kinois. This question of identity has also been addressed in a meticulous historical volume by Didier Gondola (1997a), who mirrors life in Kinshasa and Brazzaville, the capital of the Republic of Congo on the opposite bank of the emblematic Congo river.

Editing a multidisciplinary book on a single African city presents serious methodological challenges. Few anthropologists working in Africa have responded to Ulf Hannerz's plea 'to seek further illumination in the political economy of urbanism' (1980: 79), probably because the Kinshasa population is too diverse to be studied using social anthropological methods and because fieldwork conditions were difficult in the 1980s and 1990s. Economists are confronted by conceptual and methodological difficulties of studying an economy that is essentially informal. Most political scientists study the post-colonial state by looking at large geographical spaces or political entities, ranging from the African continent as a whole to geographical regions (such as West Africa or Southern Africa), and sometimes linguistic spaces (such as French-speaking or Lusophone Africa) or individual countries. In the case of Kinshasa, however, attempting to understand political dynamics and social evolution by looking at a specific urban population is pertinent for three main reasons.

First, even though Mobutu was fond of repeating *Kinshasa n'est pas le Zaïre* (Zaire is more than just Kinshasa) the evolution of the city is intimately linked to the political economy of the country as a whole. Revenues generated by the copper mines of Shaba and the diamond fields of Kasai were controlled by a Kinshasa-based political elite. The capital's predominance in terms of infrastructure, administration, employment, investment, services and image is overwhelming. Zairian identity was largely an urban phenomenon dominated by Kinshasa's image. Mobutu made some attempts to transfer the seat of power from Kinshasa to Gbadolite, his native mini-Versailles in the jungle, but was unsuccessful. The political will of the dictator was unable to match the uncontrollable dynamics of the mega-city's expansion. Kabila's 1997 march into Kinshasa and more recent jockeying for power in the framework of the Lusaka Peace Agreement also proves that the role of head of state is associated with Kinshasa, an association reinforced by international law.

Second, like Jeffery Herbst (2000) or Bierschenk and Olivier de Sardan (1997), we can consider that the degree of political control in Africa decreases in relation to the distance from the capital city. Land tenure practices in the Kinshasa hinterland support this hypothesis because traditional authority is just as important to local populations as modern law with respect to access, usufruct and ownership of real estate. In the Zaire of Mobutu, huge parts of the country were beyond the effective reach of any form of state authority, a situation exacerbated today due to war and rebellion. This reality is encapsulated in the title of Roland Pourtier's (1997) article 'Du Zaïre au Congo: un territoire en quête d'état' ('From Zaire to Congo: a territory in search of a state'). The state and, of course, foreign forces manifest themselves primarily in areas where rent-generating activities are possible.

A third factor is simply a demographic one. At least one in ten Congolese live in Kinshasa. With its approximately 6–7 million inhabitants, it is the second largest city in sub-Saharan Africa (after Lagos). It is also the second largest French-speaking city in the world, according to Paris (even though only a small percentage of Kinois speak French correctly). It is more populous than half of all African countries, a contrast admittedly exaggerated by the large number of very small African island countries (United Nations 2001).[2]

The creation of Kinshasa goes back to the early 1880s.[3] At this time, Leopoldville was a cluster of small villages. In the colonial period, the European city was organized to serve the needs of the Belgian civilizing mission and was surrounded by black townships. The spatial segregation of black and white districts was controlled as strictly as the migration from village to town. Leopoldville's formation and development have been documented in a study by Lumenganeso Kiobe (1995). This Congolese historian provides a somewhat less colonialist version of the city's expansion than Whyms's interesting but highly paternalistic interpretation (1956). The early post-colonial period was characterized by very rapid demographic growth, peaking at 9.4 per cent in 1970 (Bruneau 1995: 105). The growth rate has subsequently halved to approximately 4 per cent (United Nations 1997: 159). Like most other African cities, Kinshasa's current morphology derives from colonial planning. First, there is the former *ville blanche*,[4] which is the commercial and administrative district (where white expatriates still reside, and as a kind of historical revenge, many expatriates working in the diplomatic corps or NGO community are obliged to live there for perceived security reasons). Second, there are the planned townships or *cités planifiées*[5] (these are settlements that were occupied in the immediate post-independence first-come, first-served frenzy for land). Third, there are the anarchic extensions in the southern[6] and eastern[7] zones of the periphery that are interesting examples of urbanization without urban planning.

Key concepts: overlaps and contrasts

The implications of dictatorship and the stalemate of the two Kabila regimes have resulted in a severe crisis in the vital sectors which most urban populations take for granted. Health, education, food security, clean drinking water, public transport and housing are simply beyond the realm of most Kinois. Paradoxically, however, the relative (but not total) abdication of the state from these sectors has resulted in a process of indigenization. This refers to the ways Kinois have entered into a 'post' post-colonial phase by using their own (opposed to imported) resources, networks and ideas to adapt to adversity. The process has contributed to the unwhitening of the post-colonial political economy and social system. Public health is increasingly co-managed by the World Health Organization, along with competent Congolese staff (Persyn and Ladrière, Chapter 5). At the same time, however, there is a marked shift away from Western-style health care towards a syncretic form of healing based on faith systems and traditional pharmacopoeia. The education system that was free until the 1980s is now effectively privatized. Parents struggle to pay for school fees even though the image of the university diploma is increasingly tarnished (Tsakala and Bongo-Pasi, Chapter 6). Maractho and Trefon (Chapter 3) describe the overwhelming problem of water procurement and the multiple strategies people have invented to make up for the failures of the city's official water board.

Although there is significant overlap between chapters, there are also major contrasts and contradictions. The volume reveals this dichotomy by focusing on three broad categories: vital sectors, political and social organization, and cultural systems or popular discourses (what older-school social anthropologists referred to as belief systems). All of these chapters reflect the very high degree of complexity that characterizes people's attitudes and practices in Kinshasa. They also reveal in one way or another the capacity of Kinois to create, innovate, adapt and continue their pursuit of well-being. Their capacity perpetually to reinvent order has been sharpened over the years to adapt to political and economic adversity. The empirical data and analysis presented in the following ten chapters are a testimony to this inventiveness. Some contributors, however, also emphasize its limits. By adopting an interdisciplinary bottom-up approach, this book tells the story of how ordinary people simply get things done in what is ostensibly an unmanageable and unpredictable situation.

Survival through new dependencies

The multiform crisis that brought the near totality of Kinois to their knees during the period of post-Mobutu transition has significantly altered relations between people, between people and the state, and between people and the international community. A clear indication of this change is the way solidarity patterns have evolved (Trefon 2002a). Solidarity systems have been designed by people as a way of compensating for the failure of the Zaire of Mobutu and subsequently the Congo of Kabila *père* and *fils*. A political implication of the dynamism and multiplication of solidarity networks is the relative protection it provides to whatever group is in power because reliance on solidarity has replaced reliance on government.

While some authors in this volume challenge traditional views of solidarity, others argue that without these forms of dynamic social organization, the crisis would be much worse. They tend to agree, however, that these systems are increasingly characterized by pragmatism and that there is a marked rise of individualism. In this context de Villers has suggested that 'reciprocity' is a more appropriate term than 'solidarity' (2002: 30). While Kinois are able and willing to extend psychological support, financial and material constraints limit this solidarity, mutual dependence or reciprocal altruism to a pragmatic system of exchange. People help each other primarily if they can expect something in return. Debt, whether it be in the form of a loan, a service rendered or a favour, will ultimately have to be redeemed.

Given the precariousness of life in Kinshasa, people are forced to depend on others. Although there obviously cannot be any uniform social tissue in a city of the magnitude of Kinshasa, there are clearly identifiable patterns with respect to solidarity. According to Nzeza, everyone is subject to a perpetual bargaining system that takes place in all sectors of daily life, cutting across the entire social spectrum. This pertains to buying a bag of charcoal, applying for an administrative document or securing a seat in a taxi. In any kind of transaction there are a number of intermediaries who expect a commission, tip or bribe, euphemistically referred to as motivation. People who try to evade this form of solidarity are quickly brought to order (Ndaywel 2002: 165), usually by trickery, ruse or charm, sometimes by force, but rarely by violence (Devisch 1995a: 609–10).

While people do depend on others, they have at the same time become experts in *la débrouille* (survival by fending for yourself). Mobutu told Zairians to fend for themselves. Laurent Kabila said his government did not have the means to do much. Parents are forced to say the same thing to their children. Hardship explains the invention of *la débrouille*, the expression that Kinois always have on the tip of their tongues. Again according to Nzeza, throughout Kinshasa, from the university to the marketplace, from the home to street, individual interests have supplanted collective ones. Corruption, theft, extortion, collusion, embezzlement, fraud, counterfeiting or prostitution are the various means deployed to survive. In the same vein René Lemarchand (2002: 395) describes getting by in Kinshasa as a system in which are practised 'hustling and peddling, wheeling and dealing, whoring and pimping, swapping and smuggling, trafficking and stealing, brokering and facilitating, in short making the most of whatever opportunities arise to avoid starvation'.

Paradoxically, social pressure to share remains strong. Few people, however, have the economic ability to do so. 'Everyone has become poor' is a litany heard throughout Kinshasa. In this context, Tom De Herdt (Chapter 8) argues that the nuclear family household is still far from replacing the extended family, although contemporary consumption units are increasingly built on *vertical* (parent–child–grandchild) rather than *horizontal* family lines. His data also suggest that the understanding of solidarity varies according to a household's economic possibilities and constraints. While relatively richer families tend to conform to the conventional perception of sharing, grandchildren make up the largest part of non-nuclear-family members. Few families, in other words, can afford to feed and house distant relatives from the village as they commonly did a generation ago.

A relatively recent form of solidarity that has taken form in Kinshasa can be described as the NGOization phenomenon; the subject of the chapter by Giovannoni et al. (Chapter 7). The number of civil society associations, nongovernmental organizations (NGOs) and community-based solidarity networks exploded in Kinshasa in the early 1990s. They have become vital components of the dynamic and multiform survival strategies invented by Kinois to replace the state in many areas of public life. The phenomenon developed at this time because the country was in serious crisis and because people had to reinvent in order to survive. Congolese in general and Kinois in particular had lost hope in Mobutism and were frustrated by the fiction of democratic transition. In response to this situation, they were forced to invent new solutions based primarily on friendship, trade and profession, neighbourhood ties and religious affiliation. Ethnicity, once the foundation of associational life in Leopoldville and Kinshasa, is steadily losing its meaning as new needs and opportunities emerge. The association phenomenon is a clear example of people-based social organization driven by pragmatism and the will to survive.

Solidarity has also taken on new meaning for the international community since 1990 when Mobutu lost his political usefulness and the West abruptly stopped the flow of development assistance. Since then, donors and NGOs are increasingly acting on behalf of the state in many areas of public life. In their chapter Giovannoni et al. analyse the complexity of this new form of aid. The chapters on water distribution and public health also help understand the trend. All of these chapters take a strong position against the view that positive change can only come through outside support. Positive change is taking place in Kinshasa thanks to the Kinois' commitment to maintain the struggle for individual and collective survival. In the most recent version of donor policy, the Kinshasa-based political elite and the international community have compromised on the role of the Congo state as an 'absentee landlord' (Kobia 2002: 434).

An important but under-studied form of solidarity that contributes to the Kinshasa economy is remittances from migrants (Sumata, Trefon and Cogels 2004; Sumata 2002). The mushrooming of Western Union and similar types of cash transfer services is a reliable indicator of its importance. Congolese nationals living in Europe, the USA and Canada (and in other African countries to a lesser extent) are able to transfer money home without having to travel. Migration is increasingly practised as a strategy to diversify income and risk within households. Families are more willing to invest in the education of one family member, often the first-born boy in the hope that he will be able first to study abroad and then work abroad. In the past, students were under pressure from their families to return to Congo after having been awarded their diplomas. Now they are under pressure to earn dollars or euros and send money home. The migration process improves the standard of living of geographically fragmented families. Although fragmented, family members are today able to keep in touch from one continent to another because of mobile phones and the Internet. Migration contributes to satisfying personal ambitions and to the fulfilment of family obligations. In both cases it helps alleviate the cycle of poverty. Remittance money is used for buying a house, paying school or medical fees, or contributing to ceremonial practices such as baptisms, weddings or funerals. Remittances are also used as seed money to start up businesses.

Food and eating

Food and eating is a theme that appears regularly throughout this book. As approximately 50 per cent of Kinois eat only one meal per day and 25 per cent eat only one meal every two days, power, prestige and status increasingly derive from the ability to eat or the ability to distribute food, or money for food to others. There is strong anecdotal evidence indicating increased consumption of cat and dog. The main meal is usually eaten in late afternoon and is preceded by what Kinois tragi-comically refer to as SOPEKA (*SOmbela ngai,*

PEsa ngai et KAbela ngai – buy for me, give me, please give me). In order to forage the salt, oil or hot pepper sauce needed to put a meal together, neighbours seek and extend solidarity. More than half of most household budgets are spent on food. Food and eating are consequently the preoccupations that best accounts for why Kinois repeat *nous vivons mystérieusement* (we live mysteriously). Hunger in Kinshasa is not new: its intensity, however, has never reached such proportions as described by Tollens. Based on research carried out in the late 1940s, Suzanne Comhaire-Sylvain has already described how parents trained young children to cope with hunger (1950: 52).

Tollens's chapter focuses on the coping mechanisms, innovations and adaptations that have emerged to facilitate the city's food supply. These patterns reveal how Kinois have responded to the challenges of daily survival by developing food solutions based on trust and solidarity networks. Based on recently collected data, Tollens analyses why food security and malnutrition problems are not more severe. Despite problems of infrastructure, state services and formal private-sector operations, almost enough food is produced in and around Kinshasa or is imported there. It is transported and distributed relatively efficiently while providing employment and income for thousands of people. This miracle takes place in apparent chaos, but follows its own logic based on kinship, community, religious and commercial networks. Giovannoni et al. also address the social organization that enables this food miracle to work because the associations, networks and 'local development initiatives' they describe often revolve around food production.

In contrast to these solidarity patterns that have emerged in the food sector, Nzeza (Chapter 2) argues that the need to procure food for oneself or the family accounts for the multiple forms of *la débrouille*. For Nzeza, people bargain themselves out of hunger. Tom De Herdt's meticulous analysis of changing household composition supports this wheeling-and-dealing approach. He describes the phenomenon of hidden families, meaning children born of single mothers who continue to live with their parents. Young girls are told by their parents to find food in the streets, a suggestion to meet men who will give them money for food in exchange of sex. Nzeza gives the example of a thief caught 'red-handed' who reportedly defended himself by asking the question, 'If I don't steal, what am I going to eat?' Stealing food also appears in the de Villers and Omasombo chapter, but takes on more dramatic proportions. In their analysis of the violent and very destructive looting sprees that shook Kinshasa in 1991 and 1993, they excerpt a telling newspaper account of the looting of a cold storage warehouse:

> The warehouse ... was easily opened with machine guns. Soldiers helped themselves to sides of meat and cartons of fish. They fled, leaving little more than scraps. A group of idle onlookers – men, women, children and some old-timers – scrambled over the remains. In the midst of an overwhelming disorder, the warehouse was completely emptied in just a few moments. (*Le Potentiel*, 1 October 1991)

Food and eating as metaphor and symbol is an important dimension of Filip De Boeck's chapter on street children and witchcraft (Chapter 10). His interviews with Kinshasa street children reveal that they 'eat' their fathers and uncles to procure dollars and diamonds, while for others 'the street is ... where food, freedom, sex and money can be had'. This food can help explain why the street is seen as modern and exciting. This metaphor also appears in the Tsakala and Bongo-Pasi chapter on university education in Kinshasa. In a section on popular perceptions of higher education, they provide some Lingala expressions revealing the sentiment that study and erudition are useless, and that prestige without wealth is only false prestige. The most appropriate one here is *nakolia yo* (am I going to eat you?), which in this context means: all of your fancy intellectual talk can't put food on the table.

Faith

The nearly universal recourse to faith in the face of the despair and suffering caused by poverty and insecurity is omnipresent in Kinshasa, although detractors joke that people who live by faith die of hunger. Faith even helps achieve well-being, which is an often underestimated dimension of contemporary social dynamics in Kinshasa. The Jesus of the Belgian missionaries was replaced by African prophets such as Kimbangu (MacGaffey 1983a) and by the doctrine of Mobutism. When Mobutism failed, hope in Jesus took on new meaning, as witnessed by the mushrooming of revelation churches, pastors and prayer groups. The fact that churches may be filled on Sunday morning, however, does not mean that Kinois believe that God alone can help them mitigate their survival problems. Religious soul-searching must not be confused with material problem-solving.

Faith is given careful examination by Persyn and Ladrière (Chapter 5) with respect to faith-based healing churches because they are a significant response to failures in the modern health care system: they heal both body and soul. They help mitigate the destitution crisis in Kinshasa by placing it in a cultural and spiritual framework of solidarity. Nonetheless, while offering possible solutions, they also create new problems. These groups have created a new feeling of belonging for the street children described by De Boeck, the single mothers described by De Herdt, and other disillusioned Kinois whose dreams of post-colonial modernity have not been meet.

Popular discourses relating to faith have been given an original interpretation by Bob White (Chapter 11), who analyses rumours about witchcraft and success in the very important music business in Kinshasa. This chapter is particularly meaningful because it addresses the two forces that are widely believed to hold Congolese society together: music and religion. Both forces have helped the Congolese carve out a sense of national identity for themselves. For both White and De Boeck, understanding witchcraft beliefs and practices is useful in contextualizing the rise of Christian evangelical groups because social dynamics are best understood by looking at the thing and its opposite, or the thing and its double. The Satan of witchcraft and the God of newly formed evangelical groups are, in other words, two sides of the same coin.

Faith, or lack of faith, is a theme that characterizes state–society relations and is omnipresent throughout this volume. Kinois clearly expect very little from the state or government authorities. As expressed by de Villers and Omasombo (Chapter 9), the evolution of politics in the post-Mobutu transition has not improved living conditions and has reinforced an inherent distrust in political processes, what they have described elsewhere as an 'intransitive transition' (2002). The post-colonial state model that was designed to be a provider of social services has transformed into a social predator. People consider the lack of progress in initiating democratic institutions to be a deliberate political strategy aimed at maintaining incumbency to the detriment of social and economic priorities.

Children

Children are very well represented in many of this volume's chapters. This is hardly surprising as approximately half of all Congolese are under 15 years old, a situation characteristic of most of Africa. They are consequently important social actors and priority beneficiaries for the international donor and NGO communities. The impact that children have had on recent political events in Congo is epitomized by the *Kadogo* phenomenon (Creuzeville 2003). *Kadogos* are the child soldiers that enabled Kabila to march into Kinshasa, and into power, in May of 1997. Children are at the heart of De Boeck's chapter in which he convincingly argues:

> children and young adolescents have never before occupied a more central position in the public spaces of urban life, whether in popular music, media, churches, army, street or bed. Children are both victims and important actors in transforming Congolese society.

Focusing on witch children, he underscores the sharp contrast between children in Kinshasa and children in the West, whose social space in generally confined to the security offered by parents, school and state.

By most other accounts, however, children are quite clearly victims in Kinshasa. In the struggle to find water in the vast areas of Kinshasa that are not connected to the public water distribution system, Maractho and Trefon describe how much of the burden literally falls upon the shoulders of young girls. In their chapter on higher education, Tsakala and Bongo-Pasi describe the outrageous sacrifices made by families and students for education. While their analysis offers a tribute to professors and students for keeping the university system afloat, it also portends a serious crisis in the future because fewer and fewer qualified professionals and intellectuals are trained. Persyn and Ladrière caution that many children in Kinshasa are orphaned due to AIDS and other public health problems. Others are abandoned by their mothers, who are often teenagers themselves. Many children grow up under the dubious care of grandparents, uncles, aunts, cousins, or one of their father's co-wives. An increasing number grow up in the street, which creates a vicious circle: street children giving birth to street children who will reproduce the same pattern is an observable trend. The malnutrition problems of the city's poor, as described by Tollens, have a serious effect on children. He refers to an NGO report that found '42 per cent of children are chronically malnourished' in one of Kinshasa's poorer districts. This point is reinforced by De Herdt, whose research on children belonging to single-parent families reveals that these children are affected by adverse economic circumstances on two accounts. First, most of them grow up in a relatively poor household, which is the most important reason why they grow up in a single-parent family. Second, they grow up outside a celebrated marriage, which makes them even more vulnerable irrespective of the wealth of the household they live in.

Being Kinois

Despite all of the city's problems, Kinois tenaciously believe their city to be the capital of pleasure-seeking potential *ambiance*. This potential helps people evolve in a world beyond that of despair and sacrifice (Trefon 2002b). The sentiment of *ambiance* has completely erased the colonial perception equating Leopoldville with a city of temptation (*un lieu de perdition*). Referring to oneself as a Kinois is a sign of pride and prestige. In contrast to a generation ago, today, people clearly put forward their belonging to the human tribe known as Kinois. They are, however, simultaneously or alternatively, Kongo,[8] Pende, Yaka, Ngbandi or other ethnic groups when for reasons of social, political or economic opportunism, it is convenient to shift from one identity to another. The overlapping and multiplication of identities has helped Kinois counteract the negative effects of political oppression and economic constraints because it broadens their solidarity networks. This overlapping is a very important dimension of being Kinois and extends beyond ethnicity to all kinds of other networks, for example neighbourhood, professional or religious.

The construction of Kinois identity is based in large part on the cleavage between those who are Kinois and those who are not. *Mbokatier* and *mowuta* (Lingala slang) and *kisamamba* (Swahili) are derogatory terms used for people living in rural Congo or new immigrants who have not developed the street cunning needed to survive in Kinshasa. This negative image of the country bumpkin can be explained in part by the centralized nature of Mobutu's Second Republic. It is also a universal phenomenon of constructed urban identities: *monter à Paris* is how the French describe having succeeded in making it to Paris, in the same way that folk from New Jersey view crossing the river to New York as upward social mobility. On the opposite end of the spectrum is *Miguel:* the nickname given to Europeans or whites in general. Today, the world of *Miguel* is associated primarily with money and the status, education, health care and technology it can provide. *Lola* in Lingala is both paradise and Europe. The Kinois have amalgamated these two worlds, syncretizing the global and the local.

Another identity cleavage that has taken form is that between *mwana quartier* (neighbourhood kid) and *mwana mboka* (son of the country). The latter epithet was used by Mobutu in the spirit of Return to Authenticity (along with *citoyen* and *citoyenne*) and supplanted the unauthentic titles of Mr and Mrs. The valorization of the neighbourhood as a vital social space, in contrast to the city at large (*mwana-kin*), and in sharper contrast to the country as a whole, supports Devisch's hypothesis of the villagization of Kinshasa (Devisch 1995b, 1996).

Kinois identity is also manifested across a broad cultural spectrum. Fashion, referred to as *la sape* (Société des Ambianceurs et des Personnes Elégantes), use of Lingala slang, popular painting and music are important forms of cultural and political expression. Music, most notably, has contributed to the emergence of an urban civilization and transethnic national conscience. It also enhances the image of the Kinois well beyond their borders, as pointed out in Bob White's chapter. When a singer like Werrason, *le roi de la forêt*, fills the Bercy stadium in Paris, all Congolese appropriate his success.

At the individual level, being Kinois today means being able to brook sacrifice, adapt to adversity and perpetually reinvent one's relations with family members, neighbours and representatives of established order, be they the discredited law enforcement agents, market women, preachers, public officials or foreign NGO staff. Being Kinois also means 'doing the physically impossible and the morally unimaginable' (Nzeza, Chapter 2). At the collective level, being Kinois means taking to the streets to disobey, loot or make merry as collective catharsis and response to the state's unwillingness and inability to fulfil people's expectations of independence and development (de Villers and Omasombo). Taking to the streets is a way of refusing domination and the non-distribution of the country's potentially fabulous wealth.

In their daily quest for survival and well-being, Kinois have invented a constellation of codes, discourses, systems and practices that permit the community as a whole to ward off the long-predicted apocalypse. Despite the current context of political stalemate, economic crisis and abominable human suffering, people have appropriated the sentiment of being Kinois. Just as there is a Congolese nation, there is also a Kinois community with a powerful sense of identity and pragmatic solidarity. Conversely, crisis has also created new divisions, tensions, conflicts, betrayals and animosities. It is out of these paradoxes and contradictions that people are reinventing their state and society.

Notes

1. Lingala is one of four vehicular languages spoken in Congo. Lingala slang is the most commonly used idiom in Kinshasa.
2. Like all statistics from Congo, demographic figures need to be considered with considerable caution. The last population census was carried out in 1984, so figures are based on extrapolations that do not necessarily take into account major demographic influences like AIDS, war casualties or migration of people fleeing war and crisis in the Kivus.
3. Henry Morton Stanley established a trade outpost christened 'Leopoldville Station' on 1 December 1881. He was working for the Belgian monarch Leopold II.
4. Gombe, Limete, Ngaliema and Binza.
5. Barumbu, Kinshasa, Kintambo, Linwala, Kasa-Vubu, Ngiri-Ngiri, Banda-lungwa, Kalamu, Lemba, Matete and Ndjili.
6. Ngaliema, Selembao, Mont Ngafula, Kisenso.
7. Towards Ndjili and Maluku.
8. Approximately 40 per cent of people living in Kinshasa are members of the Kongo ethnic group.

2

The Kinshasa Bargain

Anastase Nzeza Bilakila

Na kei kobeta coop! The phrase is on the lips of millions of Kinois every morning. Translated literally, it means 'I'm going to strike a deal.' In spirit, the expression means 'I'm going to work', even though it has been many years since the idea of work has meant a secure, salaried job in the formal economy. For the vast majority of Kinois, work is any small job or activity that provides enough francs to buy a meagre meal or pay for the collective taxi fare home. Work entails breaking stones, *kobeta libanga*. This was the infamous forced labour imposed during the late Leopoldian period to build the Kinshasa–Matadi railway line: thousands of lives were lost in the process. These horrors are still very present in the Kinshasa popular imagination. Today, *kobeta libanga* means being fearless, daring to take any risk, doing the physically impossible and the morally unimaginable. The only thing that really matters is the amount of money earned, the immediate return. *Na kei kobeta coop*, like its near equivalent *kobeta libanga*, implies trickery, wheeling and dealing, acting as a go-between or bargaining. In English, the word 'bargain', used as either a noun or a verb, best captures the spirit and practice of *la coop*.

The Kinshasa bargain is an agreement between two or more parties that provides a return. It can be solicited by a beneficiary or imposed on a victim. Anyone in need of either a good or a service, or anyone who needs to resolve a problem, is invariably the 'client' of one or more go-betweens. The commission, which is generally very modest, is the stake of the bargain. This applies to dealing with a civil servant to obtain an administrative document, buying a bag of cooking charcoal or manioc or simply hailing a taxi. Given the precariousness of life in Kinshasa, people have been forced to depend on – that is, bargain with – others. Individual needs are consequently addressed best through multi-actor bargains. Every Kinois is subject to this system. It takes place in all sectors of daily life and cuts across the entire social spectrum. Those who try to evade this form of solidarity are quickly brought to order, usually by trickery but sometimes by force. As in formal economies where tax evasion is sanctioned, evasion of paying a solidarity tax in Kinshasa is also sanctioned. The dynamics, rules and paradoxes of this bargaining system, to which all Kinois are subject, are the focus of this chapter.

Anomie and the (a)morality of survival

Bargaining Kinshasa-style entails disregarding moral values. The new (a)morality in Kinshasa dictates that it is better to sell your soul to the devil than to be scrupulous. The cunning required to meet immediate needs has replaced the respect of any righteous moral code. Durkheim's theory of anomie appropriately describes this situation (1991). Anomie is a situation whereby moral, cultural and legal norms are abandoned or transformed, creating a social crisis. An imbalance exists between the desire to attain social values such as success, prestige or power, and the objective means available to individuals or groups to attain these values. This generates the sentiment that socially unacceptable behaviours such as fraud, violence or corruption are necessary and acceptable to meet vital needs.

Freud's theory of anomie is likewise applicable to the Kinshasa bargain (Thines and Lempereur 1975: 71). For Freud, anomie is the condition of individuals who perceive these forms of unacceptable social behaviour are permitted when moral norms are shattered. Serge Latouche (1998: 19), however, warns that although the informal sector is often described as being anomic, in reality it possesses an original and creative value as a socially appropriate development strategy. As a response to the anomie that characterizes the Congo on the state level, new forms of solidarity such as the Kinshasa bargain emerge on the lower level of relations between individuals. These new dynamic forms of solidarity reveal the resilience of Kinois and their capacity to adapt to and even redress broader anomic situations.

The Kinshasa lootings of 1991 and 1993 (best analysed by Devisch 1996; and de Villers and Omasombo, this volume) can be explained by the existential needs of the people and as manifestations of political rebellion. Without trying to make a perfect analogy, bargaining activities can be compared to looting because they are both manifestations of despair solidarity. The overwhelming material needs of Kinois transform anything with the slightest real or perceived value into a coveted consumer item. Office furniture, laboratory equipment, a fork or spoon in a restaurant, telephone cables, metal rods embedded in a cement wall, or light bulbs in a public area or a private *parcelle*,[1] can be the object of a Kinshasa bargain. Vigilance to protect one's property is a permanent reflex. Looting and bargaining or theft and bargaining go hand in hand because there is always a buyer. While the Kinshasa bargain is organized to help resolve the daily survival problems of the poor, it can also be a serious security threat to well-to-do individuals or public and private entities. This situation explains why private international investors still consider the Democratic Republic of Congo a high-risk country.

Acculturation brought on by colonialism and contact with Western values, particularly in urban areas, is one way of accounting for the disappearance of traditional ancestral values. Economic crisis and poverty are two other factors contributing to this attitudinal and behavioural shift. Another explanation relates to the mid-1970s' Mobutist doctrine of Return to Authenticity. This MPR (Mouvement Populaire de la Révolution) creation had the effect of undermining individual initiative because the MPR claimed to be responsible for all Zairians from cradle to grave. It was a bizarre and perverse adaptation of paternalistic policies practised during the colonial period. Some of Mobutu's aphorisms reveal how the despot perceived civic morality. This perception, which is likewise a clever form of political manipulation, is epitomized by his famous *yiba, kasi mingi te* (steal, but not too much). Another landmark political speech that foreshadowed massive nationalization of large and small foreign-owned companies, officially launched the fend-for-yourself fashion that has never lost its currency in Kinshasa. Another of Mobutu's speeches, this time to an MPR audience, had the effect of turning children away from their parents. In it Mobutu declared *soki a sakani beta ye kanon* (if your father bothers you, punch him on the nose). This MPR doctrine of authenticity contributed to the discrediting of civic respect and responsibility. When it suits their interests, Kinois can point to their political leaders as examples.

This political context helps explain the relative (but not exclusive) dishonesty of *la débrouille*, the expression that Kinois always have on the tip of their tongues. It is not uncommon to hear a thief, caught red-handed, say: *bongo nakolia yo?* (if I don't steal, what am I going to eat? You?). The need to procure food for oneself or the family is frequently the justification offered for the multiple forms of *la débrouille*. Throughout Kinshasa, from university to marketplace, individual interests have supplanted collective ones. The means – corruption, theft, extortion, collusion, embezzlement, fraud, counterfeiting or prostitution – justify the ends (survival). Fending for yourself in Congo/Zaire is a phenomenon that has already been widely described by mainly Western political scientists and anthropologists (e.g. De Boeck 1996; MacGaffey 1986, 1991a; Marysse and De Herdt 1996). Jackson (2001) provides a concise review of *débrouillez-vous* as political philosophy. The analysis and narratives of daily living conditions of Kinois in the post–Mobutu period in this chapter are intended to update these writings and provide insight into the rapidly changing urban political economy of Kinshasa.

Despite the rise of selfish individualism, Kinshasa's economic difficulties have resulted in the invention of new forms of solidarity. Poverty is psychologically transformed into despair solidarity. While the Kinois are able and willing to extend psychological support, financial and material constraints limit this solidarity to a pragmatic system of exchange. People help each other primarily if they expect something in return. Debt, whether it be in the form of a loan, a service rendered or a favour, will ultimately have to be redeemed.

The universal recourse to faith in the face of poverty's despair and suffering is prevalent in Kinshasa. One of Kinshasa's most famous Christian singers, Eva Mbikayi, sings in a popular song, *naboyi souffrance* (I reject suffering). Suffering takes the form of hunger, poor health and physical debilitation, just as it takes the form of psychological stress resulting from the complexities of survival here and now, and uncertainty about the future. The psychological constructions elaborated to refuse this suffering are indicative of the remarkable capacity of the Kinois not to give up the fight for survival. They even help to achieve well-being, which is an often overlooked or underestimated dimension of contemporary social dynamics in Kinshasa.

Recourse to the multiplicity of pastors, preachers and prophets is only one dimension of this quest for well-being. The Jesus of the Belgian missionaries was replaced by the doctrine of Mobutism. When Mobutism failed, Jesus became fashionable again. The fact that churches may be filled on Sunday morning does not, however, mean that the Kinois believe that God will help them mitigate their survival problems. Religious soul-searching must not be confused with material problem solving: hence the perpetual need to bargain. This sentiment is musically expressed by Eva Mbikayi in characteristically Kinshasa style: *Eloko na sengi yo longola mosika na ngai pauvreté. Ngai na lingi lisusu mobola te ngo Jésus, ngo papa, bateya ngai prospérité. Nkolo sunga mpo nazuva awa na se ya mozinga.* (Help me chase poverty away. I don't want to be poor anymore Jesus, my father. You told me about prosperity. Let me have it here and now!)

Despite the overwhelming number of unemployed, throngs of men, women and children flock to the commercial and administrative parts of the city. Political scientists often borrow medical terms to describe the decomposition of the Congo/Zaire state. One such term that is useful in this context is 'sthenia'. This refers to episodes of excessive or vigorous activity in a morbid state. The analogy is appropriate because from early morning to late at night the city is full of hordes of people walking along the streets, anxiously trying to get somewhere. The activity is surprising in a city where so few people appear to have jobs. Crowds walk very long distances (*la ligne 11*) or take collective taxis to destinations where they hope to earn a few francs. The mobility, density and dynamism of these groups, which set out at early dawn, is remarkable. Primary destinations are the Central Market, the principal business and administrative district of the city (Gombé) and ports along Avenue des Poids Lourds (ONATRA, Kingabwa, Ndolo, Baramoto or Marsavco), referred to as beaches. Food coming from the hinterland is discharged along these ports (see Tollens, Chapter 4). These economic spaces, like the post office, the university classroom or municipal offices, provide excellent opportunities to earn a few francs.

To portray the intricacies of how the Kinshasa bargain functions, four short narratives are presented below. They involve sectors in which bargaining and solidarity are unavoidable. Based on the author's personal observations and experiences, they have been selected less as examples of Kinshasa folklore than as examples of Kinshasa's complex contemporary social dynamics.

Les mamans manœuvres: crafty port traders

Bokole's small rowing boat is anchored approximately 150 metres downstream from the Seti beach. Some thirty *mamans manœuvres* are nervously eyeing the young man. He is concentrating on the mighty waters of the Congo river: gauging the waves, listening for movement upstream. Every time he makes a move, the women stir. Bokole's talent is his ability to detect the approaching presence of a boat or barge emanating from the food-producing interior. Today there is news that the *Ava Maria* will be reaching Kinshasa with farm produce from Bandundu. When Bokole gives the signal, the women will jump into their awaiting rowing boats and motorboats to board the still moving *Ava Maria* with amazing alacrity. They take possession of the merchandise in a kind of blitzkrieg man-oeuvre. Timing, and hence Bokole's crucial role as scout, is of the utmost importance. The first traders to board are the first to make deals with the sellers. These may be the producers themselves or *ngundeurs* (middlemen), who buy and trade agricultural produce like manioc and corn, smoked fish, bushmeat, caterpillars and traditional pharmacopoeia.

Once the merchandise is chosen, the women start negotiating with the owners. They take the offensive by combining a maternal attitude with disdain. They cultivate a relationship of superiority by treating the new arrivals with their bags of wares as naive country bumpkins (*munyenye, yuma*) who will never survive the hostile world of the port. They craftily persuade the sellers that unscrupulous port officials (or impostors claiming to be officials) will hoodwink them if they disembark their goods themselves. Sellers are reluctant, but content, to receive cash directly from the *mamans manœuvres*. The *mamans* thus take control of the incoming merchandise and establish the prices at the port market. *Mamans manœuvres* bargain on two fronts: one with the exhausted sellers coming from the hinterland (some of these people can spend up to three weeks on a boat or barge if they come from Kisangani, for example) and the other with port market traders. They can double their money in the transaction.

Although *mamans manœuvres* are broadly viewed as unscrupulous, predatory intermediaries who inflate already exorbitant prices, the perception also exists that their commission is partially justified by the complexity of the beach trading. To succeed, one needs cash for the initial investment and a reliable network of social contacts.

Traders coming into the hinterland depend on *mamans manœuvres* because they generally do not have the cash needed to pay the river transport, or the money needed to settle fees, taxes and other real and invented administrative costs. Indeed, these ports swarm with a multitude of police, coastguards, military, customs officers, and public health officials, who all try to wrest a few francs out of them. Between a swarm of real and pretend state agents and *mamans manœuvres*, the inexperienced traders see the latter as the lesser of two evils. Nonetheless, these women are considered selfish troublemakers, creating inflated prices by earning proportionally large profits.

Bemba Saolona, minister of economic affairs under President Laurent Désiré Kabila, thought that he could slow down food price increases by prohibiting the activities of *mamans manœuvres* at the Kinshasa ports. When he tried to do so, they demonstrated in front of the Kinshasa hotel de ville, chanting: *Ba papa basalaka te! Tokolesa bana ndenge nini?* (Our men don't work! How are we supposed to feed our children?) Unable to respond to this troublesome but justifiable question, the government backed down.

Money changers: outlaws or alternative bankers?

On 6 June 2001, *Palmarès*, a pro-government Kinshasa newspaper, headlined: 'The importance of street changers in Kinshasa's currency trade is slowly but surely losing ground'. Most Kinois sniggered at this. Every time the government tried to fix the value of the Congolese franc by artificially controlling exchange rates, the same prediction was made. Since implementation of monetary policy decisions never followed, this lucrative street trade continues.[2] Originally initiated by female traders who needed hard currency for their own purposes, mainly cross-river trade with Brazzaville, the activity became a full-fledged profession in the early 1990s when the entire Congolese economy entered the period of dollorization that still reigns today. Dollars replaced the Zaire currency and then Congolese francs due to hyperinflation. Euros are increasingly traded in Kinshasa as well. Although increasingly spread out all over the city, these traders have their headquarters in and around what is known as Wall Street (Avenue des Aviateurs). Although men sometimes change money, women are the principal agents. Usually assembled in small groups of two or three, they sit in front of makeshift stands composed of cardboard boxes or wooden crates. Depending on the degree of surveillance at the time, they may have 'bricks' of Congolese francs displayed openly, or they may have their cash hidden in plastic bags under their stands, pretending to be cigarette vendors. Congolese franc bills have denominations worth only a few US cents. They are bundled and tied together with hemp string into packets about the size of a brick: hence the expression bricks of francs. Policy on the legality of money changing has shifted from strictly illegal with enforcement of the law, to illegal without enforcement, to legal. In all of these cases, like mongers flogging their goods at the market, money changers accost a potential client with the chorus of 'dollars, dollars, papa?'

Although it is well known that these traders practise all kinds of tricks to take advantage of their clients, people still rely on their services. The most common tricks are not putting enough bills into the 'brick'; inserting smaller denominations than bargained for; or inserting worn-out bills. Another trick takes place when a client wishes to change, for example, a $100 bill. Here the trader will take the bill in hand, shuffle through her plastic bags of cash, and return, by use of sleight-of-hand, a counterfeit bill, claiming that she does not have enough cash on hand to make the deal. Money-changers make their best deals when the franc is devalued. On 26 May 2001, for example, the official exchange rate was CF75 for one US dollar. The street rate was CF300 for a dollar. The next day, the Central Bank liberalized the currency market and set the rate at CF314 to a dollar. Despite the efficacy of *radio trottoir*, precise financial information circulates slowly. The moneychangers, however, are very well informed (largely thanks to their mobile phones) and play upon both the ignorance of the uninitiated and the need for customers to change money. Here, the advantage of the Kinshasa bargain clearly accrues to the moneychanger. Due to the complexity and dysfunction of the official system, many categories of people have recourse to this unofficial system. They include traders who need hard currency to make purchases abroad, people with savings who seek a hedge against inflation, or individuals who have received money from a relative working abroad and need to convert it into Congolese francs. While even the wariest of Kinois have been hoodwinked in this fashion, they have to admit that at least they were hoodwinked pacifically.

Khadafis: fuel on the spot – for a price

The petrol station has been closed since 2.00 in the afternoon. Hundreds of cars and vans, mostly old jalopies, are squeezed tightly one against the other as drivers try to jockey into what they perceive as being a lucky spot once the station reopens. When it does, there may not be enough fuel for everyone. Tempers are high because scrapes, bumps and dents are frequent. In this gridlock, even the delivery trucks have problems making it to the pumps. Putting a couple of dollars' worth of fuel in the tank is one of the many all-encompassing transportation nightmares in Kinshasa.

The Congolese government sets the price of imported petroleum products in an attempt to control inflation. Once fuel prices increase, the price of many other basic commodities increases as well. Price fixing is also intended to limit the negative impact of speculation. This policy is, and always has been, unsuccessful. There is indeed both inflation and speculation. Petrol speculators have received the sobriquet of *Khadafis*. In both the Mobutu years and since the 1997 transition, Libya, unlike other exporters, has distinguished itself as a reliable supplier of petroleum products to Congo. It was easy for Kinois to apply this nickname to fuel retailers who always seem to have some petrol on hand even during the worst periods of shortages, in the most unlikely places or at any time of day or night. The *Khadafi* is a rescue service.

Petrol stations adopt a system of rationing by closing down when supplies become low, when lines get longer or when there are rumours of a price increase. Once the stations close, hordes of men, women and children appear with plastic jugs between 1 and 5 litres in size, offering fuel to the stranded drivers. The price can be up to four times the official price. In May of 2001, for example, when the petrol station price was 75 francs per litre, these *Khadafis* were selling a litre for between 250 and 300 francs. The *Khadafis'* way of bargaining, however, is not confined to marking up prices. Like money changers, they have lots of tricks up their tattered

sleeves. The most common tricks include spreading false rumours
about imminent price rises; mixing petrol with cheaper fuels such
as kerosene (even though this can cause engines to catch fire); or
selling 5-litre jugs with false bottoms of wax so the purchaser ends
up with only a portion of the amount agreed upon. One does not
necessarily have to be a *Khadafi* to earn a few francs selling fuel.
A gardener sent to buy five litres of petrol for a lawnmower immediately sold half on the street before putting the rest into the
machine. By taking advantage of his boss he feels he has accomplished
something positive. This type of pilfering is deeply engraved in the
Kinois spirit, reflecting the belief that people who do not steal when
the opportunity presents itself are poor providers to their families.
A day without stealing is perceived as a lost day.

Even though the *Khadafis* must compete among themselves to
survive, they do share an *esprit de corps*: no one would denounce a
fellow *Khadafi* who is in the process of cheating or lying to a customer. Solidarity is also manifested in cases of harassment. If police
or military try to fine or confiscate fuel from a *Khadafi*, others will
rally in support, chasing away or even beating up the official who
has tried to abuse his uniform to extort his taxi fare home or beer
money. These examples of solidarity reveal that there are elements
of order in the broader disorder. Popular wisdom has its own voice
to describe this kind of situation frequently encountered in Kinshasa:
mboka ebebi na yango; batika batu ba débrouiller (The country is a mess.
Let people make ends meet as best they can).

Facilitating public transport

An old man accosts a group of teenagers with the question, 'Kids!,
when is independence going to come to an end?' 'Why would you
want independence to come to an end, papa', they reply. 'So the
Belgians (*les nokos*) can return!' Despite this bizarre type of desperation
discourse, Kinois refuse inertia. They refuse just to sit and wait.

Packs of people assemble at bus and taxi stops at the city's major
transport nodes: Victoire, Ndjili Sainte Thérèse, Kimbondo, Bandal-
Moulaert, Gare Centrale, and the Central Market. Three key actors
in public transport are the drivers, the receivers who load passengers
on board and collect fares, and the facilitators who help unlucky
travellers find a seat, for a small commission of course. Waiting two

hours for a taxi is not uncommon (a problem that contributes to the valorization of the neighbourhood as a vital social space). During rush hours, drivers and receivers have all the reasons in the world to be frantic. Surprisingly, they remain remarkably relaxed. They pay no attention to the questions bombarded upon them by nervous commuters. There are many more passengers than seats, and lines are long. Without knowing exactly where the minibus-taxi is heading, people try to squeeze in, even before the arriving passengers have succeeded in making their way out. Finally the receiver will discreetly whisper the destination of the jalopy. Women are the first to be informed because they tend to pay their fares without trickery or major arguments. Men, whether in uniform or in civilian dress, civil servants or journalists, often try to get a free ride by brandishing some kind of vague official *laissez-passer*. The receiver's announcement inevitably sparks a scramble. Those who have neither an aggressive temperament nor physical strength, or those who simply have no tolerance for the unbearable closeness that a collective taxi ride will entail, will just have to wait for the next minibus, praying to have better luck next time. If livestock were transported to the slaughterhouse in Europe or the USA in these conditions, animal-rights activists would be up in arms!

The solution to this major transport headache is the facilitator, who bargains with both drivers and passengers. His job is to find a place for those riders who do not want to fight for a seat. He can also decide where a bus will go, as well as the tariff riders will pay. The facilitator's revenue come from two sources. The first source is the passenger who compensates him for finding a place (here the facilitator may simply remove a passenger by force from his or her seat and install his client in the thus vacated seat). The second source is the driver who compensates him for having stewarded passengers into place. In non-rush-hour travel, the facilitator cries out the taxi's destination. The driver will not depart until the vehicle is full.

The governor of the city of Kinshasa has tried to eradicate the facilitators' mediation by claiming they create additional costs for public transport users. Despite periodic crackdowns, however, these efforts have only been half-hearted. The only viable way to eliminate these bargainers would be to improve the entire public transport system in the city. Before this vast project is realized, however, the facilitator will continue to be the *chef d'orchestre* at bus and taxi stops.

For how long can this organized disorder last?

For Kinois, the Congo is a country the government is unable to manage. They see the state as unable and unwilling to make decisions or implement them in cases where they are made. Lack of progress in putting democratic institutions in place is considered a deliberate political strategy, aimed at maintaining incumbency to the detriment of social and economic priorities. The state appears to have accommodated itself to the activity of the people involved in a process of cannibalization: society is its own prey. There is a collective sense of guilt that helps explain why so many individuals see divine intervention as the only possible remedy. There is also a sense of collective social stress: people worry, but appear to be unable to transform their desires into political mobilization. Mobilization aimed at inducing change is perceived as a long-term commitment that transcends the demands of daily combat. It would require even more sacrifice, but provides no guarantees of success. At best people prefer to wait for God to liberate them from their woes. An amazing number of prophets broadcast this mystification throughout Kinshasa. Although they do not necessarily collaborate with political leaders, politicians benefit from their message. It is consequently not surprising that Dominique Sakomi, the principal political *maître penseur* of the cult of Mobutism, is one of the most popular prophets of born-again Christendom today.[3]

It is more the imperturbable thirst for life that Kinois cling to, than the deplorable economic conditions, that has generated the bargaining phenomenon. It may be interpreted as chaotic or subversive according to classic, free-market, Western norms, but in the Congo it is an immensely powerful form of social organization, inextricably linked to Kinshasa's political economy. Underestimating its significance would be a political mistake. Trying to eliminate it will be impossible before new economic opportunities are created. There are, however, no prospects in sight for re-dynamizing the economy. Indeed, all efforts taken to date to proscribe the Kinshasa bargain have either failed completely or had only short-term implications.

Despite the major obstacles described, people continue to flock to economic spaces to break stones. Criticizing or trying to circumvent the bargaining system is considered as an attack on the established social order in which solidarity is a crucial form of survival. Given thirty-two years of oppressive dictatorship, when political contest was brutally silenced, social discontent is rarely voiced, even today, against political authorities. Complaint and criticism are directed to society itself or God. Rich and poor alike participate in solidarity networks based on family ties, friendship, marriage alliances, neighbourhood groups, clan, or region of origin. These networks are dynamic and multiply themselves into new forms of organization. One political implication of this situation is the protection it provides to whatever group is in power, because reliance on solidarity has replaced reliance on government. The National Radio broadcasts programmes every day that correspond to the spirit of the people. They repeat the litany of complaints Kinois express, but invite the people to find their own solutions, claiming that the government cannot do everything. The reality of the situation is that Kinois have replaced faith in the political system with their own people-based forms of social organization.

Notes

Translated by Theodore Trefon.

1. A parcelle can be either a simple house lot or a lot upon which more than one family build and share a central courtyard.
2. For an excellent analysis of how the moneychanging sector is influenced by market forces as well as the social identity of the brokers themselves, see De Herdt and Marysse 1999.
3. It was Dominique Sakomi who conceptualized the *Voix du Zaïre* news programme that started every evening with the image of Mobutu descending from heavenly clouds. He also orchestrated the funeral of Laurent Désiré Kabila following his assassination, proving his political resiliency. Sakomi was also an outspoken proponent of the Comités du Pouvoir Populaire.

3

The Tap is on Strike:
Water Distribution and Supply Strategies

Angéline Maractho Mudzo Mwacan

and Theodore Trefon

'The tap is on strike.' 'Water is as rare in Kinshasa as it is in the Sahara.'[1] These statements resound throughout the thirsty city. While they highlight one of the major daily struggles of the population, their tone also reveals the humour and hardened resolve of the people. Rich and poor have become equals in the struggle to procure water. Water only trickles through Kinshasa's dilapidated distribution system during both dry and rainy seasons. This is ironic for a city lying along the banks of the earth's second most powerful river, a city moreover that has an annual rainfall of 1,450 mm (République Démocratique du Congo/UNDP 1998: 114). The Congo river is 4,700 kilometres long, and at Stanley Pool, located slightly upstream from Kinshasa, has a flow of 38,000 cubic metres a second (Gourou 1970: 279). Rainfall is often plentiful enough to be hazardous. In November 1999 the water level of the Congo river rose six metres above normal. Hundreds of people lost their lives and thousands more saw their homes float downstream. Although tropical rains can take on catastrophic proportions, they can also be a blessing: the capital's inhabitants painstakingly and cleverly collect rainwater to compensate for the dry tap.

The city's relentless expansion has resulted in an obvious increase in demand for water. The original system was first set up in 1950 and was designed to serve what was then a population of approximately half a million. For most families, Régie de Distribution d'Eau et d'Electricité du Pays (REGIDESO), the official state-run agency that provides water treatment and distribution service, has done little either to maintain existing infrastructure or to create new water lines or pumping stations. Aside from some investment from international donors, the distribution system largely remains a legacy of Belgium's urban development of the city. Today, approximately 2 million Kinois have no access to the REGIDESO network (Oxfam/Great Britain 2001: 31).

Water shortages in Kinshasa are a relatively recent addition to the city's multidimensional crisis. Although first apparent in the elevated parts of the city since 1985, regular shortages are now generalized all over the capital. In neighbourhoods where pipes are completely dilapidated, running water is no more than a memory. The political transition of 1997 did not improve the situation. The elevated parts of Kinshasa, such as Ngaliema, Mont Ngafula, Lemba and Kinsenso, although connected to the REDIGSO system, undergo constant shortages. The low-lying districts, comprising the *ville blanche* (old European neighbourhoods) or the planned African *cités*, are increasingly affected as well.

The struggle to find water for drinking, cooking and washing is paramount among the daily challenges confronting the women and young girls of Kinshasa. Like most other household activities, water procurement is highly gendered, though men are increasingly involved. Given the absence of public-sector investment in water, the people of Kinshasa will be thirsty for many years to come. They will also continue to be sick with water-borne intestinal diseases, for there is little hope the problems of contamination from wastewater and sewage will be resolved anytime soon. Kinois will continue to be forced to collect, store, filter and boil this vital resource.

After tracing the political and technical problems of the water distribution sector, this chapter will examine the social context of water procurement and the multiple strategies that households have invented to secure a daily supply of the vital resource. It will emphasize the state's role in providing water to the Kinshasa population, mainly focusing on the limits of the state in the sector. It will provide a counter-argument to those who claim the state is completely absent. The state's management of this theoretically public service is indisputably insufficient. Nonetheless, its role remains central to Kinshasa's water needs because it provides minimum service and oversees the international community's involvement in infrastructure maintenance, development and investment. More than anything else, this chapter is a study of social innovation: Kinois have clearly

created solutions to water procurement beyond exclusive reliance
on the state network.

REGIDESO: a stingy supplier

The REGIDESO was created in 1933 to process and distribute
water and provide electricity in the Belgian Congo, Rwanda and
Burundi. Prior to independence, Kinshasa was supplied by two
water-treatment facilities. One was located along the Lukunga river
at Kinsuka (Ngaliema district) and the other at Ngaliema bay on the
Congo river near Utexafrica (also in Ngaliema). These stations and
their accompanying conduits were built to last approximately thirty
years with normal maintenance, but they did not last that long. By
1985 the material was seriously dilapidated. A third station, built on
the Ndjili river at Kingabwa (Limete *commune*), was designed to sup-
plement the ageing first two. Financial constraints meant the work
was carried out in two phases. The first was funded by Belgium
in 1971; the second by Germany in 1982. Recourse to financial
aid from multiple Western countries was cleverly manipulated by
Mobutu to diversify the sources of his outside support. It was also a
way for the West to recycle its petrodollars while filling the coffers
of large construction and public works companies (Willame 1986).
Three other stations were eventually built: one at Maluku, another at
Kinkole and the third at Midendi. The last was built to supply the
agro-pastoral farms near Kimbondo, as well as the areas of Mitende
and Mont Ngalafula. The World Bank provided aid to replace the two
original stations and to supply large-diameter pipes for distribution,
but work stopped in 1997 when the Bank interrupted its relations
with the post-Mobutu government.

REGIDESO's production/distribution capacity falls abysmally short
of the city's needs. During the 1990s, it was estimated that only
one-third of the Kinshasa population had access to water at home.
This was down from an estimated 50 per cent in 1986 (République
Démocratique du Congo/UNDP 1998: 115). Since the early 1990s,
REGIDESO's daily output from its six processing stations has stabilized
at approximately 400,000 cubic metres (REGIDESO 1989: 39). In
addition to these six stations, there are also eleven pumping stations
dispersed along the distribution network to reinforce pressure. Daily
water needs, however, vastly outstrip production. In 1990 estimated

needs were already 1.2 million cubic metres, and daily estimates for the year 2000 were 2.4 million cubic metres. To improve production REGIDESO planned three new pumping stations. The first was built on the Lukaya river (*commune* of Mont Ngafula) and was to have a capacity of 110,000 cubic metres. It never worked, however, because its equipment and material were pillaged in 1991 (see de Villers and Omasombo in this volume). REGIDESO invested its own funds in this project but was unable to invest the amounts needed to bring the project to fruition. Promised state subsidies never materialized. The French government agreed to finance a second station at Ndjili but it was never completed either: the French broke off development aid with Mobutu in October 1991 after many years of very lucrative contracts for French companies (Trefon 1989). The third station, also planned for Ndjili, this time with Japanese funding, was never finished either. Because of the September 1991 lootings, the boat transporting all of the material made a U-turn at sea before it had reached Matadi, Congo's Atlantic seaport.

These major public works projects should have raised production capacity to 2.4 million cubic metres to meet the city's minimum needs. Failure to do so sparked a deep frustration:

> REGIDESO piping is dilapidated because it goes back to the colonial period. Why didn't our leaders do anything for the past forty years, especially when the country could have afforded to do so before the economic crisis?

As REGIDESO is a state-run monopoly, it is incumbent on the state to provide funds to finance maintenance and new investment. Although Mobutu paid lip-service to the importance of water, notably after the United Nations Conference at Mar del Plata designated the 1980s the Decade of Water, he provided no funding to the sector. It was, for example, the international donor community that funded the major water development projects carried out in the provinces of Kasai Occidental, Maniema and Equateur. Laurent Désiré Kabila's government devoted approximately 80 per cent of the national budget to the war effort, considerably limiting investment in the public-service sector. Joseph Kabila's government is apparently waiting for peace before seriously tackling the financial and technical problems of water distribution, though completing the processing station at Lukaya is a stated priority of his government. It is also a priority for the ordinary people of Kinshasa:

Our only hope is the finalization of Lukaya. Much of the western and southern parts of the city will then have water in the tap. We are even willing to participate in a special lottery for REGIDESO because we just can't cope with this situation.

Water is, theoretically, provided to different neighbourhoods on selected days or during a few hours per day. This rotating system is, however, criticized by residents of the poorer areas. They claim that authorities are guilty of favouritism towards districts where strategic public buildings are located (notably the Gombe), military camps and the university campuses.

REGIDESO also asks individuals to invest in the distribution network. Clients are sometimes asked to buy their own water pipes that the REGIDESO installs, sometimes without meters. They bitterly complain that they have to pay for pipes that are frequently empty. Clients also complain because they are sent arbitrary bills (arbitrary because there are no meters). This helps explain why 50 per cent of them pay their bills late. If they refuse to pay these bills, the company digs up and confiscates the pipes that in some cases were paid for by the client!

During our surveys in the first half of 2003, a cubic metre of water (1,000 litres) cost $0.77. According to REGIDESO, this is one of the lowest rates in Congo Basin countries, and for many of the clients with official connections the water bill represents less than 3 per cent of the household budget. Like most money matters in Kinshasa, the water tariff is arbitrary and subject to negotiation. Indeed, REGIDESO takes into account the neighbourhood, purchasing power of the customer, size of the house lot, and the amount and quality of the house.

Inflation, coupled with the relatively low price of water, poses serious financial problems for REGIDESO because the Counsel of Ministers, which establishes the price of water, reacts slowly in indexing prices. To avoid social unrest, government officials prefer to keep prices low. This creates cash-flow problems for REGIDESO, which in turn has difficulty paying its workers, purchasing chemicals for water processing, importing spare parts, and repairing machinery. Until the 1990s the company had tank lorries that were used to transport water into areas of the city not covered by the conduit system. The effort, nonetheless, was more symbolic than operational. Due to cash-flow problems these lorries were not replaced when they broke down.

To make matters worse for Kinois, obtaining an official REGIDESO connection is complicated. The company requires an ownership title for the house or building, plus a title to the land. A REGIDESO form is also required. This may seem simple, but potential customers frequently find they need one more paper or one more official stamp, a more or less normal situation when dealing with any Congolese bureaucracy. The difficulty of fulfilling these requirements helps explain why there are so few official connections. Because of inadequate production REGIDESO also deliberately tries to discourage potential clients. In 1996 there were 201,400 official connections reported in Kinshasa (République Démocratique du Congo/UNDP 1998: 115). As many families live on a single lot (*parcelle*), there are many more people using water than official REGIDESO customers. Those people who have connections sell water to neighbours who do not. Given these conditions, it is impossible to establish exactly how many people benefit from an official connection. This is similar to the pattern of electricity distribution. Many Kinois have electricity at home thanks to unofficial connections, which can be made relatively easily. It is used primarily for lighting and for listening to music. Although the SNEL (Société Nationale d'Électricité) claims to have 171,029 official subscribers (approximately 27 per cent of the city's population, assuming there are eight people to a Kinshasa household), the multiplier effect from these unofficial connections is considerable (République Démocratique du Congo/UNDP 1998: 112).

Inventive supply strategies

A study carried out in the Mont Ngafula district published in 1999 is representative of problems throughout much of the city. It reveals that only 17 out of 210 *parcelles* (8 per cent) had access to the REGIDESO network and only 30 of them (14 per cent) had wells. Of these *parcelles*, 163, a striking 78 per cent, had neither tap water nor a well (Senda Lusamba and Emina Be-Ofuriya 1999: 123). To compensate for REGIDESO's limited service, Kinois have adapted various types of supply strategy. People living in the low-lying areas of Kinshasa dig wells. Those living in the poorer peripheral extensions of the city draw river water. Everyone collects rainwater in any available plastic or metal container.

To deal with water scarcity, people have been forced to adapt, invent, innovate and sacrifice. Attitudes have evolved: as with many other basic necessities, people have simply learned to do without. Behaviours have also evolved. Kinois have drastically reduced their consumption of water because of its cost in terms of time, money, fatigue and anxiety. Tap water, when available, is reserved first for drinking, for washing food and then for cooking. Rain, river or well water is used for personal hygiene, laundry and washing the house. Water is never wasted: it can always be used one more time.

Taps are practically always dry during the day beyond the central administrative and commercial parts of the city. They work, albeit niggardly, during the night. This is due to problems of pressure. Because of greater demand during the day, pressure is reduced and the REGIDESO infrastructure is unable to pump water into the outlying districts. People keep their taps on overnight, hoping the trickle will fill their buckets or plastic jugs. Others connect rubber hoses to the tap and fill larger containers. Family members take turns performing the night watch. Each night, someone is responsible for staying up in order to make sure no water is wasted or to make sure that any opportunity to collect and stock the precious commodity is not lost. On *parcelles* inhabited by more than one family, boys tend to perform the night watch. Parents try to limit the promiscuity of their daughters by separating these daytime and night-time water chores.

During the rainy season, cuts can last up to four or five days. During the dry season, cuts can last up to two weeks. When household reserves are depleted, Kinois must walk to fetch water. One study reports that 25 per cent of Kinois have to walk more than one kilometre per day for water (Ministère de la Santé Publique 1999: 55). Another report estimates that in the very poor district of Kisenso, people have to walk up to two and a half hours per day for water (Oxfam/Great Britain 2001: 31). In our surveys, many women complained of having to trek much further than a kilometre. They either go to rivers where water is free, or to the *parcelle* of a friend or family member. Another option is buying water from individuals at *parcelles* identified by *radio trottoir* as having water available.

Getting the water home is the next ordeal. Depending on the volume of water and the distance to home, different techniques are adopted. It can be carried in buckets on the head (by women, girls and boys) or in wheelbarrows (by older boys); put in barrels and rolled along the ground (by men); or transported by car or taxi (by men or women).

Containers used to collect, carry and conserve water range from plastic buckets, to 100–200 litre drums, to 500 litre plastic cisterns or even larger 1,000–10,000 litre cisterns made of galvanized metal, cement or brick. The strategies adopted depend on the family's financial situation, as well as on the women's degree of ingenuity and organization. Although expensive, cisterns are particularly useful to collect rainwater:

> We installed a very expensive 10,000 litre cistern. It is made of brick and covered with cement. Half of it is three metres below ground; the other half is above ground. It is perfectly watertight. The lid is made of concrete. A pipe is connected to the gutters of our roof that is covered with corrugated metal sheeting and fills the tank when it rains. I even have a pump that can draw water from the REGIDESO network to the tank to make up for the low pressure. Such a system provides enough water for all our domestic needs. There are health benefits, because people are cleaner after a shower opposed to just washing up in a bucket.

Because stagnant water contaminates easily, it needs to be filtered and boiled before drinking. Thirty minutes of boiling is recommended to eliminate bacteria. Boiling water, however, raises another serious dilemma. Almost all Kinshasa families use charcoal (*makala* in Lingala) as their primary source of cooking fuel. Electric stoves are rare due to their cost and SNEL's poor distribution of electricity. Most districts are under-electrified and there are frequent blackouts. Access to *makala* is just as difficult as it is to water. Women have to make difficult strategic choices of how to use *makala*, and consequently prefer using it to cook food rather than to boil water. Despite the prevalence of water-borne intestinal diseases, boiling water is perceived as a waste of valuable *makala*. Bottled water for drinking (bottled locally in factories that also brew beer and produce soft drinks) is available but, once again, lies beyond the reach of most Kinois. One alternative to boiling water is adding chlorine or tincture of iodine tablets. Few people do this. They are not used to doing so, do not like the taste, or are afraid of being poisoned.

The price of water is thus much more costly for those Kinois who lack direct access to official connections, which amounts to nearly two-thirds of the population. To tariffs much higher than the official REGIDESO rates, they also need to add the cost of time, effort and transport. During the rainy season, lines at places where water is available are long.

> At around five o'clock in the morning I gather all my pails and those of my friends and start queuing up to have a good place in line for what we call water duty [*likelemba ya mayi*]. Tomorrow, one of my friends will get up early for *likelemba ya mayi*.

In contrast to this pragmatic solidarity, long waits can also seriously strain relations:

> High population densities in the poorer neighbourhoods create huge crowds at places where water can be found. People argue and even fight over whose turn it is next.

This situation is common at the numerous springs that exist at the foot of Kinshasa's many hills. These springs are carefully lined with rough stonework and plastic or galvanized metal pipes to avoid sediment build-up and formation of stagnant pools. These relatively clean groundwater springs are crucial to the survival of the Kinois. Equally important is the water from the numerous rivers that run through Kinshasa. These include the N'sele, Kinkole, Konde, Tshenke, Tshangu, Ndjili, Lukungu, Lukaya, Kinkusu, Yolo, Funa, Gombe, Makelele, Basoko, Kimwenza, and Mitende. River water, however, tends to be polluted with human waste. Another means of obtaining water, especially in the lower and poorer parts of the city (such as Kambanseke and Masina) is digging wells in the *parcelle*. These wells are between 2 and 6 metres deep, depending on the level of the underground water tables. They are dug by hand and are reinforced with recycled oil drums with both ends removed.

As highlighted elsewhere in this volume, a remarkable characteristic of the Kinois is their ability to capitalize on new economic opportunities, even though profit margins may be extremely low. One such opportunity is the child water carrier (*mwana ya mayi* in Lingala). Unemployed youth can earn a few francs by selling drinking water packed in little plastic bags in the administrative parts of the capital or by delivering buckets of water to homes of individuals who have placed orders. Although it may seem paradoxical, their meagre earnings are barely enough to pay for a collective taxi home after a long day's work. A slightly more profitable version of *mwana ya mayi* is carrying water to houses under construction in Kinshasa's expansion zones beyond the reach of REGIDESO. House construction requires vast amounts of water, notably to mix cement. Given the volume of water needed and the long distances that may be covered, entire families work as teams. Children reconnoitre new building sites, the father negotiates a price with the builder, and then the whole family is mobilized to fulfil the delivery. Earnings are used to buy food for the family or to buy commodities that can be resold in petty retail.

Turbid water – precarious health

The different technical steps between pumping river water and distributing it must be carried out meticulously. Although REGIDESO regularly monitors water for nitrate content, colour, smell, taste, pH level and residual chlorine, it is still unable to deliver clear, drinkable water. A 1999 study of distributed water in Mont Ngafula revealed that while some of these criteria are met, others clearly are not (Mayimunene 1999). The pH level is far below recommended norms, as is the amount of chlorine. Without sufficient chlorine, because of contamination in the pipes, clean water that comes out of a pumping station is contaminated before it reaches the tap in someone's home. This problem is exacerbated in the neighbourhoods where REGIDESO distribution is only sporadic. When cuts are frequent, the degraded pipes become vectors for various pathogens. In the household, bacterial contamination, which modifies smell and taste, develops if water is stored in containers that are not regularly cleaned. While basic hygiene dictates that these containers be sterilized, few households do so. People tend to not use their precious water to wash a container used to store water! The same attitude applies to carbon filters. These filters should be scrubbed and washed regularly and the carbon element needs to be replaced periodically. If not, they are a host to serious diseases such as typhoid, salmonella, cholera, hepatitis A, or diarrhoea and forms of shigella (or bacterial dysentery) can develop. It is estimated that 30 per cent of all registered medical visits in Kinshasa were water related (Oxfam/Great Britain 2001: 31). The same report also noted that people are unaware of the relationship between disease and unsuitable drinking water.

Spring water is generally drinkable after boiling if it is not stored for more than twelve hours. Well water, however, is almost always polluted, especially from those wells dug in a *parcelle* and thus close to human activity. It is polluted by wastewater, household refuse, garbage and excrement from humans and domestic animals. River water is also frequently polluted (Muteba 1999). Phosphates found in washing detergents (in addition to bathing, people wash their clothes in the rivers) and chemicals used for urban agriculture along their banks contaminate these rivers. Although these activities result in water pollution, there is generally no alternative.

Overwhelming water-supply and storage problems have forced families to reduce their water use severely. Although there are no comprehensive studies available indicating how much water individuals use in Kinshasa, it is estimated that consumption varies from between 20 and 80 litres per day per person. The 20-litre figure applies to those families who have to carry water home, but does not include water used at rivers for washing. The 80-litre figure applies to families with a tap and meter at home. Houses in general and toilets in particular (that are either inside the house or located in annexes dug on the *parcelle*) are not cleaned sufficiently and bodily hygiene is sacrificed. Simply washing one's hands with soap can be a problem. This situation increases the risk of contracting diseases such as gastroenteritis and onchocerciasis. Storing water in containers without lids attracts rodents and provides a propitious breeding ground for malaria-carrying mosquitoes.

Water thanks to international partnerships

Unable to resolve water processing and distribution problems, authorities have negotiated with the international community to act on their behalf. The Congo state has ceded a part of its responsibilities to international, bilateral and nongovernmental organizations that have the financial means and technical know-how to bolster the deficient REGIDESO. Nonetheless, because outside assistance tends to be based on short- to mid-term agendas (influenced by political criteria and availability of funding), the international community remains dependent, to a large extent, on Congolese ministerial personnel and REGIDESO staff. These individuals have the knowledge that is essential to the water sector. Despite their precarious economic positions these people are elements of relative stability in their sector. From 1980 until 1997, for example, Tsongo Kubila wa Ntumba was the head of REGIDESO. Removed by the first Kabila government, he has been asked to return to the water board as special advisor. Thus, while the state may well be weak or corrupt, circumventing it is not an efficacious option for donors or NGOs. The case is clear for the water sector, but the same argument can be made for other development sectors. The most important outside actors are the International Committee of the Red Cross, the European Union, OXFAM/Great Britain, and OXFAM/Quebec. Congolese ministry authorities dealing with intersectoral problems of energy, planning, reconstruction, public health, public works, urbanization and habitat all collaborate with these outside agencies.

The Water and Housing section of the International Committee for the Red Cross (ICRC) in Kinshasa offers direct assistance to the REGIDESO. This takes the form of digging wells, supplying processing chemicals, as well as maintaining, replacing and rehabilitating processing stations. A major project aimed at rehabilitating pumps at the Ndjili station, which serves 75 per cent of the city with a capacity of 260,000 cubic metres per day, is ongoing. The tragic floods of November 1999 seriously damaged this station: four of the six pumps broke down due to siltation. Work is being done to diminish future silting problems at both Ndjili and Lukunga stations. Since 1999, the ICRC has provided some 2,300 tonnes of processing chemicals worth approximately $1 million.

The European Union is active in the water sector, notably through Programme d'Appui Transitoire au secteur de la Santé (PATS), Programme d'Appui à la Réhabilitation (PAR) and Programme d'Appui au Droits de l'homme (PAD) (European Union Delegation/Kinshasa 2000). A major contribution was the financing of three processing units that transform non-iodine cooking salt into a chloride solution used in water processing at the Ndjili, Lukunga and Ngaliema stations. REGIDESO uses approximately 2.2 tonnes of this solution daily. The EU (along with a local NGO, Action Contre la Faim) is also involved in providing water pumps to communities in Kimbanseke, Kindole, Nsele and Kikimi. These communities lie beyond the reach of REGIDESO's distribution network. PATS is providing water pumps to hospitals. EU future projects in the water sector focus on identifying leaks in the network and replacing dilapidated pipes. This is of primary importance: an estimated 50 per cent of water is lost within the distribution system due to leaky pipes.

OXFAM/Great Britain has targeted high-population districts and the semi-rural extensions of the city for its work (Oxfam/Great Britain 2001). This NGO has dug wells in Mikonga, Kimbanseke and Mont Ngafula that are connected to the REGIDESO network, improving service to an estimated 150,000 customers, plus the numerous families who procure their water from these customers. OXFAM/Quebec is also involved in digging wells. OXFAM/Great Britain, along with other international actors contributing to the water sector, has also been involved in institutional support of REGIDESO. While this takes the form of funding REGIDESO activities, it also includes capacity building. Training staff and keeping them motivated to carry out their jobs is a major service to the people of Kinshasa.

A thirsty future

REGIDESO has adopted the motto 'Water is Life'. Water, however, is not available in much of the city; in most neighbourhoods taps are dry. Some neighbourhoods do not even have taps. The water sector is a poignant example of the multidimensional crisis facing Kinshasa. The challenge of satisfying this (theoretically) public service is at once political, demographic and economic. The most obvious solution to the water supply problem is increased investment in the sector, but this is an unrealistic notion. Needs surpass, to an extraordinary degree, the means that may eventually be made available by either the international community or the country's national budget once the Congolese are in a better position to manage their own economy. This is likely to be many years down the road. Yet this same sentiment of pessimism characterized the telecommunications sector in the Congo until only a few years ago. Today, through new technology and the de facto privatization of the sector, access to telephone service has expanded rapidly. Along these lines, many Congolese are calling for a partial privatization of the water sector, claiming that such a hybrid arrangement is unlikely to be worse than the current REGIDESO. This has admittedly been said about the Zaire/Congo economy since the mid-1980s, and indeed the situation has continued to worsen. Kinois still have their own inventive strategies and solutions to water procurement, although the cost in fatigue, money and public health sacrifice remains high. Most

Kinois continue to say that without water, the social and economic development of the city will continue to be compromised. The noble proclamations of the United Nations about 'water for all in the year 2000' remain a pious wish for the one out of ten Congolese who reside in Kinshasa. This tropical mega-city with huge hydraulic potential remains as thirsty as ever.

Note

1. Extracted passages are transcribed from our interviews in 2001 and 2002.

4

Food Security in Kinshasa:
Coping with Adversity

Eric Tollens

One would expect the food security situation in Kinshasa to be catastrophic. War and rebellion have cut off northern supply routes in Equateur, Orientale and Kivu provinces since 1998, roads are in deplorable condition, and the car and lorry fleet is dilapidated. Foreign aid and humanitarian organizations regularly report hunger and malnutrition. People eat only once a day or once every other day. Nonetheless, a famine situation has never developed, even during the dramatic siege of Kinshasa in August and September 1998. What does the evidence show to explain this? Is the situation indeed as catastrophic as expert reports and Western logic indicate? What are people's attitudes and practices with respect to food? How, in fact, are people feeding themselves?

This chapter attempts to address these fundamental questions. The evidence reveals that current food security is not much worse than it was at the end of Mobutu's regime in 1997. Important supply changes and innovations have taken place because of the war. Coping mechanisms, social innovations and adaptations have emerged to facilitate a continuing food supply. These have come to fill the void left by the formal private sector and compensate for the policy failures of the Laurent Kabila regime. They also help overcome the obstacles faced by the government of Joseph Kabila.

Total food imports, particularly wheat, fish (*mpiodi*),[1] rice and chicken are not less now than three years ago, despite the acute shortage of foreign exchange, particularly during the reign of Kabila *père*. A host of new food provision services have been invented.

Urban farming and peri-urban agriculture have expanded considerably. Given the deplorable state of the road between Kinshasa and Bandundu, the main supply province, new transportation routes have developed. River transport now supplies more than half of the capital's food. A new fleet of locally made wooden boats now ply the Congo river from Kinshasa to Bandundu and Kasai, just one of many adaptations to crisis.

In the war zones, by contrast, the humanitarian crisis is one of the worst in the world. Although the number is probably exaggerated, an estimated 2.5 million people have died in eastern Congo since the war began, largely as a result of malnutrition and preventable disease (IRC 2001); over 2 million people have been internally displaced. Nearer the war front in North and South Kivu and in northern Katanga, severe malnutrition of children under 5 exceeds 15 per cent and even reaches 25.8 per cent in Kiambi (Northern Katanga) (Table 4.1).

Poverty, purchasing power and hunger

Monthly income for most Kinshasa families has not changed much since 1997. (An average family is composed of between six and seven individuals.) The poorest families have a monthly income of approximately $50, which is barely enough to cover the food bill. The very poorest have about $30, clearly insufficient to make ends meet. Individuals in these families cannot attain 2,000 calories per day. Half of the population has only one meal per day; 25 per cent of the population has only one meal every two days, and the quality of food is very poor. How they cope is both mystery and miracle. It is also a good example of why Kinois often say *nous vivons mystérieusement* (we live mysteriously).

The poorest areas of Kinshasa reveal worrying levels of extreme poverty. This poverty in turn has produced a chronic state of food insecurity. Residents there live an extremely precarious existence, vulnerable to external shocks such as monetary fluctuations, illness or loss of employment. A survey conducted in the poorest parts of Kimbanseke district in April 2001 found 42 per cent of children chronically malnourished and global malnutrition rates reaching 18.3 per cent. Malnutrition rates in these areas tripled between September 1999 and January 2001 (Save the Children/Oxfam/Christian Aid). Increased malnutrition rates coincide with macroeconomic shocks – inflation or monetary reforms, for example – that impact the purchasing power of Kinois (Luzolele, De Herdt and Marysse 1999). The data show the importance of macro-economic stability and economic growth in combating malnutrition and poverty.

In 1999 Ntoto M'vubu (2001) did household budget surveys in three poor districts of Kinshasa (Kisenso, Kindele and Makala). Average monthly household income in Kisenso was the lowest: $71 for an average of eight persons. They spent 39 per cent of their income on food, 22 per cent on energy, water and soap, 12 per cent on transport, 11 per cent on housing, 8 per cent on education and 6 per cent on health. (The poorest households spend well over 50 per cent of their income on food.) Although they spent 39 per cent of their income on food, most families also grow some of their own food. Energy expenses are high because most of Kisenso is not electrified, forcing people to use charcoal or wood for cooking and petrol lamps for lighting.

Peri-urban and urban agriculture in Kinshasa is another response to poverty and food insecurity. The phenomenon is observable throughout Africa, Asia and Latin America (FAO 2000). Although several NGOs now support it, its emergence and growth in the 1990s is essentially a grassroots, bottom-up innovation. Along with household livestock breeding, it greatly reduces the food vulnerability of poor households (Trefon 2000, 2002a).

Food prices

Food prices (calculated in US$) rose by approximately 30 per cent between October 1994, when they were at their lowest in the last decade, and January 1999. Seasonal price fluctuations also increased during the same period. Due to alternating growing seasons north and south of the Equator, the seasonal variation in food prices was traditionally moderate, but this stability disappeared once food supplies from the north were stopped. Seasonal fluctuations are consequently more pronounced. Prices decline during the main Bas-Congo and Bandundu harvest periods from January to May and increase in the second half of the year, with peak cassava prices in October and November. During these peak rainy season months the drying of cassava *cossettes* (chips) is particularly difficult.

Despite supply problems, exacerbated by the war, prices started to fall in January 1999 and attained their October 1994 level in early

Table 4.1 Results of malnutrition surveys in Democratic Republic of Congo, 2000–2001

Province	Location	Age	Global (%)	Severe (%)	Date	Source
Kinshasa City	Kimbanseke district	<5	12.2	2.6	2/2001	ACF-USA
	Selembao district	<5	12.0	2.6	2/2001	ACF-USA
	Kisenso district	<5	9.4		2/2001	ACF-USA
	Masina district (Tshimungu)	<5	11.3		4/2001	SC UK
	Kimbanseke district (Lobiko)	<5	18.3		4/2001	SC UK
Bas Congo	Luozi	<5	4.6	1.3	3/2001	MSF-B
	Mangembo	<5	5.0	0.8	3/2001	MSF-B
Kasai Occidentale	Demba	<10	30.0	10.0	12/2000	Demba hospital
Province Oriental	Rimba (Ituri)	<5	8.6	2.0	3/2001	COOPI
		>5	3.2	1.3		
	Nioka	<5	10.4	15.1	3/2001	COOPI
		>5	12.6	22.8		
	Kisangani	<5	9.1	1.7	—	MSF-H
North Kivu	Goma health zone (6 aires de santé)	<5	9.3 29.3	0.9 11.9	12/2000	SC UK
	Kayna	<5	29.4	14.3	5–6/2001	Solidarités
	Kibabi (Masisi)	<5	5.7	1.3	9/2000	SC UK
	Kirolirwe (Masisi)	<5	6.7	0.3	11/2000	SC UK
South Kivu	Bitobolo/ Bunyakiri*	1–5	41.1	17.1	12/2000– 1/2001	SC UK
Maniema	Kalima	<5	14.1	8.1	1/2001	Merlin
N. Katanga	Kalemie town	<5	7.0	4.0	8/2000	Nuova Frontiera
	Nyunzu	<5	21.7	12.2	9/2000	Nuova Frontiera
	Kioko	<5	14.0	9.2	9/2000	Nuova Frontiera
	Manono	<5	23.2	19.9	3/2001	Nuova Frontiera
	Kiambi	<5	32.1	25.8	3/2001	Nuova Frontiera

Note: This covers the majority of the nutritional surveys conducted in DRC in 2000 and 2001. It is possible that some nutritional surveys may have been excluded.

* Global malnutrition rate registered by Save the Children UK during a vaccination campaign in Bunyakiri, South Kivu. The methodology used was a first screening using MUAC and oedema detection. No anthropometric measurements were taken.

Source: Save the Children/Oxfam/Christian Aid 2001.

2000, a drop of 30 per cent. Thanks to repairs on the Matadi–Kinshasa asphalt road, prices for *pondu* in early 2000 were only one-third of those in early 1999. *Pondu, a fresh cassava leaf vegetable and main source of protein, is very perishable and does not travel well over long distances.* It has to be consumed within a couple of days after being harvested. *Pondu* prices are now back to their low 1993 level.

Kinshasa maize prices in 1999 and 2000 were higher than in 1997 before the war, with very large seasonal variations (from $0.30/kg after harvest in February to $0.70/kg in December before the harvest in Bandundu. Cassava prices have been more or less stable, like those for imported rice and wheat. Prices for rice and wheat are at historically low levels (rice at about $0.50/kg and wheat flour at $0.40 to $0.50/kg). In May 2001 food prices rose significantly following economic liberalization and a fourfold increase in fuel prices. The impact on the population was severe.

Nuancing malnutrition rates

Table 4.1 reveals that global malnutrition rates among Congolese children under 5 years old range from about 10 per cent to 20 per cent according to the district. Severe malnutrition among children under 5 in Kinshasa, however, is less than 3 per cent. Kinshasa residents seem somehow better able to cope. How they do so is one of the enduring mysteries of the Kinois' capacity to survive.

While food insecurity is clearly prevalent in Kinshasa, it does not show up in the food and nutritional situation of the population (Banea-Mayambu 2001). This can be explained by practices and mechanisms that allow Kinois to manage food insecurity without too many adverse consequences. Banea-Mayambu also notes that moderate, severe and acute malnutrition rates in Kinshasa have remained relatively stable over the last ten years. Thus, in light of the deteriorating economic situation, it is clear people have learned to manage their food security more efficiently than before.

The food supply situation

Cassava roots and leaves are important sources of protein and are the cornerstone of food security in Kinshasa. Cassava alone supplies the population with more than 50 per cent of their calories. Maize,

Table 4.2 Contribution of food items in the diet of the Kinshasa population (1996)

	% of calories (out of 1,989 Cal/day)	% of weight (out of 719 g/day)
Cassava	50.0	39.0
White rice	9.5	7.4
Palm oil	9.0	2.8
Maize	6.9	5.5
Bread	5.0	3.8
Plantain	4.6	10.0
Vegetables	1.0	7.6
Fish	3.6	3.8
Beans	3.4	3.0

Source: UNDP/UNOPS 1998: 196; qualitative surveys and observations in Kinshasa in May 1996.

however, is growing in importance because it can be transported over long distances without spoiling and because it is nutritionally more complete. Table 4.2 lists the percentage of each food item in the Kinois diet.

The situation has evolved since the data in Table 4.2 were collected. Cassava flour and leaves now probably provide between 60 per cent and 65 per cent of all calories, with maize, rice and bread each probably accounting for between 5 and 10 per cent of the remaining calories. A survey of 625 households showed that 82 per cent have cassava *fufu* (dough) as their most frequent food (Banea-Mayambu 2001). This is followed by maize *fufu* (60 per cent), though it is the most frequent staple for only 11 per cent of the households. Maize flour is often added to cassava flour to improve consistency and dough volume. The mixing of cassava and maize flour in *fufu* is a relatively recent practice, brought about by food supply problems. Previously, only people from the southern savannah regions of Kasai and Katanga ate maize as their major staple, while people from the forest had cassava as theirs. The basic diet for the near totality of Kinois is thus monotonous and almost totally vegetarian. Meat is so rarely consumed that it does not appear in Table 4.2.

Cassava is usually transported as *cossettes* (chips), but these perish easily because they absorb moisture and get mouldy in only a few days. They are transported by lorry because this is faster than river transport. When cassava is transported by boat to Kinshasa it is usually in the form of paste *(kimpuka* or *bimpuka)* and is ready for processing into *chikwangue* (a form of cassava loaf).

Most vegetables, especially leafy types like Amaranthus (*bitekoteko* and *ngai ngai*), are grown in Kinshasa or in the neighbouring periphery. The more expensive vegetable condiments such as *fumbwa* (Gnetum africanum), which only grows in the wild, are flown in from Kikwit in Bandundu province. This transport occurs without state support. Indeed, one of the main constraints on trade is the state, which is very active in enforcing artificial price regulations, levying taxes and exercising extractive services.

As a result of state predation, phantom markets are now omnipresent in Kinshasa. They can be seen anywhere a lorry can park and quickly escape if tax collectors or other state agents, real or pretend, appear. For this reason large amounts of food are sold (particularly wholesale or semi-wholesale) at night or in traders' private walled *parcelles*. A similar situation exists at boat landings. These now extend as far as and beyond Maluku, and consequently beyond the easy control of predatory state inspectors. There are now a record forty-eight ports in Kinshasa (Bescoplan/GRET 2000), all of which are subject to a host of government services all trying to collect some form of duty.

Diversifying supply lines

Since the beginning of the second war in August 1998, food imports from Equateur and Orientale provinces have virtually ceased. To avoid catastrophic food shortages Kinshasa has managed to create new supply routes from Bandundu. Table 4.3 demonstrates the shift in supply sources for Kinshasa.

Compared to 1996, when 52 per cent of agricultural products arriving by boat in Kinshasa came from Equateur, between 80 and 91 per cent comes from Bandundu since 1999. Most of Equateur[2] and all of Orientale are now in occupied territory and cut off from the capital. The volume of food coming from Bandundu has more than tripled since the beginning of the second war in August 1998. Overall tonnage went up from an average 3,500 tonnes per month

Table 4.3 Percentage of agricultural tonnage supplied to Kinshasa by river boat

Province	Jan–May 1996	Jan–May 1999	Jan–May 2001
Orientale	12	0	0
Equateur	52	13	5
Bandundu	18	80	91
Kasai	18	7	4

Source: Kupay 2001.

to about 11,000 tonnes. Most of this was food; few other agricultural commodities produced in Bandundu (such as coffee or rubber) are shipped to Kinshasa by boat.

River traffic arriving in Kinshasa nearly doubled between 1990 and 1999/2000 (BESCOPLAN/GRET 2000). In 1990, 107,000 tonnes were landed at the city's ports, while 200,000 tonnes were landed in 1999/2000. In 1990, two-thirds of river traffic was transported by the parastatal ONATRA and only one-third by the private sector. Ten years later 95 per cent was transported by private operators. This remarkable redirection of river traffic from Equateur and Orientale to Bandundu is striking proof of how flexible and resilient river transporters can be when faced with problems.

About 100 to 120 wooden boats (*baleinières*) arrive in Kinshasa ports every month, each transporting between 10 and 200 tonnes, with an average of about 40 tonnes. GRET estimates the total number of wooden boats operating out of Kinshasa to be between 150 and 200. Much larger iron vessels, with powerful pusher boats to which several barges are attached, also ply between Kinshasa and Bandundu. Their average cargo exceeds 100 tonnes. This growth of wooden boats in river traffic from Bandundu and Kasai is a response to poor road conditions.

Wooden boats barely existed in the 1980s. Today they are made by craftsmen at wharfs in Eolo in Idiofa territory and at Nioki in Inongo territory. The Nioki wharf existed in colonial times but the Eolo wharf is new. It is probably the result of a boat-building project financed by USAID (United States Agency for International

Table 4.4   Number of boat arrivals registered in Kinshasa,
1996 and 1999

	1996	1999
Bandundu	130	246
Equateur	162	51
Kasaï	30	29
Province Orientale	42	0

Source: Bescoplan/GRET, September 2000, p. 63.

Development) in the 1980s as part of an agricultural marketing improvement project. An expatriate naval architect taught several local carpenters how to build wooden boats in one dimension of the project. Although criticized at the time because lorry transport seemed more logical and convenient, the project has proved to be quite successful, given the steady supply of useful and efficient new wooden boats it has created.

Road rehabilitation

While river transport has grown to accommodate urban food requirements, the road system linking Kinshasa and Bandundu has also been improved. The PAR project (Projet d'Appui à la Réhabilitation), financed by the European Union, rehabilitated the main asphalt roads between Mbanza Ngungu and Kinshasa and between Kinshasa and Mbankana in 1998 and 1999. Many feeder roads, particularly in Bandundu province, were also repaired, while roads leading to major embarkation points along the rivers in Bandundu (particularly in Idiofa zone) were improved, providing the means for alternative food sources to develop.

In 1998–99, when supplies from Equateur and Orientale were largely cut off because of the war, cassava from Bandundu replaced maize from Equateur. Supplies of palm oil, rice and groundnuts also dwindled. Palm oil, which is Kinshasa's third largest food import after cassava and maize, is still an expensive commodity in the city, sold in small plastic bags containing only 50 ml or 100 ml. Soap, derived mainly from palm oil, is so expensive it is sold in half or quarter bars. In response to economic possibilities, old natural palm oil plantations in Kwilu and Bas-Congo have been rehabilitated.

Food imports

Since the 1980s food imports, particularly wheat, rice, frozen fish (mainly *mpiodi*) and meat, have been important for Kinshasa (Goossens et al. 1994). Over 200,000 tonnes per year were imported in the late 1990s. Some of these imports are re-exported to Brazzaville and to the interior of both Congos. Local production cannot compete with such cheap imports. Repairs to the Kinshasa–Mbanza Ngungu road have facilitated these imports by lorry from the port of Matadi, but fewer animal products were imported in 2000 and 2001, particularly less poultry, because of increased price controls, hard currency shortages and a rapidly deteriorating exchange rate. The largest importer, Orgaman, reduced its imports of frozen fish and meat from 67,648 tonnes in 1999 to 62,655 tonnes in 2000. Two competing Antwerp-based Lebanese importers (Congo Futur and Socimex) increased their imports, however, providing considerable competition to Orgaman.

Since the second war began in 1998 there has been a sharp increase in dry cereal imports, particularly wheat flour and rice. The same Lebanese importers of frozen fish and meat are now very active in this trade. In 2000, over 100,000 tonnes of wheat flour were imported, and more was imported in 2001 despite a stiff 35 per cent import duty. A large percentage of these imports are fraudulent because they benefit from rapid removal procedures (*enlèvement d'urgence*) at Matadi, meaning that only part of the official duty is paid. Due to this unfair competition, MIDEMA, the traditional supplier of wheat flour in Congo with its large mills at Matadi, now produces only around 40 per cent of its capacity (110,000 tonnes in 2000).

Bread is available everywhere in Kinshasa at relatively low prices. Baguettes (between 150 and 200 grams) sell for the equivalent of around 10 US cents. Although nothing is really cheap for a family with an income of only $50 per month, these are relatively affordable and provide some nutritional value. Quo Vadis, BKTF, UPAK and Panico, the major bakeries, have sales outlets everywhere in Kinshasa. Their facilities are large-scale and efficient. Bread has consequently become a major food staple, competing with cassava and maize, both in Kinshasa and in the interior. Baguettes travel long distances and reach far into the interior, even to relatively remote villages.

To make up for supply problems from Equateur, MIDEMA has recently imported maize for its mills, and soybeans from Brazil to make chicken feed and soya milk. MIDEMA has recently opened a new feed mill in Kinshasa and over the last two years their sales of animal feed have increased by 80 per cent. The number of shops that are now visible all over the city is a reliable indicator of this trend. They mainly sell pig and poultry feed for urban and peri-urban breeding. A 1999 CEPLANUT survey found that one family out of ten raises chickens, ducks and pigeons. Indeed, livestock are now kept everywhere in Kinshasa, even in the middle of the city. Dung serves as organic fertilizer for urban market gardening.

As world prices for rice have fallen over the past few years, due to bumper harvests in Thailand and Vietnam, much more high-quality rice is being imported to Congo. Vietnam, China, Pakistan and the USA are all suppliers. Rice costs around $0.50/kg in 25 or 50 kilo bags, more when smaller quantities are bought.

Cassava crisis

The rapid spread of cassava mosaic disease (CMD) has exacerbated the already difficult food situation in Kinshasa. Although CMD is endemic and widespread in Congo, the invasion of the East African or Uganda-type virus is new. This is a more lethal and devastating virus than the existing (West African) type. Many cassava plants are now attacked by both types of virus, along with other diseases and pests like bacterial blight, green spider mite and mealy bug. The result is very low yields. Since cassava is planted everywhere in Congo, the spread of the virus by flies is facilitated. Moreover, as cassava is cultivated by planting cuttings, CMD is propagated by planting diseased stocks. In only a couple of years an entire cassava field can be affected, particularly on the poorer soils where cassava is generally planted. Farmers are now, however, planting cassava on their plots of better soils as a coping mechanism.

It is not surprising that the retail price of maize flour in Kinshasa markets is sometimes lower than that of cassava flour. Until the recent crisis, cassava flour had always been the cheapest staple, but low cassava yields in Bas-Congo and Bandundu and the increased long-distance river transport of maize explain why maize flour is now occasionally cheaper. Even imported rice is sometimes cheaper in Kinshasa markets than cassava flour. This is an unprecedented situation and a clear indication of the cassava crisis hitting the country.

Changes in cropping patterns

Important changes in Bandundu and Bas-Congo cropping patterns have taken place over the last decade. There has been a notable increase in the cultivation of cowpeas, which have become an important source of vegetable protein. Cowpea, a high-protein, short-season dry grain legume, is typical of semi-arid zones like northern Nigeria. It has now become common in the Kwango and on the dry sandy savannahs of the Bateke plateau in the Kinshasa hinterland. It is often grown as a second season crop that benefits from residual moisture in the soil. More and more millet, a Sahel crop found everywhere in southern Bandundu, is found in the dry savannahs. One also finds sesame in Kinshasa markets, again a crop of the dry savannah. In the inland valleys of Bas-Congo and in the Kwilu region of Bandundu, more and more rice is being grown.

With the Pool Malebo project, funded by Belgium in the framework of the National Rice Programme, 5,000 rice growers receive technical and financial assistance on 2,000 hectares of marshlands alongside the Congo river in Kinshasa. The project has successfully promoted locally irrigated rice production in Kinshasa. Italian cooperation is doing similar work by constructing dikes in the marshes of the Malebo pool and promoting irrigated rice production.

In Idiofa (Bandundu), where the PAR project has rehabilitated feeder roads leading to river ports, there has been a sizeable increase in maize production, which is shipped to Kinshasa and to Kasai. In general, more maize is now produced in Bandundu to counter the loss of maize supplies from Equateur province. MIDEMA, which sells improved seeds, reports growing demand for improved maize seed.

Innovations in food marketing strategies

Several innovations in Kinshasa have had positive effects on food security. They all appear to be spontaneous people-based responses to economic and political constraints, particularly the failed state and collapse of the formal private sector. Commission agents (*agents commissionaires*), for example, have become important actors in the food supply sector. They have four primary functions. One, they bulk goods to be sent to a particular destination, often in collaboration with traders. Two, they group together travellers headed for particular destinations and find vehicles going there. Three, they serve as communication facilitators, usually by radio but also increasingly by mobile phone. Four, they serve as intermediaries in sending and receiving money. This is an important service because very few banks exist today in the interior. It is thus possible to transfer money to or from any small town in the interior in a single day. There is nonetheless a high fee involved, usually 10 per cent. This innovation is always based on trust and generally on ethnicity. The commission agents are located primarily along Avenue Kianza in Kinshasa (for Bandundu) and along Avenue Kasavubu (for Bas-Congo) and have partners in the rural areas. These agents emerged in the 1990s in response to the specific need to reduce transaction costs. They did not exist in the 1980s and clearly demonstrate the Kinois capacity for spontaneous socio-economic innovation faced with the decline of formal banking and the increase of transportation problems.

The apparent chaos at Kinshasa's ports and the need to find new sources of household income have contributed to the emergence of intermediaries who facilitate the sale of food transported by river to local market women. They deal primarily in cassava and corn, but also handle smoked fish and bushmeat. These intermediaries are called *mamans manœuvres*, *mamans-bipupula* or *mamans-kabola*.[3] Although some of them have access to cash through *likelemba* and *muziki* (rotating savings and credit associations), most tend to be poor mothers who have created these facilitating services to ensure their survival and feed their families. The women collect sufficient funds among potential buyers to buy, for example, one sack of cassava *cossettes*. Then they accost incoming traders and negotiate a price. They subsequently split up the wholesale sack among the different buyers in their group. A single buyer cannot afford a sack of 50 kg, but via the intermediary *maman*, who pools money for the purchase, each buyer gets a retail-sized share. The *maman manœuvre* is remunerated by shares of *cossettes* given her by the individual buyers, plus the remaining broken fragments of cassava *cossettes* that cannot be distributed. Out of a 50 kg sack, she may end up with 2 to 3 kilos. This innovation has become so successful that the number of *mamans manœuvres* has greatly increased. As a result, each one now handles only an average of two or three sacks per day, collecting 4 to 9 kilos of *cossette* fragments. Part of this is used to feed her family and part is sold for cash.

Other jobs related to food supply have also emerged. *Chayeurs* are urban-based intermediaries who find clients, propose deals and barter goods. There are also *groupeurs* or *commissionnaires* who forage the Kinshasa hinterland for goods, reserve them for buyers, group them and store them. They are aided by *éclaireurs* (scouts) who work for particular buyers or transporters and lead them to places where deals can be made. Their major role is to provide information about where food products are available and their price. *Ngundeurs* are small-scale traders who, during the main marketing campaign, live in rural areas and seek out the cheapest prices and best deals. They may work on their own or on commission for a large-scale trader. Finally, there are *drogadeurs,* informal-sector dockers who load and unload boats in the many makeshift phantom ports that lie beyond the control of official port authorities. They also guide boats to a particular beach where they can operate without the usual administrative hassles encountered in official Kinshasa ports.

All of these new intermediary services are facilitated by the rapid spread of mobile phone usage. Although Kinshasa was one of the first large cities in Africa to have mobile phones, there has been an explosion of mobile phone companies recently. Oasis, Celtel, Comcel, Starcel, Celnet, Telecel[4] and more recently Vodacom are some of the companies competing for this lucrative market. Since many of these cell phone providers are not compatible with one another, some people now have a collection of several phones. Phone services are widely available through mobile phone kiosques (*téléboutiques*) where one can rent a phone by the minute. In some cases these *téléboutiques* also provide internet services. Some cities in the interior also have mobile phone networks. This has facilitated the emergence of many types of informal services that reduce marketing transaction costs.

The construction of the huge Marché de la Liberté is a joint state and private-sector initiative that has the potential to improve food access in Kinshasa's poorest districts. It is a retail market in Ndjili on the former site of the General Motors assembly plant. Still under construction on the 21-hectare site, Liberty Market looks set to be the largest retail market in Africa, with 7,300 stands. It will be managed by the city of Kinshasa. Bank offices, cold storage facilities, parking areas and storage chambers are also planned. The Katanga-based mining and construction firm of Georges Forrest is the contractor, apparently as part of a deal between Forrest and Congo authorities to process mine tailings in Lubumbashi and, along with Union Minière Company (Umicore) of Belgium, to produce cobalt.[5]

Food security in the war zone

It is difficult to obtain reliable information on the food security situation in Congo's interior, particularly in the war zone. Most of the information available is purely anecdotal. One has to rely mainly on materials supplied by OCHA (Office for the Coordination of Humanitarian Affairs of the UN), FAO (Coordination of Emergency Operations in Congo), ECHO (Office of Humanitarian Aid of the EU-Commission) and NGOs active in the war zone. This information is sketchy, but it points to an enormous ongoing human tragedy.

In the eastern DRC troops are slowly retreating from the front-lines, but are often redeployed to mineral-rich areas. This has led to upsurges of fighting between different armed groups, generally at the expense of local populations. One current driving force behind the conflict, which also prolongs it, is a desire to control the country's vast mineral resources of gold, diamonds and coltan (Samset 2002). This greed causes the suffering of millions. Since soldiers are not paid and do not receive food supplies, they force the local population to supply them with food, often at gunpoint. The usual reaction is to flee into the forest, thus becoming internally displaced persons. An estimated 2.05 million persons have been internally displaced in the Kivus and Katanga; an additional 328,000 have fled to neighbouring countries. Displaced populations are particularly vulnerable to severe food insecurity. An estimated 1 million people are still hiding in the forest, living in difficult circumstances. They survive by hunting and gathering and have no medical care or support. The nutritional situation, particularly of women and children, is particularly appalling.

> In rebel-held areas, the rates of global malnutrition among children under five reported in the past year have reached 41 per cent, with severe mal-nutrition rates of up to 26 per cent. These figures were recorded at the point at which the humanitarian community gained access to previously isolated communities. Consequently, it is reasonable to expect that in areas of the East, which continue to be too insecure to allow any form

of assistance to be delivered, the situation is at least as bad, and possibly worse. Displaced populations inaccessible in the forests are in a particularly bad nutritional state, as illustrated by [World Food Program] WFP's figures for South Kivu, which show that 75 per cent of malnourished children currently registered in feeding centres belong to families which have just emerged from the forests. When Manono and Kiambi [northern Katanga] became accessible in January 2001, Nuova Frontiera conducted a nutritional survey which found a global malnutrition rate among under fives of 32.07 per cent and a severe malnutrition rate of 25.79 per cent. (Save the Children/Oxfam/Christian Aid 2001: 25)

Displaced peoples living in forests mainly eat cassava roots and leaves and wild fruits. This unbalanced diet results in nutritional deficiencies and increased susceptibility to disease. Displaced persons also lack simple farming tools, seeds and planting material. They often steal food and planting material in their flight, further adding to tensions and conflict.

Humanitarian organizations active in the Congo, particularly OCHA and ECHO, seem to be well organized and efficient although they lack adequate funding. The cost of reaching displaced and vulnerable populations is very high because of long distances, poor roads and security risks for personnel. Displaced persons also tend to be afraid of foreigners and flee once again when they see them. Many are in rags or naked, so stay in hiding. One of the first things humanitarian organizations should do is distribute clothes, and then food. The distribution of seeds, planting material and farm tools can then follow.

Conclusion

Eating in Kinshasa is more of a challenge today than at any time before. It is a challenge due more to poverty than to inadequate supply. Paradoxically, this hardship is not obvious in nutritional indicators because Kinois have developed sophisticated coping mechanisms over the last decade. Despite tremendous adversity in infrastructure, state services and formal private-sector operations, almost enough food is produced in and around Kinshasa or imported to this mega-city. It gets transported and distributed relatively efficiently. In the process, it provides employment and income for thousands of poor people, particularly women farmers and traders. Food distribution networks also provide income for state officials and some revenue for the central government. This daily miracle happens in apparent chaos, but follows its own logic based on kinship, community, religious and commercial networks that sometimes span thousands of kilometres. It defies state control and the predatory tactics of those who are supposed to ensure safety and a facilitating environment.

Cassava and some maize supplies from Bandundu, mainly transported by boat, have almost fully compensated for the loss of supplies from Equateur and Orientale provinces. This is remarkable. Boat transport has more than tripled (in tonnage) during the current conflict. The rehabilitation of many feeder roads in Bandundu and the emergence of wooden boats facilitated this positive evolution. This Kinshasa miracle helps explain why food security in Kinshasa is better than expected.

All of the innovations described above reveal how Kinois have responded to the challenges of daily survival by developing their own appropriate, people-based solutions. These are not always efficient or low cost, but they tend to work. They almost always employ large numbers of people and are based on trust and solidarity networks. They can be considered as informal-sector operations, but the line between formal and informal is blurred: formal and informal generally work in tandem and in symbiosis, complementing each other in order to beat the predatory state system wherever possible. Many informal operations may have a formal façade, like the *agences commissionaires* that are commercially registered yet operate outside the formal banking and trading system. This chapter has also shown that large, formal-sector operators are increasingly operating informally or even fraudulently by, for example, importing wheat, rice, *mpiodi* or chickens partly officially and partly unofficially. In the end, the poor Kinois benefits in some small way. How else can one understand that a baguette costs only 10 cents and is found all over Kinshasa and in the interior, or that *mpiodi* can be purchased for less than $1 per kilo.

Although the food security situation in Kinshasa is dramatic, malnutrition rates today are really no worse than ten years ago. Coping strategies have been developed and honed with great skill and creativity over the last decade. The question as to how long this can situation can last, however, remains unanswered. Once peace returns, and if economic growth becomes a reality, how can these forms of social innovation become levers for economic and social development?

Notes

1. *Mpiodi* is the low-cost, low-quality fish most commonly eaten by Kinois. It was formerly called Thompson.
2. Unilever Congo has lost control of its Yaligimba plantation in Equateur province and Lokutu plantation in the Eastern province, but it still has control of the Boteka plantation in Equateur province. This is now the main supply of palm oil in Kinshasa.
3. The *mamans manœuvres* phenomenon is also addressed by Nzeza, Chapter 2 in this volume.
4. Telecel started in Kinshasa in 1985. It was the first mobile telephone company in Africa.
5. New technology has made the processing of yesterday's excavation waste profitable today. The Forrest factory in Lubumbashi is now the second largest of its kind in the world.

The Miracle of Life in Kinshasa: New Approaches to Public Health

Peter Persyn and Fabienne Ladrière

The public health sector in Kinshasa reflects the tragic destiny of the large majority of Congolese. Hygiene and housing conditions have fallen to a critical level. Public health problems are social problems and indicators of decades of political crisis. Physical suffering is widespread and affects the most vulnerable. Women and children are the first victims. It is a miracle that the population of this mega-city has not been decimated. Kinois are sick with water-related diseases and debilitated by undernourishment. They suffer a host of diseases such as malaria, tuberculosis, typhoid fever and leprosy. Other endemic diseases such as polio and haemorrhagic fever, well under control by Independence in 1960, have reappeared. The tsetse fly and sleeping sickness have made their way to the outskirts of Kinshasa (Arbyn et al. 1995; Van Nieuwenove et al. 2001). AIDS exacts a heavy toll on Kinois and has done so since it was first identified (Colenbunders et al. 1984). Since the mid-1990s, health officials have been confronted by yearly cholera epidemics in the rainy season, illustrating the poor state of the sewerage system.[1] More than elsewhere in the country, Kinshasa's colonial heritage inflated social expectations by reshaping mental frameworks and material infrastructures. Because it was dissociated from a deeper social setting, however, the hospital and doctor-centred health culture transplanted from Belgium has provoked adverse effects. Human existence in traditional rural areas was intricately embedded in a social and cosmological continuum where individual needs and desires were dependent on the larger social, natural and spiritual environment. Health was traditionally considered a reflection of the body's balance of forces within this continuum.

Post-colonial health authorities replicated the centralized colonial medical hierarchy and continued to perpetrate mistakes of the past. Emphasis on the doctor and hospital approach is one of the system's most visible failures (Médecins sans Frontières and Job 2000). Going to hospital is often a last act of faith. Kinshasa's main hospitals (General Hospital, formerly Mama Yemo; Makala; and King Baudouin) are places of death. The buildings themselves are ruins; plumbing and electricity are inadequate; material and equipment are practically non-existent. Patients go to a hospital reluctantly, and even when they can afford to go they must provide their own bedding, medicines (often outdated or counterfeit), hypodermic needles and sterile gloves. All of these supplies are sold on the streets in front of the hospital under the glaring Kinshasa sun.

These hospitals are, moreover, severely understaffed. Many Congolese doctors have left the country, frequently settling in South Africa where there was a need for qualified medical personnel in the early post-Apartheid years. Despite these conditions, however, doctors in Kinshasa can achieve remarkable results. European and American doctors who work in Kinshasa testify to the creativity and resourcefulness of Kinois doctors faced with complex medical cases. The Kinois doctor is comparable in this respect to the Kinois mechanic who can keep an old jalopy running by fixing it with pieces of string and wire, a common phenomenon throughout much of Africa.

While infectious pathology is the major public health problem in Kinshasa, Kinois are increasingly prone to modern chronic conditions such as hypertension and diabetes, a consequence of adopting sedentary habits. In terms of crude calorific intake their nutritional status may appear reasonable, but the monotony of a single meal of manioc, usually in the form of *foufou* or *chikwange* (see Tollens in this volume), alternated or complemented with bread and beans, salted fish and offal, produces chronic malnutrition (Nackers and Malengreau 1999). Ageing, along with the long-term effects of infectious strain and other poorly understood factors, such as the impact of ongoing social and mental stress on health, account for growing occurrences of cardiovascular disease in the city. Severe cases of hypertension, diabetes and stroke put additional burdens on families and the health system.

Health care is no longer perceived as a basic public service, but as a free-market commodity. Health personnel are no longer respected as community workers with a valued social mission, but as commercial service providers. Although the crisis in this vital area is alarming, Kinois have developed extraordinary strategies in their search for healing. This search for healing is the subject of this chapter, which is organized in three sections: first, a short historical survey; second, a discussion of the hybrid health care market where public and private biomedical facilities, traditional practitioners and charismatic healing movements intermingle (Persyn and Devisch 1992); and third, an analysis of the relationship between national health authorities and the international community.

Historical context

The colonial health care system

The Congo's extraordinary biodiversity, physical conditions, demography and cultural diversity help explain why many serious infectious diseases such as Ebola, AIDS, sleeping sickness, malaria, leprosy, yellow fever and tuberculosis are endemic. These conditions also explain why the Congo was perceived as a white man's graveyard in the early colonial period. Concerned about the health of their European staff and the productivity of the African labour force, colonial administrators encouraged biomedical research. Physicians and natural scientists explored every corner of the country, gathering an impressive amount of knowledge and expertise (Janssens et al. 1992). The colonial administration also invested heavily in the medical domain. Its public health campaigns organized among local populations sought primarily to avoid epidemics. Convinced of the superiority of the hospital- and doctor-centred system, Belgians transplanted it to the Congo (Van Dormael 1997). Congolese were trained as medical assistants to deliver basic care, starting in 1935. Religious congregations, historically involved in charity in Belgium, began to organize free education and medical assistance throughout the territory in the same period. In many remote areas, medical facilities were the most visible manifestation of colonization, along with schools and churches.

For the Catholic clergy, however, pagan beliefs and rituals, particularly in the highly symbolic domain of health and disease, were considered a serious threat to the Christian civilizing mission. They fought traditional healers vehemently, relegating elements of traditional culture that had proven successful for millennia to the realm of magic and sorcery. In the pre-colonial era, the highly symbolized ritual practices and sense-giving offered by the healer were deeply embedded in ancestral traditional culture. In the colonial period, the paternalistic but efficient white doctors (then considered to be white witches) stimulated potent metaphors and reinterpretations of popular imagery. Their public health discourse echoed the attitudes of colonial administrators by portraying the village as a backward social space. Its paganism, polygamy, healing practices and sorcery required conversion. Its oppressive conservatism, based on respect for elders, needed to be eradicated.

Biomedical care, pharmaceuticals and technical interventions administered in neat brick facilities rapidly became part of social expectations. People eagerly took advantage of the new approach given its seemingly practical results and availability. Childbirth and childcare, once part of the domestic realm, were also increasingly medicalized. As a consequence, effective health care was exclusively conceived of as medical care based on imported Western science and technology. This perception still prevails among health planners and intellectuals today. Nonetheless, by reinterpreting the white man's science in popular representation and imagery, most Congolese have continued to combine traditional healing practices with imported care, taking advantage of the best of both worlds (Hunt 1999).

The Zairean health care system

At independence in 1960, there were no Congolese medical school graduates, despite medical studies having been inaugurated in Kinshasa in 1954. With the abrupt withdrawal of Belgians, the health system required large numbers of new health workers. Haitian and other French-speaking experts were called in for support and many Congolese medical assistants were nominally upgraded to physicians (De Craemer and Fox 1968). Given political instability and social unrest for most of the 1960s, Mobutu did little to address the challenge of providing public health services until the early 1970s. Congolese and expatriate physicians, faced with monumental public health problems, argued that service had to be brought as close to people as possible to ensure access to good-quality care for the entire population. The ultimate goal would be an integrated health-care system. Several pioneering experiments were started, notably the Primary Health Care (*Soins de santé primaires*) scheme (Van Balen 1989). This was conceived as a bottom-up approach, with each level theoretically assuming its own tasks and responsibilities. The base of the health pyramid was the community that was to be responsible for its own health-related behaviour, environmental management, health education and promotion and preventive actions. When professional attention was needed for basic care, people went to clinics (*Centres de santé*), while patients needing specialized hospital care were referred to better equipped health centres (*Centres de santé de référence*) or to a general district hospital (*Hôpital général de référence*). In more complicated cases, transfer to specialized third-level clinics was recommended.

In administrative terms, the public health map overlapped the country's administrative divisions and replicated its hierarchy. Given the highly centralized organization of the Ministry of Health, local-level health officials had little autonomy or resources. National health officials (*Directions centrales de la santé*) designed health care policies and monitored their implementation. This strategic level was supposed to define national health priorities in response to data and demands coming from the provincial level and, theoretically, to decide strategies and budgets. Best-practice guidelines were to be developed, tested first in Kinshasa, and then extended to the district level.

While there was a huge gap between expectations and reality, the system seemed credible throughout much of the 1970s. Smallpox was eradicated and vaccination coverage for childhood diseases, a reliable indicator of preventive care performance, was 95 per cent. This was among the highest rates of all developing countries. The Zairean experience stood as an example for sub-Sahara Africa, and by the end of the decade Zaire was a leader in primary health and community health care. In 1980, the government committed itself officially to the principles of primary health care by signing the African Charter for Health for All by the year 2000. This ambitious programme was launched in the crowded central neighbourhoods of Kinshasa and its expanding peripheral districts.

The turning of the tide

By the time the government began the Health for All programme, however, the tide had turned for the Second Republic. The economy was in free fall, copper prices dropped dramatically, fuel prices rose, and the period of hyperinflation began. Zairanization, Mobutu's version of nationalization, destroyed the internal market and poisoned relations with foreign investors. Implications for the health sector were obvious: the bureaucratic–authoritarian single-party state stopped providing social and public services. Doctors, nurses and other health personnel in the public sector went unpaid, but they were still supposed to meet their official obligations, and provide for their families. As a consequence, they were forced to add private practice to their official duties. The health system had not been designed to be economically self-reliant; it was supposed to be state-financed. In this context of crisis, however, medical staff had to manage with incomes based on medical delivery. Financially unrewarding activities such as preventive care, health education and environmental measures were rapidly abandoned. Buildings and equipment were no longer repaired or replaced, and infrastructure became dilapidated without public funding.

In the absence of decent working conditions and new training opportunities, medical staff started to lose skills and motivation. Teaching standards in general, and medical training in particular, declined, and newcomers were rarely qualified for their jobs. Structural adjustment programmes (SAPs) of the International Monetary Fund exacerbated the situation. SAP-imposed salary cuts in the public sector were harshly felt in the health system. Many staff, made redundant in the process, nonetheless stayed on the job. This was typical throughout the entire public service sector. People had few other job opportunities and remained at work in hope of a turnaround. Health workers compensated for lost income, prestige and privileges by moonlighting in the expanding private medical business, and as workloads in public facilities decreased, reduced working schedules were introduced (*horaires de crise*), enabling people to be legally absent from work to make money elsewhere.

Health workers gradually began to abuse their power by requesting extra money for every service. They imposed upon patients what they themselves experienced every day in the public arena: you only get what you pay for. People in a position to pilfer anything of value followed the example given by government officials. Small office materials and medical supplies such as pharmaceuticals, laboratory equipment, surgical instruments, books and blankets simply vanished. Later, even large furniture and sophisticated machinery disappeared.

In some facilities medical staff, who had the protection of political or military authorities, diverted revenues. This kind of complicity easily led to a situation in which health workers were exploited by their bosses. They had little or no choice. They had either to accept or to sacrifice the few advantages left. Workers' unions had little impact, for there were several unions for every profession, each pretending to represent a majority of workers. Encouraging rivalry and competition between and within professions suited a government with little or nothing to offer. Eventually, distrust and contempt replaced communication and respect among professional workers.

In the late 1980s health care management in several parts of the country was virtually taken over by religious congregations such as the (Catholic) BDOM (Bureau Diocésain d'Oeuvres Médicales) and the (Protestant) Salvation Army and nongovernmental agencies like Médecins sans Frontières. They tried to maintain the primary health care system and Health for All project in Kinshasa; state health authorities reluctantly accepted this substitution. They nonetheless continued to exert political influence to ensure personal financial benefits.

In the early 1990s political events completed the disintegration of Zaire's public health system. After three decades of unconditional support during the Cold War, Belgium, France and the USA repudiated Mobutu. In 1990 Belgian official development aid abruptly ceased, ending two decades of support for the medical sector. Joint health projects collapsed, and many Congolese physicians emigrated. The lootings of 1991 and 1993 scared off what remained of the expatriate NGO medical staff.

It took several tragedies before the international humanitarian community realized this part of the world was permanently at risk from natural and man-made disasters. In 1994, the apocalyptic events in neighbouring Rwanda caused massive migrations of refugees (approximately 1 million people) and armed incursions into Congo's eastern provinces. In 1995, Ebola broke out in Kikwit, killing more than 400 people, and in the same year the biggest polio epidemic of recent history ravaged the city of Mbuyi-Mayi, taking more than 1,000 lives. These events were unmistakable warnings that the country's sanitary system was in serious trouble and could have far-reaching consequences. Huge efforts were imperative to avoid new calamities. In response, the World Health Organization (WHO), United Nations Children's Fund (UNICEF), United

Nations Development Programme (UNDP), United Nations High Commission for Refuges (UNHCR) and other agencies became increasingly involved in humanitarian aid, working in close partnership with the Ministry of Public Health. The public health situation has not, however, improved in post-Zaire Congo.

The Kinshasa health-care market today

A marketplace approach, as in most other domains of public life, has replaced long-forgotten public health services. Offer and demand, value for money and bargaining (see Nzeza in this volume) have become the basic rules of Kinshasa's health care system. A disproportionate number of medical facilities have been based in Kinshasa since the colonial period. Some of the country's major hospitals are gathered in a few square kilometres in the single health district of Kin-Malebo. Hundreds of smaller facilities, both public and private, are scattered all over the city (Simon 1996). Here, medical doctors dominate; surgery and technical interventions are more valued than equally important but financially less rewarding tasks such as basic care, prevention, health planning and awareness. Nurses, technicians, social workers and administrators do these jobs.

The presence of national elites and expatriates has meant that relatively up-to-date medical technology and services are available in Kinshasa. Only a small percentage of Kinois, however, can afford this care and only a few health facilities can fully meet modern standards. For major surgery or sophisticated medical treatment, even elites must seek care abroad, usually in South Africa or Europe. For the vast majority of people this is impossible. They have to accept poor quality care and rising costs. Given the generalized crisis situation in Kinshasa, people have to be seriously ill or incapacitated before seeking treatment.

Data on Kinshasa's 22 health districts make clear that the ideal of an integrated health system is still very distant (Miakala 2000). In 1999 only a few districts reported on care delivery: the average utilization rate is 0.19 new visits per inhabitant per year compared to a national average of 0.5. International standards for best-practice utilization are one new visit per inhabitant per year. In the official centres, only about 2 per cent of patients were referred to a higher level. In contrast, WHO recommends that referral should reach as high as 10 per cent in developing countries. The number of women visiting official facilities at least once during the last three months of pregnancy is only 16 per cent. Only one out of three districts (7 of 22) kept data on deliveries: the number of registered newborns was half of those expected, with only 1.68 per cent recorded as complicated. Maternal mortality was 0.7 per cent (70 per 100,000 deliveries); neonatal mortality 1.45 per cent. Babies under 2.5 kg represent 5.5 per cent of all births. All districts report on routine vaccination. For children under one year, tuberculosis vaccination coverage was 83 per cent (6 out of 7 babies), while coverage for other child diseases (polio, tetanus, whooping cough, diphtheria and measles) reached only about 65 per cent (2 out of 3 children). Fifteen years ago 95 per cent of children were vaccinated (République Démocratique du Congo 1999).

Proliferation of private practice is both cause and consequence of poor performance in the official integrated facilities. While 220 health centres would suffice to cover the 22 health districts of greater Kinshasa if they were adequately staffed and supplied, 1,310 private facilities were registered in 1999. These facilities were initially run by physicians working after hours. They saw private practice as proof of social success and as a means to earn extra money. Officials and entrepreneurs subsequently invested in private health care business as well, attracted by its economic potential. Lower-level medical personnel, and even unqualified employees frustrated with their petty wages, soon ventured into the sector. They started to sell their practical expertise in the back rooms of a house or rented office, but this generally proved of little use. Working without proper equipment and in poor hygienic conditions, they put the health and lives of their patients at risk for a small profit. The poor and sick of Kinshasa accept this because they have no other option.

In the West, the concept of general well-being has only recently been linked with other categories like quality of life and functional health status, concepts which take into account physical, cultural and environmental factors. For Kinois, the traditional idea of good health and well-being goes far beyond the disease-oriented focus in Western biomedicine. It more closely corresponds with the 1948 WHO definition that describes health as a complete state of physical, mental and social well-being, not merely the absence of disease (World Health Organization 1948). This helps explain why Kinois continue to adhere to traditional beliefs and attitudes even though Western biomedical services have modified health patterns and practices.

Quality of life and general well-being have decreased for most Kinois over the last two decades. The WHO concept of health for all is a distant utopia. The rapid resurgence of the major endemic diseases, eradicated or put under control in the late colonial period, results directly from economic crisis and poor sanitary conditions. These are certainly determining phenomena but they do not explain why new problems appeared so dramatically. One explanation is that the structures and strategies imported and imposed by the colonial hierarchy were culturally inappropriate and were never totally adopted psychologically and culturally by Congolese beneficiaries.

Many traditional sanitary efforts consisted of environmental measures such as keeping the neighbourhood clean and free from stagnant water. This type of surveillance does not necessarily require sophisticated technology or heavy investments; rather, it relies on community involvement. Some experts blame the colonial paternalistic hospital- and doctor-centred health-care culture, mainly because it impeded the proactive involvement of people in their own environmental and health issues (Grodos and de Béthune 1988).

Faced with bad luck, misfortune or disease, even when they understand the problem might be brought about by a microbe or an accident, people want to know more: why something happened to them, why now, and whose fault it is (who cast the spell). The mechanistic Western logic emphasizing how things are brought about is hardly satisfying. The perceived need to understand the supernatural cause of health problems eventually led many Kinois to alternative health systems. This is particularly true when a problem persists after Western-style medical treatment has failed.

AIDS and HIV

Kinshasa has been associated with HIV/AIDS since the very beginning of the pandemic. The oldest known seropositive blood sample was taken from an unknown Congolese soldier in Kinshasa in 1959 and many of the first clinical cases of AIDS described in medical literature emanated from DRC (Offenstadt et al. 1983). Epidemics often erupt at times of social and economic crisis, and AIDS is no exception. Its spread is directly linked to poverty, class and gender inequality, population movements and problems in the public health sector, making Kinshasa a perfect breeding ground (Schoepf 2002). Some HIV was probably present in rural Congo from the 1950s but by the 1980s it was primarily concentrated in urban areas. Once in Kinshasa, it spread quite rapidly, in part due to the city's rapid demographic growth. Survival sex and prostitution practised by many young women exacerbated its spread. The blood of pregnant women in Kinshasa drawn in 1970 found 0.25 per cent with HIV antibodies; by 1980 prevalence had reached 3 per cent (Desmyter et al. 1986). The progression of AIDS in Kinshasa in the 1980s created panic in the international medical field and ambiguous discourse among Congolese intellectuals.

The doomsday scenario forecast in the 1980s because of the perceived hedonistic Kinshasa way of life has not, however, come true. Although thousands of Kinois have died of AIDS and many more are seropositive (approximately 1.5 million Congolese are infected with HIV[2]), the increase in HIV has actually slowed down, in sharp contrast with its exponential rise in other sub-Saharan African countries. By 1998, antenatal clinics in Kinshasa registered rates between 4 and 6 per cent, despite a 1992 peak of nearly 10 per cent.[3] Although there are no comprehensive studies of AIDS prevalence in Kinshasa, it is estimated that the Kinshasa level is more or the less the same as estimates for the whole of Congo, which is 5 per cent.[4] (These figures need to be treated with a great deal of caution; the Congo is a country in which reliable social statistics are virtually impossible to secure.) A number of factors help explain the relative stability of HIV transmission in Kinshasa.

During the 1980s, the international biomedical research group Projet SIDA[5] carried out pioneering work in Kinshasa's Matonge district. Matonge, famous for its *ngandas* (bars) and discos, is associated with fashion, leisure and lust. It was here that researchers first recognized and warned of the pandemic potential of this new affliction, until then perceived as a gay problem (Piot et al. 1992). Projet SIDA conducted a population-based survey in Kinshasa in 1985, and found HIV in 5 per cent of blood samples taken from 5,099 healthy residents of all ages. The rate in women 15 to 29 years old was double the general rate. In the 15-to-24 age group, nearly six times more women than men were infected. Not surprisingly, poor, young, unmarried urban women are at highest risk (see De Herdt, Chapter 8). While taboos on HIV and AIDS were at least as important in DRC as elsewhere, a national programme (Programme National pour la Lutte Contre le SIDA) was set up in 1987, and preventive campaigns were launched. These initiatives took place almost a decade before similar ones in neighbouring countries.

The common form of polygamy, with two or three relatively steady partners, helps account for the surprising slowdown. Paradoxically, economic crisis has slowed transmission. As news of AIDS was spread, men remained increasingly faithful to their small circle of mistresses. Contacts with sex workers and other casual encounters diminished, as they became too expensive to maintain. At the same time, condom use increased, particularly among young educated men. Awareness campaigns targeted this group because men's risk increased with income. Educated men, for example, were much more likely to be infected than were unskilled workers.

Popular culture also spread the word. The prominent singer and celebrity Franco Luambo Makiadi warned of the risks of unsafe sex in his famous song 'Attention na sida' recorded in 1987. Franco knew what he was talking about: he died of AIDS two years later. By 1990, general awareness about AIDS was significant, even amongst Kinshasa's young and illiterate (Kamenga et al. 1991; Kyunga 1993).

New needs, expectations and strategies

HIV and other infectious diseases that threaten particularly vulnerable categories such as young children, teenagers and women create new health care needs. The growing numbers of elderly people who need chronic care also make up an important new group of patients. People suffering from rheumatic or cardiovascular diseases, increasingly present in Kinshasa, are poorly cared for, which is far from surprising when even in developed countries efficient care of chronic conditions like diabetes and hypertension is far from optimal.

Kinois prefer modern biomedical care in some cases. In emergencies such as car accidents or complicated deliveries, patients are brought to hospital when possible. Since actual demand and care-seeking behaviour are largely conditioned by the ability to pay cash for services, few Kinois can resort to first-choice solutions. Most family heads have adopted an extremely pragmatic and well-calculated approach to family survival strategies and opportunities. Strategic choices about health care (and other vital needs such as food, housing, clothing and education) are only made after the family head has shopped around and bargained to find the best deal.

Financial constraints force people to postpone professional care. In the early phases of a health problem, people try homemade remedies or drugs sold in makeshift neighbourhood pharmacies. These pharmacies are sometimes little more than roadside stands. People rarely seek professional help until they become seriously incapacitated, highlighting the subjectivity surrounding the notion of good health. Enjoying good health certainly has different meanings for a poor Kinois and a middle-class European or American. Sick people in Kinshasa endure pain, misery and suffering. When things get really bad, especially when small children or pregnant women are concerned, they will actively search for a cure. If they can find enough money for the fee required by most medical facilities (usually thanks to credit associations or family) and if time allows, choice is influenced by earlier experiences, or the advice of respected family members, neighbours, older women or midwives.

Most Kinois, however, have no other choice but to turn to a poorly staffed and underequipped public service. With their typical irony Kinois have labelled these places *lieux de la mort* (places of death). Patients who go there on their own or who are brought there by relatives know they are condemned. These people actually surrender themselves to dubious care providers. Health care has become another commodity in the Kinshasa marketplace. It is bartered just as any other good or service. Its commercialization in both the public and private sectors is cause and consequence of the rupture between technical aspects of care and its social, ritual and symbolic dimensions. For Congolese these dimensions have always been very present and very important.

Medical assistants enjoyed people's respect before and after independence, as did the various health workers involved in the promising primary-care experience of the 1970s. Whether these actors were aware of their symbolic power or not, most of them were truly caring and upheld a sense of social and professional responsibility appreciated by patients and their families. In today's Kinshasa, by contrast, caring and compassion are no longer medical priorities. Health workers are perceived as, and in reality have become, indifferent administrators of medical know-how seeking to deal with their own survival problems. This rupture helps explain why hordes of sick and disillusioned Kinois have turned to churches, charismatic cults and traditional healers in quest of healing. By rough estimates, Kinshasa's hundreds of prophetical or charismatic healing communes and churches may well comprise one-fifth of the capital's population, particularly those of matrilineal descent, such as the Kongo. More than 1 million people are thus involved.[6]

Historically, Kinshasa neighbourhoods were largely homogeneous socially and ethnically. Extending and receiving solidarity was a social norm. In the last two decades, new solidarity patterns have emerged, no longer based solely on tribal relationships or social status. People search for alliances with others they can rely on. As in the village, these new forms of solidarity are based on, for example, neighbourhood relations or a strong sense of mutual belonging, provided by community initiative or prayer groups.

Healing churches are an important and rapidly expanding dimension of this new solidarity. They also represent a significant response to failures in the modern health care system because they serve to heal both body and soul. Borrowing from both traditional and biblical elements, these church groups succeed in creating a new feeling of belonging for homeless youth, single mothers, uprooted migrants, the unemployed and disillusioned Kinois whose dreams of post-colonial modernity have not been met. They also provide a framework for giving sense and coping with hardship and suffering for thousands of people living in Kinshasa. Neighbourhood healing churches enact people's dependence upon one another. They transform the converts into agents, instead of humiliated subjects of the post-colonial state (Devisch 1996). These groups, comprising mainly women, combine spiritual sharing through prayer with solidarity at childbirth, funerals, neighbourhood sanitation, and protection from thieves. They help situate the despair of crisis in Kinshasa within a cultural and spiritual framework of solidarity.

Because they are related to the growing numbers of traditional healers (tradipraticiens), there is an important public health dimension to these healing churches. Approximately 1,000 traditional practitioners were already officially registered in Kinshasa by the late 1970s (Bibeau et al. 1979). Today the number has exploded. Traditional healers can be divided into two main categories. The most important category is women who make use of medicinal plants and substances such as water, clay, palm oil and ashes to treat a certain number of benign afflictions. The smaller second group is made up of mediumistic diviners who are consulted by both educated and illiterate people. In a trance-like state, these diviners (*nganga nkisi*) use ancestral tokens (*nkisi* or *fétiche*) to explain the root causes of health problems.

Typical afflictions treated by the first category of healers are *estomac* or *motema motu* (literally 'heartburn', but similar to gastritis), *mpasi ya mukongo* (back pain) and *mputa ya libumu* (literally 'wounds of the bowel', meaning rectal piles). The latter are often associated with impotence (Lapika 1989). Infertility and stillbirth, with their considerable psychological and social impact, are a major concern, and in Kinshasa female clients may have a long gynaecological record without the male partner having ever been seriously examined. The blame and shame of infertility are systematically put on women. Many of these women end up consulting a diviner, who tries to unravel the causal disturbance in the socio-cosmological universe (Devisch 1993). In many of these cases, biomedical approaches tend to bring only temporary relief because they do not address mental or relational factors. Explanations drawing on traditional and popular culture often seem to make more sense to those who suffer than modern forms of biomedicine.

To appeal to the growing number of Kinois born and bred in the city and unfamiliar with the ways of the village, these healers have modified discourse and practice by combining ingredients of biomedicine, Christian and Islamic liturgy, and modern media. They also combine ancestral witchcraft with Judeo-Christian notions of good and evil to explain health and social problems.

Perspectives

Despite major obstacles, national health authorities continue to play a leading role in the health-care sector. Health programmes and strategies are designed and selected in the capital by Congolese medical experts, despite the growing number of international actors involved in the Kinshasa health market. While local financial resources have been scarce for many years, authorities have still managed to influence how international funding has been spent, in large part because outside actors need the collaboration of Congolese authorities. Without an official Congolese stamp of approval, initiatives funded by foreign agencies and NGOs can easily be blocked or sabotaged.

Belgium's bilateral Cooperation Agency and other international partners, such as the World Health Organization and the United States Agency for International Development (USAID), have made major efforts in recent years to reorganize and reinforce the health sector by working with existing national structures. This approach was adopted to keep national health programmes coherent and consistent. Nonetheless, efficiency is far from optimal and low coverage within the official health system means that help benefits few Kinois. Given the poor performance of official health structures, WHO is currently putting in place a parallel strategy to be implemented by international and national experts.

Since the beginning of the second war, which started in 1998, most international NGOs prefer to work in rural areas of Congo, and particularly the east, because of the real and urgent medical needs of rural populations. Access to much of the country is, however, handicapped by the presence of hostile armed factions and poor road conditions. Many places can only be reached by plane. As a consequence, many NGOs have developed activities in the capital itself, which also has huge potential for humanitarian action. Since the late 1990s, the country has actively joined the Global Polio Eradication Program, supported by international agencies and private donors like the Bill Gates Foundation and Rotary International. While this is a justifiable worldwide priority, it creates imbalances in resource distribution in Kinshasa. Important human and financial resources are mobilized for this single particular activity without providing guarantees of a sustainable impact on national health services.

When Laurent Kabila came to power in 1997, the health department recruited serious and well-qualified technocrats. Under the current circumstances of war and continuing socio-economic crisis, most of their time and energy is spent addressing humanitarian calamities and responding to the most urgent problems to appease national and international public opinion. Official discourse emphasizes the Health Ministry's role as provider of public service and health care. In reality, however, its role has become one of coordination and balancing national priorities with the specific agendas of international donors and NGOs. Dependence on external financing creates new constraints and tensions. While logistical and financial support for specific programmes and activities proposed by international community are significant, they do not necessarily contribute to sustainable improvements in health-care delivery.

Health-care planners involved in development projects are currently contemplating the future roles and responsibilities of national health authorities, health workers, and their beneficiaries. How will they relate to each other and to the outside world in the future? How can health workers be reinserted in the social construct and regain people's confidence? The international community can help redress the public health sector, but significant change can only come from the Kinois themselves. In the meantime, they suffer. After centuries of slavery, seventy-five years of paternalistic colonial rule, and a generation sacrificed by dictatorship and failed transition, the public health situation in Congo has never been worse.

Notes

1. S. Vong, personal communication. The *Vibrion cholerae* bacterium, causal agent of the disease, has been found in up to 15 per cent of the Kinshasa open sewerage system.
2. African Press Agency (APA) wire, 10 September 2002, reporting on Programme National de Lutte contre le Sida estimations.
3. Studies reviewed by US Bureau of Census 2000.
4. United States Agency for International Development, www.usaid.gov/pop_health/aids/Countries/africa/congo_profile.pdf.
5. SIDA is the French acronym for AIDS.
6. René Devisch, personal communication.

6

The Diploma Paradox: University of Kinshasa between Crisis and Salvation

Télésphore Tsakala Munikengi and Willy Bongo-Pasi Moke Sangol

Higher education is one of many public services in the Democratic Republic of Congo characterized by the function–dysfunction paradox. Since the early 1980s, institutions have become physically dilapidated and intellectually undermined. Teaching and research capacity has declined in proportion to the shrinking and generally unpaid salaries of the academic faculty and staff. Despite this, all the actors involved in Congolese higher education, including relevant ministerial authorities, continue to assert the importance of university-level training to improve the country's development potential. In 1971, when the economy was still strong, the university system underwent an awkward, politically motivated revamping, but no one at the time seriously predicted such a rapid decline. The system is moribund today, but bankruptcy has been averted. At one level, the university has been saved by the commitment, sacrifice, pragmatism and resourcefulness of academics, administrators, students and their families. At another level, it has been salvaged because the actors involved use the university system as an opportunity to deal with the effects of the country's ongoing economic crisis. For them it is a means to achieve and capitalize on the social recognition associated with being an intellectual.

Students, academic staff and state authorities all have varying stakes in re-engineering the university system. How and why they do so is the subject of this chapter. The following analysis highlights the daily conditions of academic staff and students. It puts into perspective the challenges facing both decision-makers and Congolese youth, who will have to confront the crisis of university education before the imbalance between the 'educated' and the 'uneducated' becomes even more pronounced. While the facts and analysis presented here are largely limited to Kinshasa, the situation in the country's intellectual capital is largely representative of the function and dysfunction of universities in other Congolese cities, such as Lubumbashi, Kisangani and Mbuji-Mayi.

From Lovanium to UNAZA

Higher education has evolved rapidly in the Congo. The founding of Lovanium University in 1954 marked the birth of university education in the Congo. Inspired by its prestigious Roman Catholic namesake in the metropole, its task was to train an intellectual elite for the Belgian Congo. Its founding father, the Belgian Monsignor Luc Gillon, is credited with the university's institutional development and is still remembered as having been mentor to an entire class of Congolese intelligentsia (Gillon 1998). There were three universities at independence. Today there are more than a hundred university-level institutions. The handful of students in 1960 has grown into throngs of individuals motivated by the notion that a university diploma is the key to success, modernity and well-being. By the late 1980s, however, the race to Westernize through formal university education (as well as Christian conversion, work, urbanization, capitalist economic development and belief in the post-colonial nation-state model) was seriously put into question. This extremely rapid expansion deeply impacted on the institutions, seriously compromising the quality of teaching, research and funding, and giving rise to the conditions of dysfunction and delinquency that characterize the system today. Despite the crisis of the public and private institutions that award diplomas, the degrees themselves still remain important tickets of entrée into the shrinking but valued world of salaried employment. They signify their holders' status as intellectuals, nearly equivalent to European titles of nobility.

The first major university reform occurred in 1971. The National University of Zaire (UNAZA) was set up to regroup the three universities of Kinshasa, Lubumbashi and Kisangani and all the official Instituts Supérieurs (university-level training institutions). Lovanium was re-baptized University of Kinshasa (UNIKIN). This reform was more political than educational or administrative; its tone was characterized by a demagogy that forecast Mobutu's subsequent Return to Authenticity programme. Its primary aim was the training of patriotic, devoted, honest and militant Congolese who would adhere to the African values of solidarity and respect for authority (République du Zaïre 1996). The reform also emphasized that the best way to educate the Congolese was through the combined efforts of family, school and the Mouvement Populaire de la Révolution (MPR, or Revolutionary Popular Movement).

The MPR was the foundation of Mobutu's single-party state. University education and the politics of the single-party state were intimately intertwined. According to UNIKIN's first Congolese rector, Monsignor Tshibangu, this reform had the potentially positive effect of harmonizing the functioning of higher education establishments by standardizing curricula. In reality, he noted, it created an unmanageable bureaucracy and jurisdictional rivalries within the system's upper administrative levels (Tshibangu 1998). These problems, exacerbated by inadequate financial support and swelling student enrolments, led to the 1981 decentralization reform.

The 1981 reform claimed to re-establish the relative autonomy of higher education. Nonetheless, a single statute was elaborated to manage (i.e. straitjacket) the activities of all teaching, research, administrative and technical personnel across the country in both universities and other institutions. This led to confusion pertaining to the mandates and objectives of the two types of institution. It also created panic over pay scales by recalculating wages and benefits in ways that disregarded status and longevity in both recruitment and promotions. Traditional criteria for evaluating academic achievement were minimized, creating a new disincentive to pursue an academic career.

By the mid-1980s, these failed reforms, coupled with an inability to keep up with increased enrolments and inexorably shrinking financing from the Ministry of Higher Education, left Congolese higher education at an impasse. The idea of elaborating a master plan for university training was abandoned.

Mobutu's call for Africanization of the university system, a leitmotiv throughout much of Africa in the 1960s and 1970s, negatively impacted on the system's financial management and quality of training. Rhetoric was not supported by an appropriate redefinition of curriculum or harmonization with new development needs and social reality (Crossman 1999: 12). While Congolese intellectuals in this period thought themselves to be in touch with developments outside of the country, thanks to research and travel grants to Europe, the university system actually devolved in an introverted manner.

Financial constraints: creative responses

The degradation of the Congolese political economy has had obvious negative implications for the university system. The budget for all levels of education in the Congo has declined steadily over the years. In 1960, it represented 15 per cent of the national budget; today it is less than 1 per cent. Until the early 1990s the state budget constituted the major source of university financing, covering salaries, maintenance, overheads and some symbolic investment for research. Except for sporadic payment of salaries, there has been a clear state withdrawal from the sector since then. The authorities have justified this withdrawal by pointing to the overall economic crisis, but Congolese see the problem as an inability of the state to respect its social responsibilities. Academics have consequently been forced to find their own solutions to salvage the university system and slow down the degradation of Congolese training and education. In these efforts they were primarily motivated by the need to preserve their own jobs.

A partial solution to financing problems was found by 'privatizing' the system, mainly by introducing student tuition fees. The initiative referred to as 'salvaging the academic year' first appeared at UNIKIN in 1994 and was subsequently applied in the country's other universities. UNIKIN's academic 'year' is now eighteen months because academic staff are unable to offer their courses in the traditionally shorter period. This is representative of time management in Kinshasa in general. Lack of money, materials and infrastructure has contributed to an all-encompassing lethargy that slows everything down.

Students and parents are now the primary source of financing for what officially remains a state-run system. This has ended the once sacrosanct principle of free university education for all. The cost of tuition in Kinshasa's universities varies from $60 to $160 per year depending on the institution. Although autonomously created by the staffs of different state institutions, political authorities in the educational sector have tacitly accepted this financing strategy. If they had not, the universities would have had to close. The strategy was designed as a short-term, ad hoc solution but has turned into a permanent one with unexpected side effects. The state has disengaged even more since state officials have seen the system reinvent itself without state funds. When the state does in fact intervene, it is more as a repressive force than as an organizational support.

Although the observation is clearly applicable to the whole gamut of state–society relations in the Congo, there are a number of specific examples in the area of higher education. The most flagrant example pertains to tenure and promotion decisions. Since the 1990s governmental nominations have been politically motivated. Academic credentials and seniority have been disregarded, creating considerable disaffection within the academic staff. Authorities also carry out regular inspections aimed at intimidating what are perceived as troublesome intellectuals. They have also impeded financing initiatives and the pursuit of international development aid.

Since the 1996–97 academic year there have been nearly 26,000 registered students at the university.[1] The institution can actually absorb far fewer. Under normal circumstances there should be approximately 5,000 students at UNIKIN. In 2001 UNIKIN had 25,886 students, 482 teaching staff and 795 assistants. The male to female ratio is approximately three to one. The student to teacher ratio is twenty to one, well below UNESCO recommendations. Without these additional students, however, the institution would be unable to survive financially. UNIKIN administrators refer to the process as massification. This process has replaced the former elitist policy. Tuition fees for these student 'masses' vary between $120 and $160, depending on their department and status as graduate or undergraduate. The bulk of the tuition is paid at the beginning of the academic year and the remainder prior to the examination period. Fees must be paid in dollars, given inflation and low esteem for the Congolese franc.

These fees cover the bulk of UNIKIN's operating costs. The state did, however, provide $2.3 million for the 1996–97 academic year and approximately $1.8 million for the 1998–99 academic year. With fees paid by the students and funds provided by the state, UNIKIN has income of approximately $200 per student. This is well below the minimum baseline of $1,000, advocated by UNESCO to guarantee a satisfactory level of instruction in African universities.

The marginalization of education in the national budget and the government's failure to respect its commitments have virtually eliminated the positive initiatives taken by teachers and families to save the university system. For the university authorities this is a major problem, for without a reliable source of revenue decision-making becomes arbitrary and inefficient, undermining the university administration's credibility even further. During Laurent Désiré Kabila's rule, it was argued that all available financial resources were needed for the war effort. There has been no improvement under his successor, even though the mobilization of funds to conduct the war has diminished.

A full professor at UNIKIN earned approximately $170 per month in 2002. The official salary paid by the state is $30. The difference is a university bonus (*prime*). This bonus money comes from the fees paid directly by the student body. Teaching assistants earned approximately $60. Senior-level administrators earn less than $100. The UNIKIN financial department strictly controls tuition payment and collaborates with the personnel department to pay staff. To make ends meet, teachers work in more than one institution, take on other non-academic side jobs, or, if they have any savings, engage in small-scale trade. These living and working conditions translate into high absenteeism and a general lack of motivation. Students are the first victims because the quality of education declines.

Kinshasa academics are not naive about the prospects seeing their salary situation improve, and as a consequence they have taken the situation into their own hands, *à la* Kinois. They have sought alternative forms of material and non-material compensation. Some sell their own course material: they earn extra money and the students who pay this indirect tax are guaranteed better exam results than those who do not purchase the material. Bartering sex for exam points, although certainly not unique to Congo, is practised extensively in Kinshasa. Discourse about the practice is particularly interesting: girls who pass with good marks are accused by their peers of having slept with their teachers; those who fail say that it is because they refused to do so. Ethnic and regional favouritism can easily be transformed into social debt to benefit a teacher. Discourse on success and failure also reflects the influence of ethnicity: Kasaien students, for example, do well because of the preponderance of Kasaien teachers.

Travel by academics, like that of non-academics, is always used to supply goods and material that are desperately lacking in Kinshasa.

Academics travelling abroad to attend a conference often use their expense allowance to buy material that will generate earnings back home. A computer purchase, for example, enables them to set up a typing service for students. Acquisition of a video camera is an investment that can produce income by filming graduation ceremonies or weddings.

The state's failure to meet the financial needs of Kinshasa's universities during the Kabila *père* years was partially compensated by the Committees of Popular Powers (Comités du Pouvoir Populaire, CPPs). The CPP was a political structure created by the president and controlled directly by him. During the 1998–99 academic year, the CPP invested in the rehabilitation of UNIKIN infrastructure with positive results. The CPP subsequently failed to deliver on other promises, and monthly subsidies of $400,000 mysteriously disappeared.

The institutional context

Congo's entire university system is intimately linked to the city of Kinshasa, home to the country's oldest and largest institution. UNIKIN is referred to as Mont Amba, after the area on the southern fringe of the city where the 5-square kilometre campus is located. Despite major handicaps, UNIKIN is still the Congolese model of university education, influencing university life throughout the country. Its problems are representative of how other institutions function in the country.

In addition to UNIKIN, Kinshasa has eleven other state institutions of higher learning: one college (Institut Facultaire des Sciences de l'Information et de la Communication, IFASIC), three teacher-training institutes (Instituts Supérieurs Pédagogiques, ISPs) and seven technical institutes (Instituts Supérieurs Techniques, ISTs). The twelve institutions have a total student body of approximately 80,000. They employ nearly 3,000 academic staff and researchers, or approximately 80 per cent of the country's academics, 60 per cent of which are at UNIKIN. There are also twenty private, generally denominational, institutions of higher education in Kinshasa. The more important ones are the Catholic College of Kinshasa (Facultés Catholiques de Kinshasa), the Protestant University of Congo (Université Protestante du Congo), the William Booth University, the Simon Kimbangu

University and an agro-veterinary college (Institut Supérieur Agro-Vétérinaire).

Almost all university personnel working in Kinshasa today are Congolese. A significant expatriate teaching community worked there until the early 1990s, but once the West withdrew political support for Mobutu, expatriate academics (other than a number of Jesuit fathers) saw their funding sources dry up and left the country. The impact was particularly harsh because financial contributions to the teaching institutions were also cut. Important skills were lost when qualified expatriates were replaced by less qualified nationals, in many cases for political reasons. Funding for equipment, documentation, scholarships or training abroad disappeared. As a result of expatriate departures, imbalances in the quality of teaching and research became increasingly apparent both nationally (largely to the benefit of Kinshasa) and within institutions and even departments. With minimum funding Kinshasa academics entered a phase of isolation and were unable to take advantage of new information technologies. Only since 2000 have Internet connections become relatively available and people had email addresses. As Internet connections remain scarce at UNIKIN facilities, cybernet boutiques (which also offer phone services) provide students and teachers access to cyberspace.

A number of factors help explain the concentration of academic personnel in Kinshasa. UNIKIN's primary rival, UNILU (University of Lubumbashi), lost students and teachers who relocated to Kinshasa (as well as to South Africa) after violence between students and security forces on the UNILU campus in 1990. The incident, with its loss of life,[2] became a pretext for the West to proscribe a failing dictator who had lost his *raison d'être* after the fall of the Berlin Wall. It marked the beginning of the end of Western development cooperation with Zaire. In the early 1990s there were also inter-ethnic conflicts in Katanga, the province where UNILU is based. Provincial Governor Kyungu Wa Ku Mwanza mobilized 'native' Katangans to expel Luba back to Kasai. Many traders, academics and other professionals were part of this ethnic cleansing (Bakajika Banjikil 1997). In 1995 UNIKIN reintegrated the College of Social Science, which had been transferred to UNILU in 1971, siphoning off staff from UNILU. Since 1998, the war in the East has also contributed to this brain drain towards the capital. Economic degradation in the provinces was yet another factor that forced academics to the capital. There at least they could hope to find badly needed forms of complementary employment. As a consequence of this movement, the teacher to student ratio outside the capital has widened even more sharply than in Kinshasa's institutions.

Most Kinshasa teachers work in more than one institution. They are consequently overloaded with teaching responsibilities and unable to keep their courses up to date through research. UNIKIN provides the majority of these roving academics who teach in other institutions. They benefit from the relative prestige of being affiliated with the country's largest institution. For the newer private institutions, this prestige improves the value of diplomas and attracts paying students.

The constant need to combine activities to make ends meet, given low and sporadic academic pay, has deformed the aspirations of teachers and researchers. It distorts the objectives of higher education and whatever academic values Kinshasa educators may still cling to. This has become more manifest as ageing academics come to be replaced. As the older academics who received sound training in the early years of independence leave the university system, they are replaced by colleagues with less experience, fewer academic credentials and less attachment to the values associated with academic life. An alarming qualitative gap between older educators and their replacements has been the result.

Interviews with UNIKIN professors in May of 2001 reveal bitterness and frustration concerning the state's lack of support for higher education. Their litany of complaints includes problems about financing, mismanagement of public funds, and having to use their own money when they do carry out research (Ndundu 2001). Because the government decided to suspend granting pensions to retiring professors in 1990, the average age of academic staff at UNIKIN is high: 54 years old. Without pensions, professors cannot afford to retire. Although lacking motivation, they continue to teach. The government also stopped paying widows' pensions and end-of-career bonuses, further contributing to making an academic career less attractive.

Academics complain that the government does not respect their work. When the government does consult them, it seeks to legitimize politically motivated decisions rather than acquire expertise. This, of course, is reminiscent of the way Mobutu co-opted the country's most brilliant intellectuals, men like Maître Nimy (Mobutu's *chef de cabinet*), Professor Mpinga (prime minister under Mobutu many times) and Dominique Sakombi (MPR communication guru), into the MPR.

The student

Until the 1980s, students believed their university diplomas were equivalent to titles of nobility. Initiation into the world of academia was a crucial step towards social respectability (Rubbers 2003: 26–8). Graduation ceremonies testify to this symbolic rite of passage. By the early 1990s, however, students were brutally confronted with a new reality. Although degrees still constituted social capital, and an argument if a job opportunity did miraculously present itself, they no longer ensured automatic recruitment. In the context of all-encompassing crisis, degrees were rendered useless in helping their holders 'escape the world of the profane' (Rubbers 2002: 35).

A phenomenon now observable in Kinshasa's colleges and universities is the significant number of students who drop out before graduation. Many Congolese try their luck at university but few succeed. Since the late 1990s, approximately 120,000 individuals have graduated from secondary school in the Congo each year. This figure is remarkably low for a country with approximately 55 million people, half of whom are less than 15 years old. Although the country's university system cannot absorb more than 20,000 students because of institutional constraints, nearly 120,000 register at university. Table 6.1 shows that law and medicine are the largest colleges at UNIKIN, followed by other disciplines that allow students to dream of entering a white-collar profession. The UNIKIN distribution is representative of student choices elsewhere in the Congo (Rubbers 2002: graph 8).

There are several explanations for the university's high drop-out rate. They include, for example, the poor selection of students, for those who can afford the fees are not necessarily the most motivated. The decreasing quality of secondary-school education and the poor quality of instruction at the university itself also contribute. Over the years the image of the student as a model for Congolese youth has consequently tarnished. As in the past, students today are considered a category on their own. For both the political establishment and the population, they are perceived as being capable of the best (an elite with leadership capacity giving voice to popular sentiment)

Table 6.1   Enrolment, academic year 1999–2000

College	Enrolment
Law	7,212
Medicine	6,338
Social Science, Politics and Management	3,725
Economy	3,285
Science	1,378
Liberal Arts	1,139
Psychology and Education	953
Agronomy	728
Polytechnic	566
Pharmacy	562
Total	25,886

Source: Financial Department, UNIKIN, 2001.

and the worst (intellectual troublemakers, political instigators). For UNIKIN authorities, students are increasingly perceived as threats to the established order because they contest the way the university is run. In response to student demonstrations over tuition increases in January of 2002, soldiers entered the UNIKIN campus to re-store order. Four soldiers were killed in the fighting. The image of students as troublemakers is reminiscent of white sentiment during the colonial period when every Congolese youth was perceived as a potential delinquent (Biaya 2001). Conversely, students accuse the UNIKIN authorities of blaming the victim and place responsibility for university dysfunction on government and university authorities. For the students, these events are representative of the combat they must wage to earn their degrees.

Despite these problems, and the low probability of finding salaried work in one's field of study, many parents continue to dream of a university diploma for their children. Families strive to have at least one graduate who will add to its prestige and help it financially. Until only recently, Congolese families that had children studying in Europe or North America urged them to finish their degrees quickly and return home. Today, they urge their graduates to find jobs abroad so they can send money home.[3] The students themselves are willing to brook all kinds of material and moral hardship in order to realize this dream. Though chimerical in most cases, the status of being an intellectual justifies the sacrifice. If a student fails (*abuka bic*: literally he/she broke his/her pen, in Lingala), he or she complains that the university should nonetheless award a degree to testify to the hardship endured on the university battlefield. Failing is a tragedy for both student and family, but a tragedy justified by the host of difficulties students go through.

Living conditions are a major hardship for students. Of the approximately 80,000 students in Kinshasa, 90 per cent live off-campus. UNIKIN has only room for 2,000 residents; none of the other institutions has housing for more than 200. Although relatively few students thus live on campus, it is useful to have some impression of their living conditions. Student rooms frequently house four or five times the number officially allowed. Some students opt to live on campus to get away from their parents. Others claim that they cannot afford transportation between home and campus. The paucity of taxis and mini-buses, moreover, means that a two-hour commute, one way, is not uncommon. Those travelling from outside Kinshasa may have no other choice. In the past, students coming from the provinces could stay with a Kinshasa-based parent, but today, given the economic crisis, this form of 'traditional' hospitality has diminished. People simply do not have the financial capacity to share. University authorities turn a blind eye to the overcrowded dormitories, referred to as *maquis*. The French term has the connotation of being an inextricable and difficult predicament, generally in a war environment.

This overpopulation is the root cause of a number of serious public-health problems. Access to water is inadequate and bodily hygiene is sacrificed. Worse, plastic bags tend to be used as chamber pots and are discarded with little regard for elementary sanitation. For a number of months in 2001, 7,000 dormitory residents shared a mere seven toilets! Since the university cafeterias closed in the early 1980s, students cook and eat in their rooms, but there is insufficient water to clean up and there is no waste removal service. Cases of cholera, typhoid fever and sexually transmitted disease are frequent on campus.

Student views of professors are ambivalent. They are respectful and critical at the same time. Ndundu Nkayamene (2001) has studied UNIKIN student perceptions of their teachers. While referring to teachers in terms of respect which imply intelligence, wisdom and leadership (*mwalimu, nganga mayele, moto ya bwana, moyangeli, molakisi* and *moteyi*), students also claim teachers abuse their positions for personal aggrandisement: they are greedy for money and bargain their academic expertise to secure political appointments. Reliance on inexperienced teaching assistants is yet another frequently heard complaint. Others say it is normal that professors be underpaid because they are already lucky enough to have received intelligence from God. Jealousy is a very powerful emotion in Kinshasa, where all forms of symbolic, social or material wealth are coveted.

Beyond jealousy, there is also a sour grapes attitude harboured by those who failed to get their degrees but succeeded economically by fending for themselves. These are the graduates of the college of hard knocks. Hence the sentiment in some quarters that 'study and erudition are useless' or 'prestige without wealth is only false prestige' revealed by the following local expressions:

- *Français, frangani* (Can you turn French into francs?). Speaking French correctly is a prerequisite to being considered an intellectual.
- *Nakolia yo* (Am I going to eat you?). A common Lingala expression that in this context means 'all of your fancy intellectual talk can't put food on the table'.
- *Léisa mpunda, mpunda aleisa yo* (Feed your horse and he'll feed you). This Lingala expression was first used in the community of horse-racing gamblers. Today it is a wheeling and dealing expression that can be interpreted as meaning 'one hand rubs the other'.
- *Toka weyi, masikini* (Get lost! you're poor). A Swahili expression adopted by Kinois, meaning 'A teacher who only teaches will always be poor. You have to wheel and deal to get ahead.

University health care

One trademark of Kinois survival strategies, as revealed throughout this volume, is the combination of various activities. People cleverly capitalize on whatever assets they have. The UNIKIN College of Medicine staff are no exception. To compensate for low salaries, they make ends meet by taking advantage of the reputation, infrastructure and clientele of the university health service. This clientele comprises poor students and underpaid faculty because people from the crowded residential areas of the city avoid the university facilities. Mama Yemo, for example, the city's largest hospital, is centrally located and more accessible to an urban population that experiences serious public transportation problems. The arrangement suits university authorities because the health service compensates students for the poor quality of instruction and unpleasant campus environment.

Primary health care is administered at the Centre de Santé Universitaire. More serious health problems are addressed at the Centre Hospitalier du Mont Amba (CHMA), the Cliniques Universitaires and the Centre Neuro-Psycho-Pathologique (CNPP). Although well-qualified medical specialists are associated with these centres, they are handicapped by an insufficiency of investment and materials. Financial self-sufficiency is impossible because patients are too poor to pay for Western standards of good health (see Persyn and Ladrière in this volume). Patients tend to barter instead of paying cash for services. The medical staff take advantage of this by offering patients cheaper fees in their own off-campus private clinics. With typical Kinshasa logic, they justify this abuse of position by arguing that if they did not divert clients, money would be embezzled by UNIKIN clinic administrators (Ndaywel 2002: 144).

Thus far unsuccessful, efforts to set up a cooperative health-care fund for staff at the university have been ongoing for the past ten years. Thanks to the efforts of a European Union-funded local NGO (Horison-Santé), however, a student cooperative fund was set up in 1999. This improved access to service at the primary health Centre de Santé Universitaire. The centre now treats approximately fifty students a day. Malaria is the most commonly treated problem, followed by sexually transmitted diseases and intestinal parasites.

Perspectives

The rehabilitation of higher education in the Congo depends on modification of its governing statutes, new financing strategies, new management approaches, and updating curricula. Prerequisite as a foundation for this is an improved political and economic context. So long as the present crisis persists, the university will remain a bargaining arena. Bilateral and multilateral development aid is a key element for improving the state of university financing. It can help pay for operating costs (notably salaries), local and international scholarships, modernizing and rehabilitating infrastructure, and launching new research projects. African intellectuals have to be careful, however, not to fall into the trap of Western scientific superiority (Tuhiwai Smith 1999). During the process of reinvention of the Congolese university system, it will be crucial to strike a balance between the pertinence of local indigenous knowledge and the priorities of Western donors and partners.

Partnerships with local industries and commercial enterprises could also help. The benefits and responsibilities of research and training could be shared. Tax incentives could stimulate private capital to invest in the evolution of higher education. Unfortunately, the country's economic outlook will have to become more optimistic before this idea can take root (Bumba 1999). If the state resumes responsibility for financing the university system, it should also envisage granting greater management flexibility. This flexibility is badly needed with respect to seeking outside funding and re-establishing an efficient student–teacher ratio by reducing the number of students. Without greater state funding this imbalance will not diminish. Another strategy is through the support of private institutions of higher learning. Whatever options are chosen, it is difficult to imagine the state not being a key actor in the financial future of the sector.

Updating the legal framework of university management is another major challenge, because current rules and regulations are completely obsolete. Despite numerous efforts to reform the sector, mainly by granting institutions greater management autonomy, the state has systematically undermined them. Theoretically the state still wants to maintain control of higher education. It is able to do so by doubling up the roles of university teachers and administrators who are co-opted into the higher education ministries. The need for autonomy is crucial at the administrative level (recruitment and dismissal of staff), at the academic level (recruitment of students and curriculum) and at the cooperation level (signing agreements and contracts and hiring expatriate personnel). Without a greater level of autonomy, Congo's educational institutions will be unable to make an academic career attractive.

A further challenge pertains to harmonizing university services and products with the new priorities associated with globalization and the evolution of the international political environment. For the moment, the Congo's higher education system is completely unable to modernize because of political and financial constraints.

The curriculum is geared neither to the job market nor to the new socio-cultural realities of the country and beyond. The curriculum to train managers of small-scale companies, for which there are major demands, is simply not adapted to the country's needs. Part of the problem stems from the Congo's relative isolation in terms of information. Congolese academic and university administrators have not been able to take advantage of new information technologies until recently. In this relatively inward-looking system, universities do little more than award diplomas without worrying about the quality of training and instruction given to their graduates. The result is un- or under-employed graduates.

Conclusion: 'My pen is my shovel'

Congo's higher education system is in crisis, but like many other areas of public life it has miraculously avoided bankruptcy. Its hobbled survival can be attributed to the resourcefulness of an academic staff that has so far agreed to work, *faute de mieux*, in an environment that is intellectually diminished, financially strapped and politically dubious. This survival can also be attributed to the attachment of Congolese youth and intellectuals to the image of the university diploma, even though they are increasingly critical and sceptical about the future of what was once perceived as an avenue leading to prestige and well-being. New avenues to social recognition and wealth, like digging for diamonds or coltan, or the wheeling and dealing described by Nzeza (this volume), are gradually replacing the perceived need for a degree. The phenomenon is described clearly by the famous Kinshasa singer J.B. Mpiana, who sings of the fortunes and misfortunes of disillusioned Congolese youth who dig for diamonds in Angola: 'We've studied but our diplomas are collecting dust at home ... my pen is my shovel, my notebook is my mining pan.'[4]

Despite increasing scepticism about the future of the university system, it is clear that the financial arrangements invented and implemented by the professionals of higher education in the early 1990s were able to keep it afloat in the difficult years of democratic transition that overlapped with the twilight of the Mobutu regime. There has been little evolution under the more recent governments of Kabila *père* and *fils*. These arrangements have, however, fallen short of imagining a university system without the paradoxical involvement of the Congolese state. On the contrary, the limits of these arrangements reveal that state intervention is still very much part of the academic agenda. Over the years, the state, academics and students have accommodated themselves to a problem-ridden but workable modus vivendi. It is not, however, a system well adapted to the pressing needs of Congo's future.

Notes

Translated by Theodore Trefon.

1. Unless stated otherwise, figures in this chapter about UNIKIN were provided by the rector's office.
2. Although there was violence and at least one person killed when soldiers intervened on the campus in response to a fight between Rose Baramoto (daughter of General Baramoto, who was a key Mobutist figure) and other students, observers agree that to refer to this as the 'Lumumbashi massacre' is an exaggeration.
3. The spread of Western Union is an indicator of the importance of these remittances (Sumata 2002).
4. The song 'Bana Luunda' has been transcribed and analysed by De Boeck (2001b) and Sabakinu (2001).

Acting on Behalf (and in Spite) of the State: NGOs and Civil Society Associations in Kinshasa

Marco Giovannoni, Theodore Trefon, Jérôme Kasongo Banga, Charles Mwema

The NGOization of Kinshasa

The number of civil society associations, nongovernmental organizations (NGOs) and community-based solidarity networks exploded in Kinshasa in the early 1990s. Since then they have become vital components of the survival strategies invented by Kinois to replace the state in many areas of public life. The phenomenon developed because the country was in crisis and people had to reinvent order to survive. Congolese in general, and Kinois in particular, had lost hope in Mobutism and were frustrated by the fiction of democratic transition. They referred to basic public services as memories. In response they invented their own solutions, based primarily on friendship, professional, neighbourhood and religious ties. Ethnicity, once the foundation of associational life in Leopoldville and Kinshasa, is steadily losing its meaning as new needs and opportunities emerge. Kinshasa's association phenomenon exemplifies people-based social organization driven by pragmatism and the will to survive.

This powerful internal motivation for social invention was boosted by an external one: Zaire's international support came to an abrupt end in the early 1990s. Mobutu's erstwhile backers officially claimed that violence at the University of Lubumbashi in May of 1990 and the failed democratization process were the reasons for ending assistance. In reality, however, the dictator had outlived his usefulness following the collapse of the Soviet Union. After being a trusted ally for twenty-five years, Mobutu had become an embarrassment

(Wrong 2000). International development aid fell, as a result, from $898 million in 1990 to less than $200 million in 1993. By 1998 the amount had dropped to $126 million (André and Luzolele 2001). Recently, the trend towards cutting aid has reversed: in mid-2002 commitments have reached nearly US$1 billion, mainly from the World Bank and IMF.

The objective of this chapter is to analyse how and why these associations and NGOs were constituted, emphasizing their evolution, typology and functioning. Their paradoxical and complicated relations with the state and with the international community are also described. While the association and NGO phenomenon has a unique meaning in Kinshasa, its mechanisms and dynamics are similar to those in other African cities. The particularity of Kinshasa is the utter dependence that Kinois have on these new forms of social organization. Without them, life would be even more difficult than it is today. Given the degree of crisis in Kinshasa, it is possible the association phenomenon there may presage new forms of social organization in other cities that are increasingly confronted by new, economic, social and political challenges.

The need to get things done in the absence of public services is the primary reason why Kinois, like people living in other ostensibly ungoverned and ungovernable societies, form associations. They form NGOs, in contrast, because these provide access to international funding opportunities. This obviously simplified dichotomy needs to be explained, for there are a number of interconnected and overlapping reasons that cause Kinois to pursue both forms of social organization. Given the degree of un- and under-employment in the city, participating in an association or NGO provides hope of moving from voluntary work to gainful employment. In a society where people are forced to multiply their chances of opportunity (to find food, work, psychological sustenance), the NGO is just one more card to play. Beyond mere hope, associations and NGOs help people increase their self-esteem because work in them relieves the social burden associated with idleness. Associations and NGOs can also improve people's reputations within the community when their activities are socially useful.

In contrast to the perception of more traditional associations, Kinshasa NGOs are also identified with modernity. Although the NGO phenomenon is seen as being foreign and imported, Kinois increasingly speak of NGOization as a new form of social organization. The Kinois who farms on the outskirts of the city is apt to say that he has an agricultural NGO, opposed to merely saying that he is growing manioc to feed the family! Kinois also perceive NGOization as a new form of cultural and material dependence, given the NGO's role as the dominant model for international development aid currently in vogue (Crewe and Harrison 1998). The NGO is, in this context, both myth and nightmare.

'Association' here, as opposed to 'NGO', refers to entities that have been created by Kinois themselves with their own resources to address their own specific priorities. They are part of the internal dynamics of social organization. Common forms manifested in Kinshasa today are *likelemba* and *muziki* (Ntambwe 1983). The phenomenon encompasses all of the visible and invisible dimensions of society ranging from access to credit to the circulation of ideas and aspirations (O'deye 1985: 5). It is also a historic process intimately linked to Kinshasa's urbanization. Benoit Verhaegen (1970) documented pre-political associations based on ethnic and regional origins, professions, and school relations in colonial Leopoldville. Suzanne Comhaire-Sylvain (1968) traced the evolution of women's associations in the capital from 1945 to 1965. Pascal Elengesa Ndunguna (1997) identified leisure associations (sports, fashion and music) dating back to the 1920s and analysed their social transformation.

'NGO' has a somewhat different connotation and pertains to externally generated support structures. The distinction between association and NGO is nonetheless ambiguous because there is considerable overlap between the two. Their characteristics and motivations are often quite similar, as many associations transformed themselves into NGOs in the hope of benefiting from donor funding.

Millions of Kinois are members of at least one association or NGO. In the spirit of multiplying opportunities, many belong to different ones simultaneously. Because they are so diverse and numerous, Kinois joke, if the presidents of every association and NGO in the capital were to meet, the Palais du Peuple would not be big enough! Although it is impossible to quantify their exact number, Elikia M'Bokola has recently alluded to 1,322 NGOs (2002: 10). The number of solidarity groups is considerably higher. Many Kinshasa intellectuals today believe that associations will be in a far better position than the state to help them find peace, improved quality of life, democracy and perhaps even poverty alleviation in the years to come.

NGO Relations with the state

Despite increasing pressure on Mobutu in the early 1990s, many international and bilateral organizations continued their activities in Zaire, focusing on the allegedly politically neutral sectors of health, food security and education. To continue their work, and to reach the people most urgently needing this aid, the international community established partnerships with associations and NGOs. There were few other options given pressure to exclude the state, even though this strategy never really succeeded. The responsibility for managing development and humanitarian aid consequently shifted away from state partners to civil society partners. International NGOs and donors had to identify serious and reliable local structures to serve as intermediaries between the international community and local populations. This was crucial because navigating the bureaucratic, complex and ostensibly chaotic Kinshasa landscape is practically impossible without local partners. In many cases international NGOs created local ones to implement their projects.

Relations between the state and international NGOs became particularly complicated. Because the international community chose not to work with the Mobutist state, it normally should not have continued working with staff of decentralized state services. Nonetheless, people like school principals, doctors in officially state-run health clinics, and state agronomists working on food security projects continued to be valuable intermediaries, and it was not easy to establish working relations with these resource people without involving their ministerial hierarchy. While the problem was easier to avoid in rural areas where state meddling was less present, doing so in Kinshasa could not be done without respecting administrative procedures. Despite a policy of not working with the state, some international NGOs made official agreements with administrative authorities to facilitate specific programme priorities.

The health sector offers a clear example. The European Union (EU), via its health programme, Programme Appui Transitoire à la Santé (PATS), provided funding to European NGOs[1] to support decentralized health facilities (Zones de Santé) without working directly with the Health Ministry itself. The NGOs supplied and distributed pharmaceutical products, trained medical assistants, provided logistical support, contributed to operating costs and even helped pay the salaries of ministerial health workers in the form of bonuses (*les primes*). The irony of this arrangement is that the EU, in conjunction with the international NGOs that implemented its programmes, reinforced the upper echelons of the Health Ministry, which inevitably claimed credit for the work being carried out by their decentralized agents. The loyalty of these agents, moreover, while manifested towards the NGOs that pay their salaries, is also directed to their hierarchical chiefs, with whom they maintain complex patron–client relations.

In another form of ambiguous state–NGO relations, local and international NGOs use the state administration as a reservoir from which qualified personnel can be recruited or state infrastructure obtained. Employees of the Ministry of Public Works, the National Rice Programme or the National Seed Service, for example, are frequently recruited and put under contract by these NGOs because their expertise corresponds to NGO or donor priorities. In some cases, their buildings or facilities are also rented by the NGO.

State officials were quick to criticize donors for providing NGOs with funds destined to improve the living conditions of the Congolese people without involving political authorities in the decision-making process or choice of priorities, especially when ministerial employees would be used. This remains an important but unresolved debate among development strategists. The Kinshasa experience reveals that it is not a question of supporting either the state *or* civil society. The real problem is how to support both state *and* civil society. Even in what is perceived as a failed state, like the Congo, results are best achieved by dealing with both. This option has pragmatic benefits because it has maintained qualified staff in their agencies. Without such support, these people would probably have been forced to engage in other survival activities having nothing to do with their areas of competence. Outside funding used to rent state infrastructure, such as buildings, also had the pragmatic benefit of slowing down their deterioration.

Despite the advantages of this type of accommodation, a number of problems resulted. The system provoked rivalries and tensions among state employees: those who worked for an externally funded project earned much more than those who did not. A skilled worker like an agronomist or doctor can earn $300 a month with an international NGO, and up to $1,500 with an international body such as the EU, United Nations, World Health Organization or Food and Agricultural Organization. This contrasts sharply with the $20 to $30 they earn as a ministry employee. Such salary imbalances disrupt the work environment, for the best workers neglect their administrative functions if they find NGO work. In addition to creating rivalries *within* ministries, this system also creates rivalries *between* ministries. Not all administrative sectors are priorities for externally funded projects, so those unable to tap into NGO wealth are left to fend for themselves.

Another serious problem results from the resentment of state officials who were not able to find NGO work. They have become bitter opponents of NGOs and do whatever they can to sabotage or hamper projects being set up. As most NGO projects will eventually need some kind of official bureaucratic support in the form of authorization, information or conflict resolution between workers, a bitter bureaucrat can easily enjoy revenge at some point. The problem is so widespread that it constitutes one of the major preoccupations of project officers. To circumvent the problem, NGO project officers try to co-opt senior officials by involving them early in a project. This again contributes to the paradox of state workers participating in or implementing NGO activities.

Despite the relatively low sense of state found at the ministerial level, officials tend to perceive NGOs as troublesome rivals or unfair competitors. Officials and NGOs compete when funding mechanisms allow government agencies to bid for contracts. They also compete for recognition. During the Mobutu transition and the government of Laurent Kabila, this type of competition was not very pronounced. Now that Joseph Kabila is trying to improve his relations with the Western donor community and encourage donors to support state institution building, this competition has become a serious handicap. At the same time, authorities are increasingly accepting NGOs as useful partners. A spirit of cooperation between officials and NGOs paradoxically exists alongside the atmosphere of tension and rivalry.

There are other problems that flow from the intermingling of state and NGO activity. In recent years, officials have asked NGOs for humanitarian aid to provide assistance after the August/September 1998 Kinshasa war, and after the November 1999 floods when thousands of people were displaced (and many killed), and to provide medical assistance following the explosion at Ndjili airport in early 2000. When large amounts of money reached Kinshasa to respond to these crises, however, there was a problem of absorption capacity: there were not enough experienced NGOs to deal with the demands.

NGOs have also experienced serious problems with traditional authorities (*le pouvoir coutumier*), particularly in the Kinshasa hinterland where numerous initiatives are being carried out in the food security and health sectors. Governance in these areas is extremely complex. Even during the highly centralized Mobutu years, a hybrid power-sharing arrangement between state and traditional authority was maintained. The presence of new administrative structures in the politically complex Kinshasa periphery threatens the authority and credibility of traditional chiefs, especially when the NGO or project officers lack understanding of this hybrid system. Some local authorities resent the way NGOs create disorder in what they consider as their social spaces: without the accord of the local chief, the project objectives can be easily undermined.

NGOs associated with the political opposition (or those that were perceived as such) have been major beneficiaries of international support, notably in the early phases of the democratic transition. The opposition's practice of working with (and in some cases taking the form of) development NGOs was facilitated by the National Conference. It was the Conference that gave them visibility and the contacts needed to promote their development and humanitarian agendas. It can be assumed, however, that these groups sacrificed some of their political autonomy through association with international donors. Donors had a twofold reason to use opposition NGOs as conduits for development funds. One, it was a way of putting pressure on Mobutu and his supporters, and two, it was a means of creating new political alliances that could be useful once the opposition came to power. At the time of the Conference many Kinois had faith in opposition promises that the transition process would be fairly rapid. This was the prevailing sentiment from the early 1990s until the war of liberation started in the east in 1996.

Types of NGOs

Given the overwhelming needs and problems of the ordinary people of Kinshasa, every activity, trade, political formation, ethnic group and religious community has an NGO to defend its interests or solicit funding. Much NGO work focuses on health, education and livelihood strategies. These are the stated priorities for both Kinois and international donors. Other NGOs go to the Congo with an imported agenda focusing on children and women, the environment or human rights, for example, even though these are considered secondary priorities by Kinois. Regardless of their goals, however, when a donor arrives with a new credit line, NGOs react rapidly. In a very short time, they are able to submit projects according to the donor's specific guidelines. When it started work in 1996, for example, the Programme d'Appui à la Réhabilitation, one of the European Union's largest projects in the Congo, received hundreds of funding requests in just a few months.

'Governmental' NGOs

When the Alliance des Forces Démocratiques pour la Libération du Congo (AFDL) was still a rebel movement in the bush, it created an NGO called Solidarité Entre Nous. Once in power, this NGO sought to accomplish the AFDL's objectives of dominating the political NGO sector and having access to international funds. Donors accurately saw this as a political strategy designed by Laurent Kabila to consolidate the position of his government and refused to be straitjacketed into a relationship with a government-imposed NGO. The bizarre fiction of a 'governmental' nongovernmental organization rapidly became apparent, and Solidarité Entre Nous has now been forgotten by most Kinois. There are other examples where Mobutu and Kabila co-opted or established NGOs to expand their political power bases. Moziki 100 kg and AMACCO (Association des Mamans Commerçantes du Congo) were women's traders groups closely associated with Mobutu's MPR. REFECO (Regroupement des Femmes Congolaises) and BNPS (Bureau Nationale pour la Promotion Sociale) were initiatives supported by Laurent Kabila. REFECO benefited from an association with the famous Congolese singer Tshiala Mwana, allegedly one of Kabila's mistresses.

There is considerable straddling of NGO and political interests. Some NGO heads have put themselves at the state's disposal, either out of political affinity or to achieve political power. Pierre Lumbi, who headed Solidarité Paysanne with its important rural power base, was promoted Minister of Foreign Affairs and subsequently Minister of Post and Telecommunications under Prime Minister Tshisekedi. The head of GRATEC (Groupe pour la Revalorisation des Aliments

Traditionnels et l'Eco-développement des Communautés de base), Mbemba Fundu, was Tshisekedi's national education minister and then governor of Kinshasa under Kabila *père* before serving as a close aid to Joseph Kabila. As head of the National Women's Union (UNAF), Marie Ange Mufwankole was a logical candidate to manage the Ministry of Labour and Social Security (Ministère du Travail et Prévoyance Sociale), first as vice-minister under Kabila *père* and then as minister under Kabila *fils*. Along the same lines, Manoka Nzuzi of the NGO Coorporation pour le Développement des Travailleurs served as Joseph Kabila's vice-minister of international cooperation and Masiala ma Solo of the Centre Congolais pour l'Enfant et la Famille served as Joseph Kabila's vice-minister of national education.

Local branches of international NGOs

Many international NGOs have set up local branches to carry out their activities in Kinshasa. The Congolese Red Cross is part of the International Federation of the Red Cross and International Committee of the Red Cross. Caritas–Congo is heavily supported by Caritas–Europe and by Christian Relief Service, an American association of bishops. Other Congolese-registered charities such as CDI Bwamanda (Comité de Développement Intégral de Bwamanda)[2] have their directors and fundraising networks in Europe. These groups cleverly portray themselves as having European management discipline, while respecting local priorities. The international NGO that funds the local one and the activities it commissions contributes to capacity building and infrastructure support, both of which are badly needed in Kinshasa.

Religious ONGs

All Kinshasa's major religious communities have development NGOs. The Catholic Church has several. Some, such as Caritas, have become powerful development actors because they can count on a steady flow of financial contributions from fellow believers in Europe and the United States. Religious NGOs that have remained present and active in Kinshasa, despite political obstacles, personal insecurity and looting, have achieved considerable credibility and respect from the beneficiaries for their work. At the international level, donors (and not only religious ones) view them as reliable channels for development aid.

Prayer groups are another form of religious social organization but have different objectives from religious NGOs. Prayer groups are smaller and more closely embedded in community-level solidarity systems. Although prayer groups can be mobilized to start up small-scale economic activities, they are generally organized to help members access micro-credit for social and cultural activities such as weddings or funeral ceremonies.

Ethnic NGOs

Despite serious social and political tension in Kinshasa, many people appear to be motivated by the sincere desire to improve living conditions, but mainly within carefully circumscribed groups. This is particularly obvious in the area of kinship. Urban migration disrupted many kin-based social institutions characteristic of rural Africa; these have been replaced by associations and NGOs. Manifestations of this in Kinshasa are frequent informal meetings and moral support in case of hardship and, sometimes, material support. Since Kinshasa is a melting pot of migrants who maintain strong feelings of regional and ethnic identity, associations and NGOs provide the means to extend solidarity. This has been a phenomenon from the earliest phases of urbanization all over Africa. In the Congo political parties at independence were extensions of such cultural associations. Notable examples include ABAKO, Association des Bakongo, BALUBAKAT, Baluba du Katanga and CONAKAT Conféderation des Associations Ethniques du Katanga (Verhaegen 1970).

Solidarity, however, is generally pragmatic. While the spirit of solidarity is both real and stereotypical, that there are decreasing opportunities for people to manifest it is a cause of stress and frustration. One indicator of this is the way people have stopped sharing meals. Shared meals were common until the mid-1990s, but as the crisis deepened, and access to food has become more and more difficult, this form of socializing has declined significantly.

NGOs based on ethnic and regional affiliations developed to facilitate specific ethnic priorities. These NGOs tend to be headed by important traditional figures, such as chiefs or elders based in Kinshasa, or by well-to-do individuals from an ethic group. Some of these NGOs trace their origins to ethnic associations going back to the early colonial period when they were called *mutualistes*. The real strength of ethnic NGOs is their degree of solidarity, especially among adults who migrated to Kinshasa and helped each other in the urban integration process. The solidarity within the Kinshasa community can be extended to the community's place of origin outside the city. The image successful Kinois cultivate for themselves, and export to their village or region of origin, is an important motivation to participate in associations and NGOs. They become the vehicles to diffuse an image of real and relative success.

Ethnic NGOs are nonetheless subject to a serious generational gap. Gobalized Kinois youth tend to see ethnic affiliation as more a social constraint than an opportunity for solidarity. In part, this can be explained by the poverty that provokes an every-man-for-himself attitude rather than social solidarity. Families increasingly find themselves alone when it comes to dealing with daily survival. It can also be explained by the shift from kinship solidarity to solidarity within prayer communities, and by the replacement of ethnic patriarchs by younger educated or richer elites.

Project-related NGOs

Some NGOs have been established to respond to the specific demands of development activities and short-term goals of humanitarian organizations. Transportation, sanitation and health care services, for example, are implemented with international funding by businesses that have, or claim to have, the required expertise and infrastructure. They tend to be devoid of any real social commitment and disappear once the project ends. A similar category of NGO is the opportunistic one that designs projects to suit a specific donor. The NGO solicits, for example, the Red Cross to provide pharmaceuticals; the Food and Agricultural Organization (FAO) to support agricultural activities; UNICEF to help street children (called *phaseurs* or *sheges*; see De Boeck in this volume), or the Belgian Cooperation to invest in social activities. Cynics joke that these types of NGOs are not non-profit organizations but profitable organizations without objectives.[3]

Fakes and frauds

The NGO flurry has also provided opportunities for individuals to propose fictional services to potential donors. In 1999 a USAID-funded environment project (Central African Programme for the Environment, CARPE) sought to identify viable environmental NGOs in and around Kinshasa and to reinforce their effectiveness. When the CARPE project officer visited alleged sites for verification, she encountered numerous cases where the supposed beneficiaries of an NGO reported that someone came to take pictures of their work, but had no idea that they were part of an NGO activity.[4] It is not uncommon for the results of a legitimate NGO to be presented as the results of a briefcase NGO. The term refers to the NGO representative who can pull out of a briefcase neatly designed brochures and calling cards with pictures of field activities to accommodate any request a donor may formulate.

NGO federations

Given their huge numbers, and the consequent problems of gaining visibility and access to outside funding, many NGOs have grouped into federations to harmonize and defend their activities and interests. The most notable example is the CNONGD (Conseil National des ONG de Développement). CNONGD represents its members to both donors and Kinshasa authorities. While the federation is not conflict-free, it is a functioning example of representative civil society. CNONGD has used its federating capacity to create specific sectoral subdivisions. It has set up, for example, RAUKIN (Réseau pour l'agriculture urbaine à Kinshasa). It has also inspired donors to reproduce the federating pattern. The German cooperation agency GTZ created FOLECO (Fédération des ONG laïques à but économique), which is particularly dynamic in and around Kinshasa, and the Belgian cooperation created ROSAL (Réseau des ONG pour la sécurité alimentaire).

NGO (mis)management

Most Kinshasa NGOs are created and controlled by a single individual whose primary tasks are fundraising and project management. These presidents and directors generally have leadership capacity, speak French well, and have good communication skills. They tend to enjoy community respect, which facilitates public relations and networking. Academics, lawyers and university graduates in general, generically referred to as intellectuals in Kinshasa, head NGOs. Many of these intellectuals are civil servants, which constitutes another bridge between the state and NGOs.

The NGO boss relies on assistants (e.g. agronomists, engineers, social workers, psychologists) for specific technical questions, but the influence of these latter within the NGO decision-making process is generally limited. The management structure tends to be top-down. Democratization within the NGO community has made no more progress than democratization at the national political level.

The top-down approach can also be explained by the tendency throughout sub-Saharan Africa to associate power with 'big man' networks and hierarchies, as opposed to Western-style collective systems governed by power-sharing and checks and balances. This situation causes tensions with project officers from the funding agency, because they prefer to work directly with competent technical staff instead of the chief, who often does not master the pertinent issues. The absence of internal democracy reflects the fact that the director or president does most of the promotional work, while the members passively wait for their chief to secure the funding that will ensure them work. Although Congolese society is generally very hierarchical, once a contract is signed and funds are liberated, NGO members frequently (and often justifiably) accuse their chiefs of embezzling or stealing money – accusations which provoke all kinds of insults, divisions, struggles and expulsions within groups. It is not uncommon for NGOs to disintegrate once they receive funding, for they are often unable to deal with the demands and tensions of managing the transition from project elaboration to project implementation.

NGO management problems, in addition to the lack of transparency and democracy, are obstacles to project implementation as scheduled by international donors. They are, however, easily understandable. For years Kinois saw huge amounts of Western aid pour into their country without being able to participate in discussions on how it was to be used. Although loans were designed to support Mobutu and his cronies for geostrategic rather than development reasons, the international community still expects the Congolese to repay these politically motivated loans. Given the rapid shift from state structures to generally young, inexperienced and fragile NGOs, following the collapse of the Mobutu regime, management problems have been frequent. These problems are as basic as maintaining accurate accounting records, managing human resources or dealing with the administration. For nearly a generation people saw their leaders appropriate outside funds for personal use without any accountability. As ministry officials who experienced this misappropriation first-hand are in many cases the heads of NGOs today, the survival of this form of Mobutist neo-patrimonialism is not surprising.

The competitive nature of inter-NGO relations is another cause of short-sighted management strategy. Hundreds of Kinshasa NGOs compete for funding offered by only a few donor agencies. Securing an appointment with a project officer of one of these is a major accomplishment given this imbalance. Instead of joining forces to create synergies and provide added value to the NGO process (as advocated by CNONGD), a dirty-tricks mentality prevails. Accusing rival NGOs of falling into the fakes and frauds category is one negotiation strategy adopted. To become the favourite partner of a donor and eventually monopolize its funding mechanisms is the objective of this strategy. Where NGOs benefit from strong political or ministerial support, bullying and other forms of aggressive manoeuvring are employed to guarantee this monopoly.

NGO survivability and perspectives

Despite these examples of mismanagement and short-sighted tactics, many NGOs have proven to be professional, transparent and capable of maintaining long-term relations with the international community. Others have succeeded in sustaining their activities over time by combining outside funding, social capital and market forces. The following example reveals how these three different dynamics have been cleverly harmonized.

> Madame Elise farms a small plot of land near her house. Many other women throughout Kinshasa do the same. As it was difficult to buy seeds and fertilizers in the neighbourhood because no local shops sold them, she decided to buy these products and distribute them to her neighbours. Unable to pay for them in cash, her neighbours agreed to give part of their harvest to Madame Elise. Madame Elise also has a sense of community solidarity and wanted to help undernourished children. She gave the vegetables she received in payment for the fertilizers and seeds to the mothers of hungry children in exchange for a $10 IOU. These mothers sold some of the vegetables at a local market and were

able to develop and maintain buying and selling activities. They reimbursed Madame Elise $2 or $3 per week until they paid back the $10 debt. Once this was achieved, they continued to pay her a few dollars per week as savings. Madame Elise used this money to finance other women, who were sponsored by three or four women already part of the group. These sponsors had to make sure their friends paid back the money owed to Madame Elise or pay it back themselves. The network has grown into an organization with approximately 200 farmers and 140 market women. Madame Elise presents it as an NGO and consequently benefits from FAO programmes that distribute seeds and fertilizers free of charge. This aid reinforces a grassroots dynamic that would continue to exist with or without the support of the FAO.

This example can be interpreted as either a carefully designed system of solidarity or one of exploitation of vulnerable women. Whatever the interpretation, it is a telling example of social vitality that combines solidarity, traditional mechanisms of self-help, agricultural micro-credit, financial micro-credit and the use of social pressure. This form of organization has proven much more appropriate in addressing Kinshasa's food security needs than, for example, the co-operatives that were initiated by international donors in the 1980s. These co-operatives failed not only because of the looting in the early 1990s and the withdrawal of Western aid, but, more significantly, because they did not capitalize on local social systems.

The presence of major international NGOs throughout the Democratic Republic of Congo in general, and in Kinshasa (and Kivu) in particular, has helped save an incalculable number of lives in recent years. Without this form of international solidarity, hunger and sickness would be even worse than it is now. Suffering and sacrifice would be more widespread. This relief, however, has come at a price. NGO money and specific agendas have perverted the dynamics of Kinshasa's associational life, vital to the longer-term interests of the population. The depth and duration of crisis in Kinshasa have forced people to invent all kinds of strategies to organize their activities as individuals, families and groups. This started well before the NGO rush to Kinshasa. Many of the problems that characterize the way local NGOs function can be attributed to the presence of international NGOs in Kinshasa. Given fundamentally different priorities, philosophies and operating procedures, the NGOization of Kinshasa is perceived as an imported phenomenon that does not always take into account local attitudes and practices. As a consequence, many civil society developments and initiatives that had emerged in the late Mobutu period lost some momentum.

New forms of social organization have developed, however, and appear to be strengthening, perhaps due to problems inherent in the more formal NGO-type structures. The social organizations that address the most pressing needs of Kinois are known at the grassroots level as neither associations nor NGOs. They are quite simply called groups, generally of friends or neighbours. Expatriates working in humanitarian aid have labelled them Local Development Initiatives (LDIs). A group of women living in the same neighbourhood, for example, forms to cultivate a plot of land. They prepare the field, pitch in money to buy seeds or plants, help each other by carrying water, share whatever tools they might have and stand guard over the produce when harvest time is near. Another group can form to repair a road or clean gutters. Other people collectively decide to buy a bag of manioc wholesale and divide it up in order to reduce the retail cost of amounts consumed by individual families. These arrangements emerge in a relatively informal and spontaneous way when a group of individuals believes that collective initiative can be more efficient than individual struggle or sacrifice. These groups tend to be small and based on shared objectives and trust. They have neither statutes nor governing assemblies like most of the NGOs described above. Benefits are distributed equally, in a manner that is reminiscent of village distribution. These manifestations of social collaboration, where communities act collectively to respond to specific problems, counter the image of Kinshasa as a city in social crisis. Groups are certainly the form of collective action that has already enabled Kinois, and will enable them in the future, to address their most pressing needs. These groups increasingly redefine the deep meaning of Kinois identity. Their real strength derives from their autonomy and local nature. In the future, once social energy can concentrate on issues other than basic survival, they may also be the basis of political mobilization.

Notes

1. These include Médecins Sans Frontières Belgium, the Belgian Red Cross, Médecins Sans Frontières France, and the Italian Nuova Frontiera and Istituto Cooperazione Universitaria.

2. This NGO is supported by Flemish Catholic missionaries and remains close to former Mobutist groups.
3. The cynicism in French is more poignant: *association sans but lucratif/association lucrative sans but.*
4. Personal communication, Mrs Evelyne Samu, CARPE project officer, Kinshasa.

Hidden Families, Single Mothers and *Cibalabala*: Economic Regress and Changing Household Composition in Kinshasa

Tom De Herdt

What is the meaning of 'household' in Kinshasa? What is the meaning of 'family'? How many people are there in these units? How are they adapting to economic crisis and political and social change? These were some of the general questions raised in a 1997 household survey in the Matete district of Kinshasa.[1] One particularly surprising finding pertained to the size of households. In some cases, households comprised up to thirty-two members! Although we were aware that average household size in Kinshasa has been increasing over recent decades,[2] we did not expect to obtain an average household size of 9.8. This was a sharp increase from D'Souza et al.'s (1995) survey result in the same district two years earlier and consequently led to further questions.[3] What is the relationship between this increase and deepening socio-economic crisis? How does increase in household size influence survival strategies, and, conversely, how do survival strategies influence household size? Is the trend part of the so-called Kinshasa miracle or is it just another part of the economic nightmare? What is the well-being status of the additional household members? These are the underlying questions addressed in this chapter. The facts presented below can be interpreted as a Cinderella story – without a happy ending.

Further scrutiny of the composition of households in our sample revealed a phenomenon Caroline Moser had observed in other urban Third World contexts (Moser 1996): a variety of economic circumstances forced more and more people, particularly women, to stay with their parents even after having children. In many

Table 8.1 Hidden households in Matete, Kinshasa 1996

	Child of the household head?				
Yes			**No**		
52 (45%)			65 (55%)		
Father present?		**Type of family**			
Yes	No	Biparental	Single parent		No parents
44 (95%)	3 (6%)	17 (26%)	35 (54%)		13 (20%)
			Father only	Mother only	
			4 (11%)	31 (89%)	

Source: Matete survey 1996.

cases, such 'hidden families' were single-parent families headed by lone mothers who live with their children in their parents' home. In Matete, this phenomenon took on very important proportions. Table 8.1 categorizes children aged under 6 years old according to whether they were the biological child of the household head and whether their father or mother was absent. Of the 117 children in our sample, more than half belong to a hidden family within the household. In a quarter of these cases, the child is living with both parents in a household headed by a non-parent; more than half of them lack one parent. One-fifth of them lack both parents, a category referred to as 'entrusted children' (Lututala et al. 1999). Of the 35 children who lack one parent, almost all of them are living with their unmarried mother.

Some of these hidden families could also be considered as households in themselves, depending on the way household is defined. In many cases they cook their own meals, even though there are other indications that they clearly belong to the same household.[4]

In some respects Matete is exceptional. It is a comparatively older district, built in 1955 by colonial planners as a residential area for *évolués*.[5] Houses are relatively large and well-built. It is more accessible by public transportation than many other districts in Kinshasa. In other respects, however, Matete is not very exceptional. Lututala and Mukeni (1996), for instance, do not report specifically about hidden families but they do claim that in a sample of children between 6 and 24 years old, only 55 per cent live with both parents: 21 per cent live in single-parent families and 25 per cent are entrusted to other households. Further, the latest UNICEF survey reports a shift in the women's average age of first marriage or union from 18.4 to 21.5 years between 1955 and 1995 and a 'difficult to explain' (UNICEF 1996: 56) increase in fertility from 4.9 to 7.3 children per woman during the same period. Based on a much broader sample from throughout Kinshasa (all districts), de Saint Moulin (1996) reports a decrease in the percentage of married/attached adult women (older than 17 years) from 75 per cent in 1967 to 44 per cent in 1996. This contrasts with an increase in fertility from 5.85 to 7.4 during the same period (Houyoux et al. 1986: 114; UNICEF 1996: 55). The most likely interpretation of these figures is an increasing number of children born and raised outside bi-parental households.

The explanation for the increasing percentage of unmarried women was until recently the increasing rate of schooling (de Saint-Moulin 1996; Houyoux et al. 1986). As women spent more years in school they waited longer before starting a household. This explanation is consistent with the relationship between level of schooling and age of marriage in the 1975 survey (Houyoux and Kinavwuidi Niwembo 1986: 109) and in the 1984 census (Shapiro and Tambashe 1997: Table 6). Nonetheless, this explanation is increasingly less convincing today because there has been a spectacular decrease in school attendance, especially of girls (UNICEF 1996: 65; Lututala and Mukeni 1996) since the early 1990s. It appears simply that more and more children are born outside marriage.

The well-being implications of this phenomenon for mother and child is considered in the first part of this chapter. We draw on data from another survey that combined socio-economic and anthropometric data on children living in the sampled households. This survey, carried out in the district of Kisenso in 1997, enabled us to measure well-being in terms of nutritional status.[6] It is important to note here that the circumstances in which the inhabitants of Kisenso live are more or less representative of those of one-third of Kinshasa's population. Qualitative evidence that explains the hidden family phenomenon in the context of economic regress is presented in a second section. Some theoretical issues that will help understand the empirical data are addressed in the following section.

Theorizing households and marriages

While economists have made considerable progress in drawing on interdisciplinary research to analyse the household as an economic unit, many problems still remain. First, economists tend to analyse households independently of other related social constructs. They analyse households as complete institutions in the sense that their collective behaviour can be explained by the rational behaviour of individual household members. By contrast, anthropologists studying Congolese cultures always had problems with the concept of a household as being an independent sociological entity endowed with its own logic. Instead, lineage has been proposed as the major socio-economic unit of decision-making (e.g. MacGaffey 1983b). The cultural heritage of the Bakongo, for instance, is viri-local and matrilineal: people belong first of all to their mother's lineage (headed by their mother's oldest brother), while the household itself is hosted by the territory of the father's lineage. While this type of culture undoubtedly dominates Kinshasa (because approximately 40 per cent of Kinois have Kongo origins), some viri-local patrilineal cultures (e.g. from the Kasai provinces) are present as well. A marriage is not so much the foundation of a household but a strategic connection between different families.

The role of non-household members in decision-making cannot be underestimated in contemporary Kinshasa, in sharp contrast to Western systems where household decisions are made nearly exclusively at the household level. Sorcery practices, for example, which were initially restricted to the domain of lineages, are now increasingly seen as forces that can affect family as well as non-family members (De Herdt 1997). This is only one of the more spectacular signs of a world-view where many accidental phenomena (from a Western point of view) are interpreted as consequences of some lineage members' disloyal behaviour. In some respects, however, this cultural framework is probably outdated and certainly only partially pertinent. Whether or not the institution of a lineage made sense in earlier periods (see Collier and Gunning 1999), life in contemporary Kinshasa provides for a different social and economic setting. Life in Kinshasa offers new risks and opportunities, which helps explain why the old lineage heads are no longer able to protect their members. An indication of this is the organization of funerals by socio-economic groups like neighbourhood or prayer groups, where the role of the deceased's family in the ceremony is marginalized (Grootaers 1998a).

Mianda (1997) has given specific examples of changing patterns of household decision-making strategies. Some couples, for example, bypass their respective lineages' customary entitlements to guarantee a heritage for their children. By default, all the households' properties return to the husband's lineage when he dies. In Kinshasa, however, this custom can imply that the widow and/or the orphaned children are disinherited. The problem is solved by providing children with at least part of the properties without offending the husband's family, as described in the narrative below:

> As parents, we have to think about the future of our children. If something serious happens to papa, who is going to take care of all of these kids? His family [that of the husband] is going to show up and say 'give us our brother's belongings'. We have three lots of land, so decided to put one in papa's name [the husband] in case his family demands it. The other two are in my name and will go to our children. His family can't get hold of them. (Maman Fı, cited in Mianda 1997: 136)

Although it seems that the independent decision-making aspect of households has been overemphasized in household economics literature, it also seems that attributing the ultimate decision-making power to the lineage head is also exaggerated. Neither institution has overriding decision-making power. Individuals from inside and outside the household compete among themselves and bargain to further their own ends. As a result, the effect of a shift in someone's power position on a particular household member's well-being will depend on the effect of this shift on the overall power constellation in a particular local context. It is difficult to predict the outcome in advance.

A second and related weakness of current household economic analysis is the absence of a distinction between an *empirical household* (defined as a consumption unit) and the *ideal household* as a socially accepted form of living together. The economic literature makes no conceptual distinction between households and married couples in analysing intra-household allocation. Of course, for those households that consist of a husband, the wife to whom he is married and their legal children, this weakness is not too problematic. This situation, however, is uncommon in Kinshasa. Unless we consider people as irrational, mechanical norm followers, the marriage ritual must have an importance in its own right.[7] In general, rituals and ceremonies are turning points during which identities are redefined and social and family relations are altered. Though usually planned far in advance, these rites of passage can be compared to disasters. They are emotional moments for the community that redefine the roles and responsibilities of each member. Through the marriage ritual, for example, *non*-household members establish control over the couple. What was previously a private intimate relationship becomes an affair of the broader family after marriage. The couple is summoned to assume its responsibilities vis-à-vis this public.[8] It can be supposed that whatever happens outside marriage lacks this public character and is consequently lived out in a totally different way. The main difference is that the relationship remains private.

The next example focuses on what are referred to as natural children, for lack of a better term. These are children born of an extramarital relationship. These children and their mothers experience a difficult social existence in customary world-views. A single mother loses her quality as *mushika nkunde*, a thread that weaves together the tissues representing the two lineages (Devisch 1993). Her child is called *cibalabala* (in Tshiluba), literally maize stalk or 'one who lacks deep roots' (Biaya 1994: 91–2). These girls eventually escape from social death in the countryside by becoming *ndumba* (free women) in the city (Biaya 1994; De Herdt 2002). There are, however, no such customary practices that condemn a biological father to social death.

Households, families and impoverishment

Table 8.2 presents data on the family structure of households in Kisenso and the relationship between family structure and wealth.[9] These data focus on expenses rather than income and include an imputed rent for house-owners in order to obtain 'total household expenses'. Further, 'wealth' corrects for the effects of varying member- ship and household scale (cf. Annex I).

According to Table 8.2, an average household in Kisenso comprises 7.8 members. One-fifth of all household members do not belong to the nuclear family that makes up the centre of each household. This nuclear family is defined as the family composed of the close relatives of the household head. Whenever the household centre is

Table 8.2 Variation in family structure and household wealth ($\alpha=.7$, $\theta=.85$)

	Variable	Poorest tercile	Middle tercile	Richest tercile	Total	F-value
1	No. of cases	59	61	60	180	
2	Total population	9.3	7.6	6.6	7.8	10.9[*]
3	Extended family members	2.6	1.8	1.0	1.8	7.2[†]
	Family household structure (av.):					
4	Head's child	4.8	4.0	3.7	4.2	2.9
5	Head's son/daughter in law	0.17	0.08	0.13	0.13	0.6
6	Head's parent	0.07	0.02	0.03	0.04	1.1
7	Head's brother/sister	0.24	0.10	0.10	0.14	1.2
8	Head's brother/sister in law	0.02	0.10	0.07	0.06	1.3
9	Head's grandchildren	1.73	1.08	0.40	1.07	7.85[*]
10	Children ≤ 6 years (av.)	1.9	1.8	1.3	1.7	6.0[†]
	of whom:					
11	% head's children	52	61	73	62	2.4
12	% head's grandchildren	47	35	22	35	3.73[‡]
13	% living without father	39	33	21	31	2.2
14	Children living w/out father (av.)	0.75	0.64	0.23	0.54	4.8[†]

‡ p<.05   † p<.01   * p<.001

Source: Kisenso survey 1997.

composed of a bi-parental nuclear family, the household head is male. This is the case in approximately 90 per cent of all bi-parental households.

The statistical weight of non-nuclear-family members within a household could be interpreted as a reflection of the sociological importance of lineage over and above the household. Nonetheless, the data suggest a more complex situation because there seems to be a direct relationship between the percentage of non-nuclear-family members in a household and the level of wealth. If indeed the lineage logic governs the allocation of its members among the several consumption units (i.e. households) it can dispose of, the outcome seems to be very inefficient. The most impoverished households end up hosting most non-nuclear family members (a quarter of their members) while the least impoverished households host only half of them (12 per cent). The remaining variables help identify the family relationships between household members in more detail.

In a second set of variables, all members have been identified in relation to the household head. There is never a significant difference in the average amount of extended-family members, except in the case of grandchildren. The number of sons/daughters-in-law, parents, or brother/sisters-in-law, is only marginal in absolute terms. It is also unrelated to wealth. This implies that their relative weight in the total household population decreases in poorer households. Indeed, when we combine variables 5 through 8 and compare the result to variable 3 (number of extended-family members), the weight of these types of extended-family members decreases from one-third to one-fifth. In sharp contrast, the relative importance of grandchildren (variable 9) increases from two-fifths to two-thirds (1.73/2.6). In other words, the category of extended family masks many subcategories whose importance varies in different ways as household wealth declines.

A third set of variables details the category of household members less than 6 years old. On average only two-thirds of them are the biological children of the household head. This ratio varies from nearly three-quarters to one-half as we move from the richest to the poorest tercile (p<.10). According to Table 8.2, most non-nuclear below-6-year-old children are grandchildren. Their percentage increases to over 50 per cent for the category of most impoverished households. The percentage of children without their biological father living in the same household reveals a similar pattern.

These data suggest that the understanding of solidarity varies according to a household's economic possibilities and constraints. In the richer layers, extended-family members tend to conform to the conventional idea we have of them. The head's brothers and sisters, his parents and in-laws, are relatively important (one-third of all extended-family members). Even in these richer layers, however, grandchildren already make up the largest part of non-nuclear-family members. It can be supposed that as a household impoverishes, the head's children have difficulty starting their own household once grown up, even though at the same time this does not rule out the possibility of them having children. As a result, the nuclear family to

Table 8.3   Child–parent relationships, Kisenso 1997

Mother's relation to household head	No.	Married father present	Married father absent	Divorced	Widow	Single mother
Wife	109	109				
Daughter	56	5	21	13	3	14
Daughter-in-law	12	12				
Sister	1		1			
Sister-in-law	2	2				
Head	2				2	
Mother absent	11	4		7		
Total	193	132		61		

Source: Kinsenso survey 1997.

which children younger than 6 belong is hidden in the household of one of its parent's parents. Three generations live under the same roof under these circumstances. Concomitantly, the probability that children are part of a single-parent hidden family also increases with impoverishment.

Table 8.3 provides data on children less than 6 years old and their relationship with other household members. It illustrates the family ties on which the household is constructed in more detail.

Only 56 per cent of all children (109/193) are born in families where the mother is married to the household head. This percentage increases to two-thirds (128/193) if we add the children belonging to two-parent hidden households. Most often, this group consists of the head's grandchildren. In most of these cases (12 compared to 5), women live in the family of the father of their child, revealing that the principle of viri-locality still applies. However of the (65) women living de facto separated from their children's father, the majority live at their parents' house. Only one has moved in with her brother and only two have become household heads themselves. Only a minority of women do not live in the same household as their child. Though we lack information about them, on the basis of other variables it could be verified that in 7 out of 11 cases their father is also absent, and in 9 out of 11 cases the children are grandchildren of the household head. In 2 cases they live with their widowed father who is household head.

These data help clarify the ways in which Kinshasa solidarity works at the household level. Although all members of the same lineage are brothers and sisters in principle, contemporary households rarely mirror this. First, although the nuclear family is still far from replacing the extended family, contemporary consumption units are built on vertical (parent–child–grandchild) rather than horizontal family lines. Second, the principle of viri-locality is not respected in all cases where the mother and the father of the child are living separately. Children living with their mother's family tend to disregard the role of the father's lineage. In terms of traditional concepts, approximately one-third of all children can be qualified as uprooted because their mothers cease to be *mushika nkunde* (the thread that weaves together two lineages).

Table 8.4 measures the results of the different family configurations in terms of a child's well-being, based on its nutritional status (weight for age and height for age) (Annex II).

A distinction is made in Table 8.4 between children whose mother is absent and those whose mother is present. Within the latter group, a distinction is made between those whose father is either living elsewhere or deceased and those who are living in a two-parent family (the father being present). Finally, within the latter group, a distinction is made between the children of the family head and those belonging to hidden families.

It appears from Table 8.4 that the first and most important cause of malnutrition is the absence of the child's mother in the same household. Her absence implies a one-fifth decrease in the child's well-being in terms of weight and a decrease of almost 50 per cent in terms of height (referred to as stunting). Further, the decrease in well-being as a result of the father's absence is statistically significant as well because it causes well-being indicators to decrease by .07–.08 points. Finally, there is no significant difference within the group of children whose parents are effectively married: it seems to make no difference whether or not the father is also household head.

Table 8.4 identifies the *de facto* orphans or entrusted children as being the principal victims of the actual economic crisis. If undernourishment in general has been fairly low in Kinshasa (De Herdt

Table 8.4 Child under-nutrition and family configuration of household, Kisenso 1997

Mother	Father	Child of head?	No. of cases	$B_{\text{weight-for age}}$	$B_{\text{height-for-age}}$
Present	Present	Yes	106	.78	.70
		No	20	.79	.74
	Mean difference (t-test)			−.01 (−.32)	−.04 (−.63)
		Absent	52	.70	.64
	Mean difference (t-test)			.08 (2.42)	.07 (1.63)
Absent			11	.63	.36
	Mean difference (t-test)			.12 (1.82)	.32 (3.88)
Total			189	.75	.67

Source: Kinseno survey 1997.

and Marysse 1996; De Herdt 2001; Tollens, this volume), children growing up with only one or even neither of their biological parents appear to constitute an exceptional category. Nonetheless, it cannot be concluded from Table 8.4 that this is so only because they are *de facto* orphans. Two alternative hypotheses exist.

First, higher-aged under-5s are more undernourished than under-1-year-olds because of breast-feeding. Infants are usually breast-fed up to their first birthday and are consequently much less vulnerable to malnutrition. As older children run a higher risk of growing up in a household without either mother or father, the observed differences in nutritional status as presented in Table 8.4 could be partly due to differences in the proportion of breast-fed children between each of the categories.

Table 8.5 shows that the percentage of children living with both parents decreases as the children grow older, even though the details reveal some complexities. First, most children growing up without their mother are concentrated in the 4- to 5-year-old category. It could consequently be hypothesized that the relatively high rate of undernourishment in the category of 4- to 5-year-olds is caused by this absence rather than by any other external variable. Conversely, it appears that the percentage of children growing up without a father

Table 8.5 Relation between age of child and absence/presence of parents, Kisenso 1997

Child		≤1 year	2–4 years	4–5 years
Mother present				
	Father present	74	68	61
	Father absent	23	28	27
Mother absent		3	4	11
Total		100	100	100

Source: Kisenso survey 1997.

is in fact lower in the group of children younger than 1 year, if compared to the other age groups. Given that there are independent causes to explain the relatively high well-being of children before their first birthday, part of the effect of an absent father, as observed in Table 8.4, can thus have been explained by breast-feeding rather than by the presence or absence of the father.

Furthermore, on the basis of Table 8.2 it can also be deducted that the family configuration is partly explained by economic wealth. Therefore, wealth rather than the child's family status itself would be the major underlying cause of malnutrition. This means that the importance of each of the variables discussed so far should be judged within a multivariate framework that incorporates all of them.

This exercise is produced in Annex II. Here, we summarize the main results tested in two models. The first model explains child well-being based on weight-for-height, wealth, breast-feeding and the child's status. The model can explain 26.3 per cent of the original variation, which is considerable given the relatively small sample. The negative effect of an absent father (–.24) is higher than the positive effect of breastfeeding (+.17). In addition, the effect of poverty on a child's well-being is significantly higher when a child's father is absent. If a decrease in wealth of $100 implies a decrease in the child's well-being with .02 for children with father present, it implies a decrease with .08 for children whose father is absent.

The second model repeats the exercise by opting for height–for-age as the basis to proxy child well-being. Wealth now apparently influences child well-being only in an indirect way, causing the head's daughters to stay at home and have children themselves without necessarily being married. In a final version of the model, we eliminated the wealth variable again. The model is now capable of explaining 24 per cent of the original variance. Wealth seems to be significant only when the child grows up without his or her father. Note also that the coefficients relating the absent-father variables to child well-being are more or less comparable with those of the previous model. It is noteworthy that the father's presence is more important than the mother's and both are more important than breast-feeding as determinants of well-being.

The main conclusion from this exercise is that a child's state of well-being is affected primarily by the absence or presence of (one or both) of its parents. It may be true that absence or presence is the consequence of poverty, but poverty does not explain why and to what degree a child is malnourished. This depends directly on the child's family status rather than on anything else.

Discussion

Post-colonial Kinshasa witnessed a general collapse of the economic apparatus inherited from the colonial period, and this economic regression was accompanied by several significant demographic trends. Age at marriage has increased over the last thirty years; the percentage of married adult women decreased; and, somewhat paradoxically perhaps, there has been a concomitant increase in fertility and an increase in household size. The empirical material gathered in Kisenso provides more insight into the links between these phenomena.

First, the combined effects of a decreasing percentage of married adult women and an increase in fertility are reflected in an important category of natural children in our survey samples. Approximately one-third of children living in Kisenso are growing up in the absence of a father. Further, these children grow up in single-parent families, not necessarily single-parent households. Usually, the family nucleus of unmarried daughters and their children is hidden inside the household headed by the daughter's father. Thus, though the frontiers of Kinois households typically extend beyond the mere nuclear family, in contemporary Kinshasa households non-nuclear family members are predominantly grandchildren. Family solidarity, as observed in the Kisenso survey, follows vertical rather than horizontal lines.

In addition, the profile of households hiding the daughter's single-parent family is more prevalent among the poorer levels. If we assume that cross-sectional wealth differences shed some light on inter-temporal wealth differences, we can argue that impoverishment has caused marriages not to take place or to be postponed, with a resulting increase in hidden families.

Finally, it has been deduced that children belonging to such single-parent hidden families are affected by adverse economic circumstances in two ways. First, most of them grow up in a relatively poor household, which is the most important reason why they grow up in a single-parent family. Second, they grow up outside a celebrated marriage, which makes them even more vulnerable irrespective of the wealth of the household they live in.

How can we understand these phenomena?

An important clue can be found in some open interviews Laurent Luzolele carried out in households during the Matete-survey (Luzolele and De Herdt 1999a, 1999b). His findings point to what he refers to as the 'centrifugal force of poverty' (1999b: annex 5, 43), meaning the pressure it puts on traditional social practices interpreted as expressions of solidarity.

As a general rule it is unthinkable to refuse hospitality to extended family members. This supposedly age-old social norm, however, has been reinvented recently by other, secondary norms, which provide loopholes to the general rule. Visitors accept that they cannot accept hospitality for long periods of time. The Kikongo proverb *nsudi nwa kutisana* (in order not to smell the other's bad breath, one needs breathing space) is often used in this respect. The pressure of poverty tends to restrict household-level solidarity to nuclear-family members. Another innovation is that guests are expected to provide their own food: at best, hospitality is limited to providing a bed and a roof. The problem of food access is considerable, as revealed by this widespread sentiment: 'There isn't enough food for everyone. You girls are big, don't the men that you meet give you money?' (narrated in Luzolele and De Herdt 1999b: 53).

This situation is reminiscent of the lifeboat predicament where two men must make a tragic decision about the use of an amount of food that is enough for only one of them (Dasgupta 1993: 30; Elster 1992: 9). But once the same problem takes place in a less abstract setting, numerous criteria emerge that allow decision-makers to keep a clear conscience and make a reasonable choice. The decision to give the lowest priority to grown-up girls in case there is not enough food is increasingly frequent. Nonetheless, from the point of view of established role-expectations, such a decision by a father is quite revolutionary because it is generally perceived that a girl's place is in the house not in the streets: 'wandering around and meeting men is not done; it is tantamount to prostitution.' Moreover, the decision to urge girls to let the men they meet give them money increases the risk of unwanted pregnancy. Consequently:

> We prefer welcoming boys opposed to girls. We don't like taking in girls from other families because they frequently get pregnant. We prefer taking in boys because even if they cause problems and get girls pregnant, the life of a girl from our own family is not wasted [*mwana abebi*, literally the girl has lost her worth]. The boy's life isn't wasted. If a girl we have taken in gets pregnant, that causes problems with other family members. (adapted from Luzolele and De Herdt 1999b: 57)

A wasted life has several meanings in this context. First, the girl's life is wasted because she cannot proceed with her studies and will probably not find a husband. Second, the girl is wasted for the family because she cannot marry and receive bride wealth for the family. This is important because bride wealth (to be paid by the groom's family) easily amounts to the equivalent of $500, approximately half the price of the total marriage. $500 is more than the average per adult yearly income! Biaya writes that by migrating to the city and earning a living for herself as a *femme libre*, the unmarried rural mother was able to constitute her own bride wealth and fulfil her duty to her family (Biaya 1994: 94). Similarly, the urban single mother is expected to take care of herself and her children even if she continues to sleep at her parents' house. This results in the reduction of pooled resources, one of the most crucial elements of a household. Ultimately, the problem of poverty is transferred not only to the single mother but also to the next generation.

Emerging economic patterns have had an ambiguous impact on the maintenance of the social norms and role expectations of family members. Extending unconditional hospitality towards extended-family members seems to be a norm modified by secondary loopholes and the norm that 'girls shouldn't walk freely in the streets' (*kotambola mpamba mpamba*, literally 'to wander back and forth') is replaced by emphasizing the responsibilities of the men the girls meet. In addition, the traditional concept of a wasted girl is revised, resulting in further decline of family-based solidarity. The 'centrifugal force of poverty' is not exclusively a household problem. Poverty may be the primary cause, but it is the interplay between economic constraints and the existing set of social norms that determines who will be the ultimate victim.

Conclusion

In what is considered a pioneering contribution to household economics, Paul Samuelson outlined the hypothesis of a consistent family consensus on intra-household resource allocation. Everyone has their own preferences, but 'since blood is thicker than water, the preferences of the different members are interrelated by what might be called a "consensus" or "social welfare function" which takes into account the deservingness or ethical worth of the consumption levels of each of the members' (1956: 10). Although it is often the fate of pioneering contributions to be discredited by subsequent developments, research results about households in Kinshasa are very similar to those of Samuelson. Even without confusing blood ties with altruism, this chapter shows that living together is difficult to imagine without a minimal consensus about 'deservingness and ethical worth of the consumption levels of each of the members'. If blood is thicker than water, it implies more clearly defined role expectations about each family member's rights and duties than about those of non-family members. It is thus logical that the 'ideal family' will play a role in 'ideal allocation' of resources. Conversely, it cannot be expected that such norms are developed within each household and independently of other households and other institutions such as lineages. A notable difference also exists between an essentially local 'consensus' about fair allocation and optimal 'social welfare' more broadly conceived. In the local case, the consensus is only a thin veil to mask a tragic choice in favour of one household member to the very serious detriment of another.

In light of these data, interpreting the relationship between economic decline in Kinshasa and increasing household size has become clearer. Both trends are obviously more than coincidental. Increasing poverty seems to have altered existing role expectations in several, divergent ways. First, some norms, such as the one on universal and unconditional hospitality vis-à-vis other members of the lineage, have been eroded by emerging norms. Second, given economic constraints, some norms, such as that girls should not appear 'free' in public life, have simply been replaced by others. Third, some traditional practices have been reinforced, such as the expectation that unmarried mothers should repair their transgression by earning their own bride wealth.

It is the interplay between economic constraints and expected practices that determines the profile of the new victims of contemporary socio-economic turmoil in Kinshasa. In this case, young girls in poor families seem to be squeezed between the necessity to look for male benefactors and the general public's opinion that unmarried mothers are wasted. Ultimately, children living in single-parent families hidden in the household of their (generally maternal) grandfather are among the most conspicuous victims in contemporary Kinshasa. Increasing household size is clearly the result of an increasing number of hidden, single-parent families, implying that intra-household consumption inequality has probably increased rather than decreased. Although increasing household size is an effect of individual strategies to cope with crisis and is therefore part of the Kinshasa miracle, this is not inconsistent with the opposite reality that increased household size is a serious nightmare for others.

Annex I   Construction of indicators of wealth and well-being

Ia   Household wealth

$$W(\alpha, \theta)_h = \frac{Y_h}{(A_h + \alpha C_h)^\theta}$$

with

Y_h = total household outlays of household h

A_h = adult members of household h

C_h children (up to 6 years old) belonging to household h

α =   the equivalence factor to express children's consumption in terms of adults' consumption, $0 < \alpha < 1$

θ =   the factor accounting for economies of scale, $0 < \theta < 1$.

The most reasonable 'default' values of α and θ are .7 and .85 respectively (Drèze and Srinivasan 1997). In Annex II, the regression results are tested on their sensitivity to changes in α and θ

Ib   Child well-being

$$B_i(\gamma) = 1 - |((z_i - 1)/5)^\gamma|$$

with

z_i = weight (in the case of *underweight*) or height (in the case of *stunting*) of a child in comparison with the average child of the same sex and age, in terms of z-scores,

i = type of indicator (weight-to-age or height-to-age)

We considered $\gamma = 2$ as a reasonable default value. As in the case of the wealth indicator retained, we will test the sensitivity of our results to changes in this parameter.

This approach differs from other more common ones that either posit $B_i = z_i$ or define malnutrition in an all-or-nothing way by specifying a threshold value (usually -2 z-scores). Neither alternative gives due account, if at all, to the non-linear character of the indicator, or to the fact that there is an optimal nutritional state in-between the extremes of either under- or over-nutrition.

Annex II   Multivariate regression results

In Tables 8.6 and 8.7 we summarize the outcomes of several multivariate linear regression models with well-being based on weight-to-age and height-to-age. In each case, we reduced the age-factor to a dummy that distinguishes the newborns ≤ 14 months from other under-5s. The cut-off point of 14 months seemed to be harmonious with other studies on breast-feeding practices in Kinshasa (UNICEF 1996). Each model is tested in several versions, so as to look at the interaction between different variables, and at the sensitivity of the results to changes in the parameters we defined in Annex I.

Table 8.6 Regression results: determinants of underweight children

No.	γ	α	θ	1 (dummy yes = 1) Children ≤14m	Children (numeric) Wealth	Child w/out father (dummy yes = 1)	Child w/out father × wealth (dummy yes = wealth)	Max. C.I.	R^2_{adj} (%)
1	2	.7	.85	.71‡ (.01)	.18‡ (.03)	.0002‡ (.0000)				14.0
2	2	.7	.85	.59‡ (.03)	.19‡ (.03)	.0003‡ (.0000)	−.24‡ (.08)			23.1
3	**2**	**.7**	**.85**	**.64‡ (.04)**	**.17‡ (.03)**	**.0002‡ (.0000)**	**−.24‡ (.08)**	**.0006‡ (.0000)**	**8.9**	**26.3**
					Sensitivity-tests of γ, α and θ				
4	2	.5	.85	.65‡ (.04)	.17‡ (.03)	.0002‡ (.0000)	−.25‡ (.08)	.0006‡ (.0000)	8.9	26.4
5	2	1.0	.85	.70‡ (.04)	.17‡ (.03)	.0001 (.0001)	−.29‡ (.08)	.0007‡ (.0000)	8.2	23.1
6	2	.7	.75	.64‡ (.04)	.17‡ (.03)	.0002‡ (.0000)	−.24‡ (.08)	.0004* (.0000)	9.2	26.1
7	2	.5	.75	.64‡ (.04)	.17‡ (.03)	.0002‡ (.0000)	−.25‡ (.08)	.0004‡ (.0000)	9.2	26.2
8	2	1.0	.75	.69‡ (.03)	.17‡ (.03)	.0001 (.0001)	−.28‡ (.08)	.0006‡ (.0000)	8.4	23.1
9	2	.7	1.00	.65‡ (.03)	.17‡ (.03)	.0003‡ (.0000)	−.25‡ (.08)	.0008‡ (.0000)	8.4	26.4
10	2	.5	1.00	.65‡ (.03)	.17‡ (.03)	.0002‡ (.0000)	−.26‡ (.08)	.0008† (.0000)	8.4	26.4
11	2	1.0	1.00	.71‡ (.03)	.17‡ (.03)	.0001 (.0001)	−.30† (.07)	.001† (.0003)	7.5	22.8
12	3	.7	.85	.77‡ (.03)	.13‡ (.03)	.0002† (.0001)	−.22† (.07)	.0005† (.0003)	8.9	23.9
13	1	.7	.85	.42‡ (.04)	.21‡ (.03)	.0003† (.0001)	−.21* (.09)	.0005* (.0002)	8.9	25.9

* p<.05 † p<.01 ‡ p<.001

Source: Kisenso survey 1997.

Table 8.7 Regression results: determinants of well-being based on height-to-age

	Parameters of wealth and well-being			Coefficients of …						Max. C.I.	R²adj (%)
	γ	α	θ	1	Children ≤14m (dummy yes = 1)	Wealth (numeric)	Child w/out mother (dummy yes = 1)	Child w/out father (dummy yes = 1)	Child w/out father × wealth (dummy yes = wealth)		
1	2	.7	.85	.63‡ (.02)	.20† (.04)	.0003† (.0001)					11.0
2	2	.7	.85	.51‡ (.04)	.21† (.04)	.0003† (.0001)				5.0	15.9
3	2	.7	.85	.54‡ (.04)	.20† (.04)	.0003‡ (.0001)	-.298‡ (.072)			5.1	23.1
4	2	.7	.85	.60‡ (.05)	.19† (.04)	.0002 (.0001)	-.282‡ (.072)	-.248* (.101)	.0006* (.0003)	9.2	25.0
5	**2**	**.7**	**.85**	**.67‡ (.02)**	**.18† (.04)**		**-.291‡ (.073)**	**-.316† (.092)**	**.0007† (.0000)**	**7.0**	**24.0**
							Sensitivity-tests of γ α and θ				
6	2	.5	.85	.67‡ (.02)	.18† (.04)		-.287‡ (.073)	-.326‡ (.093)	.0007† (.0003)	8.9	26.4
7	2	1.0	.85	.67‡ (.02)	.18† (.04)		-.297‡ (.072)	-.318‡ (.092)	.0008† (.0003)	8.2	23.1
8	2	.7	.75	.67‡ (.02)	.18† (.04)		-.293‡ (.073)	-.318‡ (.094)	.0006† (.0003)	9.2	26.1
9	2	.5	.75	.67‡ (.02)	.18† (.04)		-.289‡ (.073)	-.327‡ (.095)	.0006† (.0003)	9.2	26.2
10	2	1.0	.75	.67‡ (.02)	.18† (.04)		-.298‡ (.073)	-.319† (.094)	.0007† (.0003)	8.4	23.1
11	2	.7	1.00	.67‡ (.02)	.18† (.04)		-.289‡ (.073)	-.308‡ (.088)	.0010† (.0003)	8.4	26.4
12	2	.5	1.00	.67‡ (.02)	.18† (.04)		-.285‡ (.073)	-.317‡ (.089)	.0010† (.0003)	8.4	26.4
13	2	1.0	1.00	.67‡ (.02)	.18† (.04)		-.295‡ (.072)	-.312‡ (.089)	.0010† (.0003)	7.5	22.8
14	1	.7	.85	.47‡ (.02)	.18† (.04)		-.242‡ (.071)	-.278† (.090)	.0007† (.0003)	8.9	23.9
15	3	.7	.85	.78‡ (.02)	.16† (.04)		-.293‡ (.068)	-.314‡ (.086)	.0007† (.0002)	8.9	25.9

* p<.05 † p<.01 ‡ p<.001

Source: Kisenso survey 1997.

Notes

1. The fieldwork reported in this chapter was carried out with institutional support from the University Foundation for Development Cooperation and the Facultés Catholiques de Kinshasa. The author thanks Stefaan Marysse and Laurent Luzolele for helpful comments on earlier versions of this text.

2. Earlier budget surveys observe an increase in average household size from 5.8 in 1975 (SICAI 1976) to 7.3 in 1986 (Houyoux et al. 1986), which is not entirely compatible with Lututula and Mukeni (1996), who claim that 'average household size in Kinshasa is eight people (compared to six approximately ten years ago' (1996: 105), but nevertheless expresses the same trend.

3. D'Souza (1995) identified 8.0 members per household.

4. The classical statisticians' definition of a household implies sleeping under one roof and eating from the same cooking pot. The discussion suggests that the second criterion is somewhat problematic.

5. *Evolués* were mainly urban Africans who had received some education, spoke French and had renounced polygamy. They were to constitute the emerging middle class encouraged by Belgian policymakers in the late colonial period.

6. For a discussion of the selection of the zone, as well as for the sampling procedure and practical difficulties in data-gathering, see De Herdt 2000.

7. Interesting in this respect is Gambetta's (1993) suggestion, as concerns an initiation ritual in a mafia group, that precisely because a ritual is so 'ir-rational' that it succeeds in impressing rational individuals, 'while the rational goal of the ritual is clear to the participant – "I undergo the ritual because if I want to become a mafioso, I want to get from A to B" – the actual sequence of symbolic steps which fulfils this logical aim has no intrinsic meaning: it is beyond rationality. The friction between explicit aspiration and symbolic meaninglessness sparks a daunting reverence: "If what took me from A to B is so mysterious, how can I possibly part from B without incurring the wrath of mysterious forces?" The ritual undermines rational expectations' (Gambetta 1993: 152).

8. This suggestion is inspired, inter alia, by Granovetter (1993: 26) and Burt's insights on re-embedding (1992).

9. A detailed discussion on the construction of a good wealth indicator is presented elsewhere (De Herdt 2000).

9

When Kinois Take to the Streets

Gauthier de Villers and
Jean Omasombo Tshonda

Crowds and might

Martyrs for independence

The Leopoldville riots of 4, 5 and 6 January 1959 were the most brutal manifestations of urban violence ever experienced in the Belgian Congo. Virtually the entire black population of the city took to the streets. The catalyst was undeniably political. ABAKO, the Kongo cultural and political association, organized a public meeting that had to be postponed at the last minute when the Leopoldville mayor refused authorization. The decision to postpone, however, was taken too late. ABAKO militants and sympathizers had already started to congregate. The situation exploded when police intervened to disperse the crowd. The riots were a decisive step towards independence and foreshadowed the 'revolution without revolutionaries' that was to follow in 1960 (Young 1968: 149).

Originally a cultural association of Leopoldville-based Kongo peoples, ABAKO had became the most radical and nationalist political association in the Congo by the late 1950s. It was the first group to demand immediate independence, a slogan embraced by the rioters and demonstrators, as well as other Congolese leaders. Patrice Lumumba, president of the Mouvement National Congolais (MNC), for example, held a popular rally on 28 December 1958. It was his first in the capital and its impact helps explain the success of the ABAKO demonstration in terms of nationalist sentiment and multi-ethnic support (Mutamba 1998: 383). Lumumba captivated the crowd by declaring: 'It is time for the Congolese to wake up, speak up and be brave. It is time to prove peacefully, but with resolution, that we are partners. We cannot wait for independence and liberty any longer. The Congo is ours' (Mutamba 1998: 363).

The January riots started as a demonstration and ended in a looting spree. In the first hours, the commercial district of Foncobel, a Greek and Portuguese enclave in the African *cité*, was looted. The looters subsequently attacked the symbols of colonial domination. Stones were thrown at administrative buildings and police stations; shops were emptied; Catholic schools and churches were wrecked, and the Belgian flag was burned (Ndaywel 1998a: 536–7; CRISP 1959: 12). Violence was not directed solely against things and symbols: people were attacked as well. Numerous nuns and other European women were allegedly raped (Mutamba 1998: 371). In a radio interview at the time of the forty-year independence celebrations, the musician Mathieu Kuka recalled that everything white was subject to attack.[1]

Social and economic factors also contributed to the start and spread of the riots. After many years of strong economic growth and improved standards of living, the Belgian Congo went into economic recession in 1957–58. City dwellers were particularly hard hit by job losses (Mutamba 1998: 346). Gangs of unemployed youth who were not able to attend school played a major role in the destruction (*La Libre Belgique*, 12 January 1959). Their involvement can be understood in the context of the Bill movement that had developed in Leopoldville a few years earlier. This movement took its name from the Wild West hero Buffalo Bill and represented a subculture of marginalized youth on the verge of deviance and delinquency (Gondola 1997a: 311).

The riots were, however, much more than the expression of social discontent. Elias Canetti, in his monumental study of mass psychology, *Crowds and Power* (1998) elaborates a classification of mass phenomena based on what he refers to as 'prevailing emotions'. The classification includes 'baiting', 'flight', 'prohibition', 'feast' and 'reversal' crowds (Canetti 1998: 58 and passim). Several of these are useful in analysing and understanding political events in Kinshasa. A reversal crowd, for example, is one 'whose discharge consists mainly in its collective deliverance from the stings of command' (Canetti 1998: 58–9). Its 'discharge' is 'the moment when all who belong to the crowd get rid of their differences and feel equal' (Canetti 1998: 17). According to Canetti,

> A reversal crowd comes into existence for the joint liberation of a large number of people from the stings of command they cannot hope to get rid of alone. They unite to turn on some group of other people whom they see as the originators of all the commands they have borne so long. If they are soldiers, any officer can stand for those under whose command they actually were. (Canetti 1998: 328)

'Independence' for the rioters of January 1959 meant freedom to disobey. An unrelated (but simultaneous) event fuelled the unrest: a football game at the Kalamu stadium (now Tata Raphaël stadium). The spectators were frustrated because their favourite team had lost. Leaving the stadium, they joined the demonstration (Mutamba 1998: 371). Mathieu Kuka told his version of what happened when people left the stadium:

> That team was really beaten badly. People were angry. A police officer tried to maintain order. 'You there! Wait! Not that way. Come this way' he ordered. The spectators didn't pay any attention. The officer shot into the air. The shots surprised people. 'Hey! What's that noise? We are minding our own business. What is he shooting for?' He was knocked over in a flash. But doing that to a police officer means trouble! It was every-man-for-himself. Things were in a state of panic.

The repression carried out by the police and military officially resulted in the death of 47 Congolese and 241 wounded. No whites were killed but 49 were wounded. The real number of Congolese victims, however, was probably many times the official number (Ndaywel 1998a: 537).

The suddenness and scope of the rioting shocked the white community of Leopoldville. Governor-General Cornelis wept in front of the press. While some Europeans chose to flee, others took up arms. Extremists set up *comités de salut public* like their *pied-noir* counterparts did the year before in French Algeria (Marrès and Devos 1959). Leopoldville's spontaneous and leaderless riots resemble the revolutionary situation characteristic of Canetti's reversal crowd. 'The lower class, which is in revolt, forms a single, cohesive crowd; the higher one, which is threatened and outnumbered and surrounded, forms a series of frightened packs, bent on flight' (Canetti 1998: 328). The 'colonial imagination', according to Jean-Luc Vellut (1987: 39), probably once again exaggerated the significance of these events. It seems that the demonstrators had no clear idea of what independence really meant. It is less certain whether or not the looters were inspired by this slogan. After three days of rioting, the population returned to an uneasy calm.

When Governor-General Cornelis regained his composure, he sought to downplay the political importance of the rioting, which he called an 'accident'. It was, however, an accident that Belgium did not view with levity (Pétillon 1967: 238). Belgium had already accepted the principle of Congolese independence and would proceed 'without distressing delay but without reckless haste either', in the words of King Baudouin. The riots did, however, accelerate the independence timetable. When the Congo became independent on 30 June 1960, 4 January was chosen as the national holiday. Laurent Kabila later recognized the importance of the demonstrations by including the date in his list of five important national and patriotic holidays in his February 1999 constitution project: 4 January was to be the Martyrs for Independence holiday.

Looters and martyrs for democracy

Thirty years went by before such politically significant events were to once again rock the Congolese capital, this time during the period cynically identified as 'democratic transition'. During Zaire's Second Republic, the only large-scale mass events were those orchestrated by Mobutu himself. Huge crowds of up to 100,000 people attended these events. The masses were summoned, manipulated and subjugated. They were 'bewitched' by the show of power and by the illusion of being associated with that power. The illusion was cultivated through a ritual dialogue that Mobutu had with the crowd: *Bomba bomba? Mabe!* (Should I hide the truth? No! That's bad!), *Nasakola? Sakola!* (Should I speak? Yes you should!), *Nasilisa? Silisa!* (Must I say everything? Yes! You must!) (Manwana 1972: 126). In these settings, Mobutu was remarkably effective. Elements of charisma were present in his communion with the assembled crowd, and he invariably dominated the crowd by force of personality, the charm of his direct and seemingly candid oratorical style, and the aura of majesty which surrounds political power (Young and Turner 1985: 170–71).

Like all great orators, as Canetti notes, Mobutu was capable of 'compressing all his aims into slogans' (Canetti 1998: 311). Some of Mobutu's more famous aphorisms were 'Let's roll up our sleeves'

(*Retroussons les manches*), 'One country, one people, one chief' (*Un seul pays, un seul people, un seul chef!*), and 'Everything must change! Everything will change!' (*Tout doit changer! Tout va changer!*). Thanks to his charisma and magical way with words, Mobutu 'created' the crowd and 'ke[pt] it alive by a comprehensive command from above.... A speaker can insult and threaten an assemblage of people in the most terrible way and they will still love him if, by doing so, he succeeds in forming them into a crowd' (Canetti 1998: 311). In his famous *mal zaïrois* speech, Mobutu complained that the international image of Zaire was one of a tragicomic blend of musicians, dancers, opportunists, incompetents and braggarts.

The decline of Mobutu's reign, characterized by the collapse of state institutions and the formal economy, began in the mid-1970s. Kinois started to lose faith in their Supreme Leader but their disillusion remained passive. The population seemed to circumvent the state by taking refuge in alternative social and economic systems. People remained docile as long as key staples remained affordable: the state did all it could to make sure that rice and beer, for example, were never unavailable at the same time (Ilunga 1984: 18). Student groups alone dared to express their revolt, but their initiatives received little support from the broader population. The regime's brutality against students seemed to be aimed at convincing other groups to remain passive.

Kinois did not turn into rebels until the democratic transition period of the early 1990s, by which time living conditions had become unbearable. On 24 April 1990 Mobutu solemnly admitted the failure of the Second Republic. The announcement opened the floodgates of change the population had so patiently awaited in silence. Shortly after, the social situation exploded. In September of 1991 Kinshasa was looted; in February 1992 Kinois took to the streets in what became known as the Christian March or March of Hope. Both were related to the democratic transition process.

The National Conference, which sought to define the mechanisms of transition, opened on 7 August 1991. It was immediately subject to argumentation and confusion, its atmosphere characterized by little more than 'mitigated hope' (Willame 1991; de Villers and Omasombo 1997). On 19 August, the opposition Sacred Union left the Conference in protest. On 21 August, Etienne Tshisekedi was sacked. This was three weeks after this opposition leader had assumed the premiership.

Exasperated by low pay and high inflation, the 31st Brigade of the Zairian Air Force mutinied on 23 September 1991. It was quickly nicknamed the 'People's Army' (Kisukula 2001: 18). As they marched towards the city centre soldiers harangued the population, urging them to join the looting. Men, women and children eagerly followed in their footsteps. The soldiers broke down doors, smashed locks and helped themselves to what they wanted. Their civilian comrades took what remained. Nothing was spared. After money and other valuables, television sets, freezers, air conditioners, electrical appliances and equipment were all carted off. Administrative buildings, shops, cold-storage warehouses, private homes of well-to-do Zairians and expatriates were looted. Booty was not the sole objective of the rioters. Violent destruction was another motivation. In some cases, they sought political targets, such as the houses of Mobutu's cronies and the former headquarters of the MPR. 'All's bad that ends bad' was the epitaph scribbled on this edifice. After being looted, shops were sometimes set ablaze (Kalulambi 1999: 551). After the centre was devastated, the movement spread to the city's popular districts. The 'official' death tally was 117 (*La Référence Plus*, 2 October 1991), most of which resulted from accidents such as electrocution or stray bullets.

Standing in marked contrast to these events was the Christian March some five months later. Mobutu's mandate was supposed to have expired at midnight on 4 December 1991 but he unilaterally decided to remain head of state. Nguz a Karl I Bond, the new prime minister, suspended the National Conference on 19 January 1992. The March was a political reaction to Nguz's decision, taken in a very tense social context, and sought to put the National Conference back on the political agenda (de Dorlodot 1994).

The Christian March was organized by a small group of Christian militants and took place on 16 February 1992. Tens of thousands of demonstrators gathered at Catholic parishes all over the city. With bibles, chaplets, crosses and palm branches in hand, the numerous groups looked more like a religious procession than a political demonstration. As the authorities had prohibited the March, the military used their guns to prevent groups from congregating. The following account reveals the pacific nature of the marchers' response to military repression:

> In response to the shots, we sat down on the road in unison. For around three minutes the sound of gunfire was deafening. When the noise

stopped, we began chanting and praying. *Mandoki oyo ekotikala na mokili oyo. Kolo Yesu akumisama.* (These guns will stay on Earth. Glory to Jesus!) *Mbongo oyo ekotikala na mokili oyo. Kolo Yesu akumisama.* (This money will stay on Earth. Glory to Jesus!) *Biloko nionso ekotikala na mokili oyo. Kolo Yesu akumisama.* (All these things will stay on Earth. Glory to Jesus!) People were entranced. The shooting started up again in heavy volleys. We remained seated in order to avoid the bullets flying over our heads. (Mata Bafwidinsoni 1992)

The obviously underestimated death count amounted to sixteen.

Canetti, crowds and inflation

Kinshasa's September 1991 disorder and looting were to be repeated elsewhere. The economy of pillage spread throughout the country, and resurfaced in late 1992 and early 1993. Besides frustration over delays in radical political change, these later events are associated with the particularly severe hyperinflation that set in during the third quarter of 1990. From 56 per cent in 1989, the annual inflation rate progressed to 233 per cent in 1990, 3,642 per cent in 1991, 2,989 per cent in 1992, 4,652 per cent in 1993 and a startling 9,797 per cent in 1994 (Kabuya and Matata 1999: 50). Hyperinflation, unemployment and the shrinking of the formal economic sector were accompanied by the emergence of short-lived but devastating pyramid investment schemes (de Villers 1992; Gondola 1997b). Mr Bindo Bolembe organized the most famous scam of this type. In exchange for a cash investment, players were to receive forty-five days later sums of money (or goods such as televisions) worth much more than their initial investment. In May 1991 Bindo went broke and the pyramid collapsed. The anger of the naive victims, many of whom were students, translated into violence, vandalism and looting.

In the first half of the 1980s in Zaire, hyperinflation was caused by a decrease in production and exports and by the government's excessive recourse to printing more zaires. The abrupt depreciation of the zaire was to contribute to the delegitimization of presidential power and the power of the transitional governments, with the exception of the one formed by Étienne Tshisekedi in August 1992.

In addition to being an economic and political phenomenon, inflation is also a social one. It 'devalues' crowds of people: 'as the millions mount up', Canetti observes (1998: 94), 'a whole people, numbered in millions, becomes nothing'. When 'inflation occurs, it is men who are depreciated until they find themselves in formations which can only be equated with flight-crowds, characterized by fear and danger' (Canetti 1998: 90). Canetti probably refers to the panic phenomenon that 'possesses' people when they rush to banks to withdraw their savings. This 'flight crowd' is the most comprehensive type because 'in their flight all the distances between them disappear (Canetti 1998: 53). As a consequence of inflation, Kinois often say that 'everyone has become poor', a situation also described by Canetti: 'An inflation cancels out distinctions between men which had seemed eternal and brings together in the same inflation crowd people who before would scarcely have nodded to each other in the street' (Canetti 1998: 187).

Canetti's concept of 'baiting crowds' is also useful in understanding the Kinshasa riots of 1991. The distinguishing characteristic of this type of crowd is its intention to kill. As with looting, there is booty, but it is the human victim who becomes the booty. 'Hunting crowds' are the precursors to 'baiting crowds' that 'divvy up' their prey according to pre-established rules. If these rules are not respected, the division of spoils results in further bloodshed (Canetti 1998: 98). In the 1991 riots, the spoils were distributed according to power, not rules. The strongest elements of the crowd had first pick, while the weaker elements had to satisfy themselves with leftovers. A newspaper account of the looting of a cold-storage warehouse is illustrative:

> The warehouse, located in the vicinity of Mont Ngafula, was easily opened with machine guns. Soldiers helped themselves to sides of meat and cartons of fish. They fled, leaving little more than scraps. A group of idle on-lookers – men, women, children and some old-timers – scrambled over the remains. In the midst of an overwhelming disorder, the warehouse was completely emptied in just a few moments. (*Le Potentiel*, 1 October 1991)

During the looting of another cold-storage warehouse in 1990 a similar scene was described. In this case, however, the journalist notes the shift from an initial every-man-for-himself sentiment to a 'poverty solidarity' whereby the spoils were shared (*Le Potentiel*, 11 December 1990). René Devisch also emphasizes this form of solidarity in cases of looting:

> Despite the confusion and avidity of the onslaught, relatively little blood was spilt. This can probably be best explained by a combination of factors such as the regulating influence of 'poverty solidarity', the carnival-like ambiance and the overall feeling of frenzy and euphoria. (1995a: 607)

This interpretation is further supported by an account given by a soldier who participated in a September 1991 looting spree in Kisangani:

> When I returned to the military camp with my spoils, I was worried that they would be taken from me, that I would be arrested, or that my house would be searched after a couple of days to steal my booty. Thank goodness! There was such a festive ambiance in the camp that I got away with impunity.[2]

The violence of looting was primarily aimed at material goods rather than people. Looters vandalized what they were unable to carry off. In the longer term, destructive violence had a suicidal aspect because it contributed to the further ruin of the economy and aggravated the general suffering of people. The September 1991 riots were acts of absolute and desperate revolt. 'The ... pillaging did not lead to a new day of regeneration and order, but rather to a regression into the imaginary world of the night with its curses, sorcery, and misfortune' (Devisch 1995a: 607).

The 'imaginary world' of the Kinshasa looting crowd contrasts sharply with the 'imaginary world' of the Christian Marchers. In the Christian March of February 1992, people chanted psalms and demonstrated with Bible in hand. They were motivated by the hope of a new Christian reign. A special chant was composed for the event: 'Stand up! Jesus is coming. He's coming today, to fight against Satan. We shall stand with courage' (Ndaywel 1993: 7). This Catholic crowd had the deliberation, calm and peacefulness of what Canetti calls a procession (1998: 154). Its strength was belief rather than politics. While looting can be interpreted as a convulsion marking a rupture with Mobutu's Zaire, the Christian March can be seen as a chosen people's struggle to flee Egypt, explaining why Étienne Tshisekedi was nicknamed Moses.

Crowds and violence

According to Congolese historian Isidore Ndaywel, violence during the period of democratic transition was unilateral, a monopoly of the regime.[3] He emphasizes the bloody repression of student protest at the University of Lubumbashi in May 1990, the repression of the Christian March, and the murders carried out by Mobutu's *hiboux* (nocturnal executioners) (1998b). Memories of post-independence bloodbaths, the massacres of the two Shaba wars, and the collective view that violence from below cannot measure up to violence from above help explain the relative nonviolent and passive public attitudes and behaviours of Kinois. Nonviolence was the policy of the major political parties of the radical opposition such as Tshisekedi's Union pour la Démocratie et Progrès Social (UDPS), just as it had been for Lumumba's MNC following independence.

The radical opposition chose the strategy of *journée ville morte* to fight Mobutu. Literally translated as 'dead city days', the objective of *ville morte* is to bring a city to a halt. People were called upon simply to stay home. The symbolism of *ville morte* is appropriate, for the concept of death describes the spirit of the city's inhabitants (Yoka 1995: 93). It is a peaceful and passive form of protest. Barricades were set up nonetheless, and stones were thrown as warnings to people who did not respect the call to stay home. The efficacy of such a strategy is obviously mitigated in a city 'where workers do not work, students do not study, ministers do not administer and educators do not educate' (Yoka 1995: 16). Indeed, the strategy of interrupting the work of fending for one's self is more detrimental to the struggling masses than to the better off.

The *journées ville morte*, like the looting sprees, reveal more despair and collective impotence than constructive capacity for political mobilization. The crucial day of 5 December 1991 proves this point. At midnight, President Mobutu's term expired. A few hours before, however, he announced his intention not to step down, basing his decision on a recent and controversial constitutional amendment. The radical opposition of the Sacred Union responded at midnight of the 4th with a concert of bells, drums, whistles and rattles. On the 5th they called for a *journée ville morte*. On the 7th a general strike was called to last until Mobutu would step down (*La Conscience*, 10–17 December 1991). Both calls were respected, but the general strike had little impact. Mobutu remained in control. On a subsequent *journée ville morte* (18 December 1992) demonstrators were brutally repressed as they ritually assassinated Mobutu by burning his portrait and other symbols of the MPR (*La Référence Plus*, 21 December 1992).

The nonviolent political discourse and the nonviolent nature of the Christian March of early 1992 stand in sharp contrast to increased social violence throughout the 1990s. Most notable was the violence associated with student actions. This included the heavy-handed requisitioning of vehicles for transportation to class; different forms of punishment and retaliation of academic authorities accused of poor management or betrayal of the common cause. There were also political and regional confrontations within the student body and violence-prone rivalries between branches of study.

The intensity of violence also heightened. The lootings of January and February 1993 were committed by men in uniform; mainly unpaid soldiers and gendarmes. Repressive violence and vicious acts were not uncommon (de Villers and Omasombo 1997: 137). These events were far more violent than the looting of September 1991. Numerous women were raped and between 136 and 500 people were killed, according to various human rights organizations. This politically uncontrollable explosion was directly linked to the introduction of the 5 million zaire banknote. Soldiers were paid with these new notes, though the Tshisekedi government refused to consider them as legal tender. According to the most widely accepted interpretation of events, soldiers mutinied because people who supported Tshisekedi and the radical opposition refused the notes. It has also been suggested that some military units who supported the opposition refused to be paid with the notes and mutinied. Families of mutinous soldiers also joined the looting, as the following narrative describes:

> A gendarme gave uniforms and bayonets to two of his sons. Dressed as soldiers, they looted shops around the Kinshasa Central Market, hiding their booty in the *cité* with a relative. The gendarme himself, his wife, son-in-law and other children went on a rampage stealing clothes, medicines, food, a radio and a TV. Civilians helped the soldiers by carrying their booty or by showing them houses of the well to do, or where people they had a grudge with lived.[4]

As in 1991, civilians helped themselves to the leftovers.

Another type of violence that occurred in Kinshasa is associated with mourning. Since the mid-1980s funeral ceremonies have increasingly been characterized by violence and delinquency. Groups of young children join funeral processions, the domain of the dead governed by ancestors and the authority of social elders. At the same time, they disrupt the procession by harassing its participants. They beg for money and accuse them of causing the death of the mourned person through witchcraft (Vangu 1997: 23; Grootaers 1998a). A specific example of crowd mobilization in this context was the funeral of Joseph Diangienda, spiritual leader of the Kimbanguist church. The body of the deceased (who died in Switzerland) was repatriated to Kinshasa on 10 July 1992. A crowd of officials and Kimbanguist followers met the corpse at the airport amid songs and lamentations. When the procession reached Kingasani, one of the city's poorest and most populous districts, it became the target of stone throwing, jeering and insults (Vangu 1997: 90–92). The anger of some is partially explained by the refusal of the Kibanguists to participate in the Christian March a few months earlier. Others responded to rumours of witchcraft that associated Diangienda with a series of tragic events in the city where people previously lost their lives.

These examples reveal the multiform nature of violence in Kinshasa. Violence is political, embedded in the confrontation of social class and generation, and is associated with witchcraft and banditry. It can be sheer violence characterized by hate, cruelty, destruction and revelry. It can target material goods and infrastructure, symbols and people – both alive and dead.

The ADFL's war of liberation and violence

The 1996–97 war of liberation led by Laurent Kabila's Alliance des Forces Démocratiques pour la Libération du Congo-Zaïre (ADFL) ushered in a new level of political violence not seen since the post-independence bloodbaths. This new political violence intensified pre-existing forms of social violence. One of the worst sequences unfolded in August 1998. Kabila dismissed certain troops and foreign military advisors on 27 July, primarily Rwandans and Tutsi elements of the Congolese army. The Rwandans withdrew, only to return shortly after in an attempt to topple the Kabila government. They invaded Kivu in the East and flew an invasion force to Bas-Congo in the West. The Bas-Congo invasion quickly proved unrealistic and turned into a fiasco. Invading soldiers were forced out of the province towards Kinshasa, even though they had been able to take control of the Inga dam for approximately two weeks. This seriously disrupted electricity supplies in Kinshasa, fraying peoples' nerves.

The Kinshasa war was launched when remnants of the invasion force reached the poor, populous districts of the capital. From 26 August through early September, Kinois ferreted out any Rwandan and Congolese Tutsi, along with former Mobutu soldiers (the ex-FAZ) who managed to infiltrate the city. Looking like a Tutsi, or simply being unkempt and dirty (due to the long march from Bas-Congo), was enough to be lynched. In an atmosphere of merrymaking, real invaders and presumed Tutsis were given the necklace – execution by having a tyre burnt around the neck. Crowds danced and sang around the charred bodies of their victims.

Like these Kinshasa mobs, Canetti's notion of the 'hunting crowd' is a collective assassin, and their use of fire also finds a parallel in his analysis. For Canetti, fire

> represents the multitude which desires the condemned person's death. The victim is assailed from all sides by the flames, which set on him simultaneously and kill him. The religions of hell go further. Collective killing by fire (fire stands as a symbol for the crowd) is associated with the idea of expulsion, namely, expulsion to hell. (1998: 50)

The symbolic meaning of death by fire extends beyond these 'religions of hell'. 'While dancing and singing,' writes T.K. Biaya,

> young Kinois carried out a kind of collective catharsis. It consisted in burning bodies over and over again as a means of marking their victory over the foreigner.... In African animist culture, burning a body means killing its soul and humanity. It breaks the reincarnation cycle and consequently access to the status of ancestor in the hereafter. (2000: 21–22)

Several factors explain the extreme violence that left an undetermined number of dead. Patriotism was one: the patriotism of being Kinois and the patriotism of being Congolese; then there was anti-Tutsi racism; fear of a return to Mobutism; and lust for revenge, exacerbated by water and electricity cuts in Kinshasa when the rebels took control and shut down the Inga dam. Another factor is the violent search for money, similar to the predatory violence previously described. Rumours (apparently well-founded) were spread that the invaders had their pockets stuffed with wads of money, supplied by their foreign sponsors.

Crowds and power

The first case of popular looting in Kinshasa in early December 1990 took place after similar incidents in Goma, but before those of Matadi, Bukavu and Lubumbashi. It was a 'bloody warning', according to the headlines in *Le Potentiel* of 11 December. Young civilians were the protagonists, targeting Lebanese, Pakistani and West African shops. Hyperinflation and Mobutu's attempts to undermine the democratization process were the cause of public frustration. The opposition did not give in. A first victory was the promulgation (on 18 December) of a law allowing unrestricted multipartism. Mobutu had tried to limit the number of parties to three. The opposition remained firm in its determination to hold a National Conference despite Mobutu's decision to hold a constitutional conference. Tshisekedi consolidated his leadership and popularity by insisting Mobutu step down, either voluntarily or by force. He denied Mobutu the compromise option of ruling without governing.

After a three-month visit in Europe and the United States, Tshisekedi returned to Kinshasa on 24 February 1991. Kinois welcomed him 'like they had welcomed the Pope ten years earlier' (*La Référence Plus*, 8 March 1991).

> Crowds formed to acknowledge his passage and legitimize his political actions. Approximately 200,000 people gathered between the airport and his headquarters in Kinshasa. Due to the density of the crowd, it took six hours to cover the distance. Zaire had not seen such a charismatic leader since the 1960s, when politicians were still able to hypnotize the crowd. (*Le Potentiel*, 27 February 1991)

Umoja (7 March 1991) emphasized the theatrical aspect of the *lider maximo*'s welcome: 'Mr Tshisekedi wa Mulumba's welcome was a real show – collective, spontaneous and disorganized.... It was characterized by a message of historic and irreversible truth.' Groups of children, described by the journalist as 'carnavalesque merry-makers', played out sketches as they accompanied the procession. In one such sketch, a picture of a fallen leopard was desecrated with a white chalk cross. Suddenly the children pointed to the animal while chanting: *Yaya Noa, assassin!... chaîne ekatana!* (Big brother Noah, assassin! Break the chains!) This was the period when Mobutu (whose symbol was the leopard) was living on his yacht, moored in the river near Kinshasa. He was seen as a selfish Noah who tried to escape the deluge alone. The sketch also recalls Mobutu's leitmotif: *après moi le déluge* (me or chaos).[5] The demystification of Mobutu intersected with the consecration of Tshisekedi. The populace of Kinshasa had found the Moses who would help them cross the Red Sea of transition.

On 22 August 1996 Mobutu was operated on for prostate cancer in Geneva. The end of the same month saw the outbreak of the Kivu war that was to bring Laurent Désiré Kabila to power in Kinshasa in May 1997. It was not until the end of September that Kinois learned that Mobutu was seriously ill. Masses were said for him in the Kinshasa churches. Tshisekedi prayed for his convalescence. 'Zaïre is thrust into panic' was the headline of *La Référence Plus*, 18 September 1996. Although an exaggeration, the headline revealed the apprehension sparked by the prospect of Mobutu's eventual demise. The chief became once again the chief. Maybe there would be chaos without him, a fear exacerbated by the new invasion from the east.

Much to the surprise of his partisans, Tshisekedi journeyed to France to meet with the ailing dictator on 21 November. Tshisekedi reported that Mobutu would reinstate him as prime minister. Mobutu did not comment. On 27 November, Tshisekedi returned to Kinshasa. His welcome was once again triumphal. The scapegoat this time was not Mobutu, but his prime minister, Kengo wa Dondo, along with his special advisor, Honoré N'Gbanda, who announced on national radio that Mobutu did not in fact agree to reinstate Tshisekedi as head of government.

On 17 December Mobutu returned to Kinshasa. Since the early months of the transition, he had spent very little time there, preferring the isolation of Gbadolite or his yacht. Kinois nicknamed him 'the neighbour'. His welcoming crowd was probably not as huge as Tshisekedi's but it was still impressive. It was also deferential and warm. 'Everyone was looking at this myth of a 66-year old man.... Weary from 31 years of power and prostate cancer... he was still the centre of attention' (*La Référence Plus*, 19 December 1996). 'He drove through the crowded neighbourhoods of Kingasani, Masina and Limete in a convertible. No Mobutist had dared to set foot in these social hot spots in years', wrote *Le Soft* (18 December 1996). 'Zairians realize the mistake of trying to kill this myth. They now have to bring it back and find refuge in it' (17 December 1996). This reversal of popular esteem can be explained by the intransitive nature of the political transition and fear of the Tutsi/Rwandan rebellion/invasion. Unable to cross the Red Sea, Zairians and Kinois remained trapped in Egypt. The miracle they believed in at this point was reconciliation between Mobutu the Pharaoh and Moses Tshisekedi. Of course it never happened. A few days after his return to Kinshasa, Mobutu asked the much-disdained Kengo to form a new government. Kinois called him 'Kengo the Tutsi' because of his mother's origins.

Before returning to Europe from Gbadolite for further medical treatment, Mobutu passed through Kinshasa once again. This time (26 December), his cortège was spurned. Women exposed themselves as a sign of contempt (*La Référence Plus*, 27 December 1996). The point of no return had been reached. Mobutu Sese Seko died in exile on 7 September 1997, four months after having been chased from power.

> The myth was dead and buried. The people, who Mobutu said owed him everything, refused him access to the Hall of Fame. It was a logical settling of accounts between a chief who considered himself indispensable and a population crippled by misery. (Vata 1997: 493)

When the AFDL marched into Kinshasa on 17 May 1997, there was little fighting. Kinois were relieved by the discipline of the *kadogos* (child soldiers). People gathered to welcome their liberators but huge crowds did not form. Retreating FAZ soldiers looted what they could; civilians, as usual, finished the job. There were approximately 200 casualties in Kinshasa's capture (the figure needs to be viewed with caution), mainly looters who were slain by AFDL troops (*La Référence Plus*, 20 May 1997).

Laurent Désiré Kabila gradually earned the popularity of the Kinois. Within a year, more people said they would vote for him in a presidential election than for Tshisekedi.[6] His few public appearances, however, were never big crowd gatherers. The Stade des Martyrs was only half full for the one-year liberation ceremony. He was only able to attract the masses twice: just after the Kinshasa war in August 1998 and for his funeral.

President Kabila monitored the unfolding of the Kinshasa war from Lubumbashi. Once it was over, while the Kinois were enjoying their victory, he returned to the capital, receiving a warm but ambiguous welcome on 9 September. It was ambiguous because by acclaiming Kabila, Kinois were indirectly celebrating their own popular victory. They felt that they had liberated themselves from their liberators. 'Those so-called Congolese Tutsis and foreigners got rid of Mobutu just so they could put us under their heel and the heel of those people from Katanga (Kabila's region of origin). But we taught them a lesson!' (de Villers et al. 2001). A week later,

Kabila held his first and last rally in Kinshasa. It was the only one that could be compared with one of Mobutu's MPR rallies.

Laurent Désiré Kabila was fatally shot on 16 January 2001. Dying, or perhaps already dead, he was flown to Harare in Zimbabwe. His body was repatriated to Kinshasa on 21 January, where people were 'dizzy with sorrow' (*Le Soir*, 22 January 2001). Huge crowds formed to look at or accompany the procession between the airport and a chapel set up near the Palais du Peuple.

People were everywhere. Men looked haggard, the women listless. Children wove tree branches. It was difficult to comprehend the chanting and lamenting because of the emotion in peoples' voices. Between the sobs, expressions of condolence could be heard: *Kende malamu papa* (Rest in peace father), *Papa akeyi na ye* (Father has left us), *Babomeli bizo Mzee* (They've killed our *Mzee*).[7] Others merely repeated '*Mzee*' or 'father' (*La Référence Plus*, 22 January 2001).

In the months preceding the assassination, Kinois had run out of patience and trust in what they considered a bankrupt regime. The Day of Patriotic Awakening (23 December), for example, was a failure: the Stade des Martyrs was 70 per cent empty (*Le Potentiel*, 26 December 2000). This was particularly humiliating because more than 80,000 people squeezed into the same stadium the next day to pray with the Army of the Eternal evangelist Sony Kafuta (*La Référence Plus*, 27 December 2000). Georges Buse, Kabila's cabinet director, celebrated the 41st Martyrs of Independence anniversary a week later in the same stadium and declared that 'the army, government and even the administration is full of enemies and traitors' (*La Tempête des Tropiques*, 5 January 2001). The stadium was two-thirds empty.

Kabila's killing traumatized Kinshasa. Although it distracted people from their daily worries, they suddenly felt implicated in the history of their country, a country in ruins, divided and invaded. The assassinated president was considered as a tragic hero who was the only person capable of ridding the Congo of its enemies. The association with Lumumba, who was killed on almost the same date forty years earlier, boosted Kabila's posthumous prestige. The importance of ancestor worship and consequently the world of the dead in African culture help explain peoples' shock and exaltation. Martin Ekwa, a Jesuit Father, explained this belief system in an interview shortly after the assassination:

The Congolese consider the dead to be extremely powerful. It is therefore necessary to be on good terms with the dead; if not, their spirits
can be very malicious. In the case of someone like Kabila, this force is
particularly powerful. If he returned as an unfriendly spirit, the country
would suffer new misfortunes. (*La Libre Belgique*, 24 January 2000)

Boyikasse Buafomo commented along the same lines:

Burying the dead with dignity is crucial in the tribal nations of Black
Africa. The dead cannot rest in peace if they are not buried in their own
land. If they feel that they were not buried with respect, they will come
back to haunt the living. (*La Libre Belgique*, 23 February 2001)

Boyikasse further emphasized that none of Congo's post-colonial
leaders was buried with due honours. After dying as a political has-
been in Boma, where he was living under house arrest, Joseph Kasa-
Vubu was buried in his native village. (Mobutu did, however, authorize
a public homage in Kinshasa to the first president of independent
Congo.) The ashes of Lumumba's incinerated body were spread out
in an isolated part of Katanga. Moïse Tshombe, who died in prison
in Algeria, is buried in Brussels. Mobutu died in exile in Morocco,
where he is buried. Perhaps the emotional crowd that mourned
Laurent Désiré Kabila was also trying to exorcize the demons and
malicious spirits that haunt the tragic history of Congo/Zaire.

Notes

Translated by Theodore Trefon.

1. Radio report by E. D'Agostino and F. Ryckmans. For the transcription, see
   /www2.rtbf.be/jp/matin/congo/accueil.html.
2. Jean Omasombo Tshonda coordinated a team of researchers to gather narratives on the January 1993 looting in Kinshasa. Archives of Institut Africain–CEDAF.
3. This is an opinion to which we only partially subscribe.
4. Archives of Institut Africain–CEDAF.
5. The play on words works better in French because *déluge* also translates as
   'flood'.
6. According to the Kinshasa-based polling service BERCI. Archives of Institut
   Africain–CEDAF.
7. *Mzee* is a Swahili term of respect for an elder.

On Being *Shege* in Kinshasa: Children, the Occult and the Street

Filip De Boeck

Children and second world realities

The urban landscape of Kinshasa, where the frenetic construction of local modernities goes hand in hand with the expectations of a millennial capitalism, is the ethnographic setting of this chapter. As elsewhere in sub-Saharan Africa, this is expressed in the thousands of independent churches operating in urban Congo (Van Dijk 2000). Time and space, heritage and innovation, and rural and urban realities of the Congolese and global worlds are imagined and reinvented in these churches. Children increasingly emerge as the focal point of all of these social and cultural interactions. They are the human intersections where the ruptures and fault lines of an African world in transition are manifested in both crisis and renewal. Children are at the frontier where the geographies of public and private inclusion and exclusion are reconfigured within the wider multiform transformation of Kinshasa.

This chapter addresses some of the internal dynamics of young people's lives in Kinshasa. What is their view of a 'good life'? What is their 'cultural politics'? How are these concepts located and imagined? How do young Kinois live the ruptures and breaches in their lives caused by decolonization, warfare and global capitalism? How do they integrate disruption and fragmentation into their lives? The voices, fears and aspirations of these young people have not been sufficiently heard. In spite of a growing body of literature on children in Africa, we know remarkably little about them. Children have often remained our 'silent others', our speechless *enfants terribles* (Caputo 1995; Hirschfeld 1999). When they are given voice, it is frequently constructed from outside and above, as a 'problem', a 'lost generation' (Cruise O'Brien 1996), or as a dead society. Despite these exclusions and silences, many young people in Africa are engaged in multifaceted social, political, cultural and economic activities that demonstrate tremendous creativity in making a living in a climate of conflict and social instability.

Street children are not new to Kinshasa. Today, however, their numbers have increased dramatically. A changing pattern of witch-craft accusations has greatly contributed to this phenomenon. The incessant reinvention of the Central African urban experience is largely enacted and produced in the enchanting spaces of Christian fundamentalism with their frenzied production of discourses and practices surrounding witchcraft. They are intimately related. One disconcerting aspect of this evolution is the central role of children in these witchcraft discourses and practices (De Boeck 2000a). In contemporary Kinshasa, thousands of children are implicated in witchcraft accusations, and, as a result, often end up on the street. They find themselves, as a consequence, at the heart of a dramatic social transformation (*Le Potentiel*, 4 September 2000), characterized by the changing relationship between the worlds of the visible and the invisible, life and death, daily reality and its nocturnal double. In Kinshasa, as elsewhere in Africa, beneath the surface of visible reality another reality has always lurked. Today, however, this 'second world', 'second city', pandemonium world', or 'fourth dimension' (one of numerous invisible worlds) increasingly seems to overwhelm the first world of daily reality. Street children, who largely live dur-ing the night, sleeping, eating and living in cemeteries, have come to exemplify the permeability of the borderlines between day and night, life and death, public and private, order and disorder. They become the embodiment of a growing alienation of the order of the visible.

After a brief description of the child witchcraft phenomenon in the streets, homes and churches of Kinshasa, it is argued that children and young adolescents have never before occupied a more central position in the public spaces of urban life, whether in popular music, media, churches, army, street or bed. Children are both victims and important actors in transforming Congolese society. This central but ambivalent status of children seems to have crystallized most clearly around the figure of the witch, a materialization of the intersection of power and sexuality. With the increasing impact of globalization, new tensions between traditions and modernities are being defined, and sometimes resolved, in the field of witchcraft.

Both the heritage of colonialist modernity, as embodied by the post-colonial state, and the current forces of globalization are some-times perceived as a source of witchcraft and evil in themselves. Conversely, there is not only the witchcraft of modernity but, as noted by Geschiere (1997), witchcraft practices in Africa have also gradually been reformulated to represent one of the major gate-ways to modernity. In the rapid growth of urban expectations and desires, an 'economy of the occult' (Comaroff and Comaroff 1999) has become the means to win 'the war of dreams' (Augé 1997). This nocturnal economy of desire, linking a fast-growing local economy of violence and the violence of a penetrating global economy, is increasingly experienced and shaped by the young. Children have begun to occupy a more central position in the public realm. Here, they appear not only as passive consumers as in the West, but also as major players with access to new global economic arenas, often in direct opposition to the generations that precede them.

The economic crisis in Kinshasa has also caused a profound transformation of existing idioms of witchcraft. The ever-increasing poverty of Kinshasa and other cities and towns throughout the vast country is accentuated by conflict in the eastern provinces. This puts further pressure on kin-based solidarity systems in the capital. The linkage between children and witches is related to a profound destructuring and restructuring of the notions of motherhood, gerontocracy, authority and kinship itself. The chapter concludes by addressing a further question: are these transformations that are embedded in the profound crisis that punctuates urban life repre-sentative of a crisis of the logic of reciprocity and gift-giving that underpins the broader field of kinship?

Children, witchcraft and the street in Kinshasa

My name is Mamuya. I am 14 years old. I became a witch because of Komazulu, my boyfriend. One day he gave me a mango. The follow-ing night he came to visit me in my parents' house and threatened that he would kill me if I didn't offer him human meat in return for the mango. From that moment I entered his group of witches and became his nocturnal companion. I didn't tell my mother. There are three members in our group. At night we fly to the houses of our victims with our aeroplane that we make from the bark of a mango-tree. When we fly out at night I transform myself into a cockroach. Komazulu is the pilot of our plane. He is the one who kills. He gives me some meat and some blood and then I eat and drink. Sometimes he gives me an arm, sometimes a leg. Personally I prefer to eat buttocks. I keep a part of the meat to give to my grandmother, who is a witch too. Komazulu is a colonel in the second world and he has offered me the grade of captain for sacrificing my baby brother. I killed him by giving him diarrhoea. With our group we have already killed eight people. Now I have come out of the world of shadows thanks to the prayer of the preacher who treats me in church. But the others who are still in the second world keep pulling at me. They want to kill me now for fear that I will betray them. (Interview in the Church of the Holy Spirit, Selembao, Kinshasa, September 1999)

By 1999 such stories of rumours and accusations had become common in Kinshasa. One immediate effect has been that the city streets are increasingly filled with growing groups of street children, referred to as monks (*moines*), sparrows (*moineaux*), *phaseurs* or *bashege* (sing. *shege/chégué*). Until recently the phenomenon of street children was restricted to the busy commercial and administrative Gombe district. Large groups of children live and roam through some of the public spaces of this area, like the central market, the space around the post office along Gombe's main boulevard, the square in front of the railway station, abandoned government buildings, and the cemetery of Gombe. Most of these spaces are linked to specific activities and are therefore occupied by children only during specific moments of the day or times of the week. Their activities are largely nomadic. During the day, many live on top of the market pavilions, which are referred to as *planète* or *Golgotha*. They sleep there and let 'their body and their sex rest'. For most, the market is a space of opportunity associated with 'a whole lot of money' (*libulu ya mbongo*) and 'similar to Tshikapa' (a Congolese diamond-mining town). Some, especially boys, have small jobs or run errands for shop owners while others beg or look for anything they can pick up from the street to sell or eat. In the afternoons they *donker* (look for an opportunity to get money) and steal (*koyiba, kokota tarmac, koluka* or *attaquer*). According to Trésor, who was then 12 years old: 'stealing is my job, I steal from everybody. Whites and blacks! I was even able to send my brother to Europe by means of the money I stole in the street.'

When the market empties towards evening, children start to become more active. Boys gather, wash in the open market gutters (what they call 'the river') and move to other places where they congregate to cook, play and spend the money earned during the day. They buy clothes, tickets for the movie theatre or a football game. Most street children, however, spend their money on drinks (beer and locally distilled alcohol), drugs – mostly Valium, marijuana (*nwa, diamba, likaya*, either in the form of powder, *pimbo*, or as leaves, *pelouse*) and glue, but increasingly heroin and cocaine. Drugs and alcohol play an important role in street life. They help one sleep and become strong; they get rid of headaches, chase away shame, make one's heart bad in order to steal or give one a healthy appetite. They serve to intoxicate (*kwiti*), to think (*kobouler, kokanisa*), to reflect (*mpo na kokotisa idéologie, mpo na kokotisa mayele*), to make ideology or wisdom enter the brain, to make memory come back (*kozongisa mémoire*) and to be calm and aware of oneself. Children use drugs and alcohol to attain the state of *dédoublement,* which can be interpreted as leaving one's own body to observe oneself.

Girls, some as young as five or six, work the streets as prostitutes at night (*koroder*), because the body is a shop, it is money and merchandise (*nzoto eza magasin, eza mbongo, eza lokola marchandise*). Among these young prostitutes several categories are distinguished: *fioti-fioti* (little little one or dancer); *nionio* (girls with firm breasts – *nionio* is the word for very small diamonds); *makoma* (girls with large breasts, named after the successful religious family gospel band Makoma, whose female lead singers are second-generation Congolese teenagers living in the Netherlands); *mabata rouges* (filthy prostitutes, literally red ducks); *ancien de Saio* (an old, worn-out prostitute, after the veterans of the Force Publique who fought in Saio during World War II); *kamoke* (little one). Often very young girls (*bakamoke*) work as assistants to older girls if the price offered by a customer is not enough.

In recent years street children have become a familiar aspect of street life all over Kinshasa. Previously concentrated in Gombe, they can be observed near the football stadiums, under bridges, in shacks and cardboard boxes (referred to as *baguesta* – from 'guesthouse'), along railroad tracks and rivers. Many of these children were forced to take to the street after being accused by family members of being witches. Such accusations against children within their own families have become a common occurrence, transcending class and ethnic divisions. Increasingly, children are accused of causing problems such as job loss or the illness or death of other family members or neighbours. In other cases young girls are suspected of transforming themselves into stunningly beautiful women to lure their fathers and uncles into their bed to snatch away their testicles or penis, make them impotent or even kill them. Illustrating the fact that Congo's current social crisis is also a crisis of cause-seeking, children are believed to be at the origin of madness, cancer or heart attacks among their relatives and parents. Other children appear to be 3- or 4-year-olds in the first world, but in the nocturnal second world they have already given birth to many children. These in turn become witch-children roaming through the streets of Kinshasa. Other girls are believed to transform into mystic serpents, crocodiles or *mami wata* sirens.

Inside the accused child's family, suspicions and accusations often erupt in violent conflict. The child can be severely beaten and in extreme cases killed by family members or neighbours. Most of these children, however, are disowned. Displaced, disenfranchised, but feared by most, the alleged witch-children (called *sheta* or *tsor*, from French *sorcier*) end up on the street. They eventually team up in a stable (*écurie*), meaning a gang of other abandoned children. This is usually a group of up to seven members that can stay together for some weeks or months but rarely longer than a year. Various stables often associate to form a larger, more loosely knit group. Most of these gangs (amongst the best known are États-Unis, Jamaïk, Temps Mauvais) are organized around age and gender with clearly separated groups of older and younger boys and girls. Mixed groups are quite uncommon.

Groups constitute cooperative units where members share the money they make, the goods they steal (such as clothes) and the food they found during the day. Group members often roam around together. They defend and protect each other against outside threats. Most male groups have strongly established hierarchies with a clear pecking order and a recognized leader. Many of the girls' groups, usually smaller, are organized around a slightly older girl called 'mother' and who acts as the 'madam' for the two or three younger girls under her protection. Although there is often solidarity among members of the group, there is also peer pressure, control and intimidation. Boys say, for example, *omoni, oyibi* (if you see me steal, steal as well), meaning: do not denounce me, or you will suffer the consequences. It is extremely important not to be seen as weak, as a *fopaner* (a poor thief who only steals during daytime), a *mbakasa* (someone who is afraid and who doesn't know how to find money) or a *yuma* (idiot). One has to be a *yanké* (a strong person, derived from Yankee), an *actionnaire* (a capable thief who also enters people's homes at night), someone who has *face* (who is street wise) and has the heart and the spirit of *zembe* (someone who doesn't fear policemen or soldiers). One has to possess *lupemba*, meaning whiteness and good luck (see White in this volume).

Interaction within and between gangs is violent. It ranges from fistfights and beatings, to physical mutilation by means of pieces of glass or razor blades, to rape and gang rape of younger girls and boys by older boys. The intra- and inter-group violence is frequently related to initiatory practices to make *zembe* enter your body and teach you how to endure, how to be hard, patient and without pity. Initiation into magical knowledge related to the street also involves various forms of violence.

Although girls often have a *mukukule* (a special street boyfriend with whom gifts, love, sex and friendship are shared), the existence of nuclear street families is quite rare. Children who end up on the street have often occupied secondary positions in their own family. Kazadi, for example, is an 18-year-old who has been living on the street since the age of 11. His mother died when he was 10. His father remarried, causing a dispute with his deceased wife's sisters. One day his older brother was sent by their father to the market to buy some goods. On the way, he lost his father's money and for fear of being punished decided not to return home. Because his father's new wife mistreated him, Kazadi soon followed his brother onto the street. Tabuki has a similar narrative. She is 16 and has been on the street for a year, where she works as a prostitute:

> My mother died and my father is in Bukavu. I came to Kinshasa with my paternal uncle because of the war. When Kabila entered the city I was still in school. My older brother was a Kabila soldier who lived in Camp Kokolo (military garrison). After a while my paternal uncle stopped feeling responsible for me. He refused to give me money and sent me to my brother in Camp Kokolo. But my brother was often absent. Sometimes I stayed in his house on my own for two days or more. That is how I started seeing husbands. One of them, a petty shop owner, paid my school fees. When my brother heard about this he beat me up. Out of fear of what he might do, I ran away and started living on the street.

Many street children were orphaned at a very early age because of AIDS and other public-health problems. Others were abandoned by their mothers, often teenagers themselves, and grew up with relatives such as grandparents, uncles, aunts, cousins or one of their father's co-wives. When one or both parents are still alive, they are often absent. This absence increasingly results from patterns of displacement and migration caused by political instability, war and economic factors.

Churches and child-witches

The spiral of violence that erupts within the kinship group following witchcraft accusations against children is partly countered by church and prayer movements that flourish throughout Kinshasa. Fundamentalist churches – primarily Pentecostal churches and apocalyptic movements – devote considerable attention to the struggle between Good and Evil, demons and Satan (De Boeck 2001a; Meyer 1999). This emphasis plays a crucial role in developing the figure of the witch, which is increasingly central to the collective imagination of Congolese society. Simultaneously, society itself is being restructured in terms of an Armageddon or second world in which demons have gathered in an all-out war against God (Book of Revelation 16:16).

Paradoxically, the demonization of the witch in church discourse makes the witch itself more omnipresent in the social field. The churches' position on evil, straightforward as it may seem at first sight, produces contradictory tensions. The churches' role vis-à-vis the child-witch phenomenon is equally ambivalent, making them both part of the witchcraft problem and its local solution. On the one hand the churches' space is one of the most prominent sites where the figures of witch and child coincide. During masses and group prayers, children are urged to make a public confession to reveal their true nature as a witch and confess the number of their victims. The naming of the witch offers an opportunity to solve the crisis as it has always done in traditional settings. Before this public moment they have usually been identified as witches by preachers during more private consultations. In these meetings, more traditional divinatory models are often blended with church discourse to create a ritualized moment of witch-finding. As a result of these denunciations, however, international aid agencies and NGOs such as Save the Children accuse the preachers of child abuse. These organizations usually treat the issue of witch-children in Kinshasa as a humanitarian problem of street children, while choosing to disregard the cultural implications of witchcraft. One could argue, however, that the churches, in providing and authorizing this type of diagnosis, offer an alternative to the violence that occurs in the family following a witchcraft accusation.

The preachers do not themselves produce these accusations. They merely confirm and thereby legitimize them. In doing so, the healing church relocates and reformulates the physical and psychological violence that accused children undergo within their kin-group. The child is subsequently removed from the threatening family context where its place has become highly problematic and is left in the care of a preacher. Here the generally tough treatment starts with an initial period of seclusion, either individually or collectively, with other child-witches. Some churches receive up to a hundred children a week. Children usually live in very poor conditions in terms of food and hygiene during the period of seclusion, which may last from a couple of days to some weeks or even months, depending on the seriousness of the case. They are subjected to a period of fasting and ritual purification when in seclusion. A lavish administration of laxatives and emetics aims at cleansing the meat of the victims they ate from the witch-children's bodies. Undigested pieces of meat and bone and other alleged pieces of evidence are displayed as having come from the children's vomit and excrement. This is proof to corroborate the children's narratives of cannibalistic practices during their public confessions before the church congregation. During the period of seclusion the children are regularly subjected to interrogations, sometimes alone, at other times in the presence of one or both of the child's parents or other related adults, if they are willing to cooperate. Many adults, though, are too afraid of their children to confront them in this context.

Some days after the crucial moment of public confession the preacher organizes a number of exorcizing moments, referred to as deliverance or soul-healing. This ritualized exorcism is carried out in prayer groups under the guidance of female church members known as *intercesseuses*. The child is placed in the middle of a circle of praying women who regularly lapse into glossolalia, which is a sign of the Holy Spirit's presence. The focus of this powerful praying ritual is the child, who is repeatedly subjected to exorcizing prayer. One woman takes the lead in prayer while the others assist her by regularly punctuating her preaching with religious songs and hymns. Depending on the type of church, these praying sessions unfold in collaboration with the child's mother or relatives in the hope of reintegrating the cleansed witch-child into its family. In many cases, though, parents are not very collaborative and reintegration remains difficult. Because relatives remain too afraid to accept such children back in their midst, they are often forced to take to the street.

Geographies of inclusion and exclusion

Children in the West are usually viewed as dependants who are not ready to act responsibly (De Boeck and Honwana 2000). Their social space is confined to family and school. Those who do not correspond to this image are immediately perceived as potential victims in need of help. In sub-Saharan Africa the situation is radically different. Few children enjoy the luxury of security offered by parents, school and state. From a Western perspective, it is not difficult to document how children are victimized by the political, economic, social, psychological and sexual violence that pervades the African continent. This general victimizing discourse is nonetheless short-sighted because African children are not merely vulnerable and passive victims, subjected to socio-economic and political processes. They are also active subjects, 'makers and breakers' of reality. Children in these worlds often have the capacity to act forcefully on the world in which they live. In line with local notions of agency, children in Kinshasa are not considered as future or proto-adults; nor do they regard themselves is this way. They are seen, and see themselves, as actors in the present with crucial social roles. They appear as Janus-like double-faced figures, embodying a frontier dynamic of mutation and border-crossing which has become an essential aspect of the central African post-colonial space (De Boeck 2000b).

Children in Kinshasa are increasingly relegated to sites of exclusion. They are expelled from the kin group, chased onto the street and secluded in churches. Never before, however, have they been so prominently present in urban public space. There is the very real and violent barrel-of-the-gun power that child-soldiers have come to represent. In 1997 when these *kadogos* (some of whom were no more than 10) made their entry into Kinshasa when Kabila seized power, most of the capital's inhabitants perceived this as something totally new and shocking.

On the economic front, young adolescents also occupy an increasingly central position. Throughout the 1990s, large numbers of Kinois youth became *bana Lunda* (children of Lunda); trekking to the Angolan province of Lunda Norte in search of diamonds and dollars. These youngsters often acquired wealth far beyond that of their parents. Upon returning to Kinshasa, their money allowed them to access versions of a modern life from which their parents were excluded. In Kinshasa today, it is said that money makes one a *patron* or a *mwana ya kilo* (a child with clout), regardless of age. Financial independence (and responsibility) bestowed social power on these youngsters.

In the context of family and kin, this power gave rise to intergenerational conflicts. Diamond-related witchcraft accusations triggered disputes over redistribution of the new wealth. Rumours abound of witch children of Lunda who have sex with their mothers or kill and metaphorically eat their fathers and uncles in return for diamonds and dollars (De Boeck 1999a, 1999b, 2001b). In these contexts, the empowering witchcraft idiom of eating, formerly the prerogative of elders, fully illustrates the nocturnal possibilities of immediate access to modernity. Eating in Congo's popular imagination also refers to a broad range of social realities and practices: eating money means having money to spend and give to others, eating one's wife means making love to her, just as eating power has specific political connotations (Bayart 1992). One 12-year-old boy describes why he likes eating human meat:

> In the human body, everything is useful. The blood is fuel, diesel, kerosene and red wine; the water that may be found in the body is motor oil, brake oil, perfume, drinking water, medical syrup, and other medicine like cream to rub on your body. The backbone is a radio, a satellite telephone, a radio transmitter; the head is a cooking pot, the glass from which the big guys drink, a swimming pool, a bucket which you can use to wash yourself in. The eyes are a mirror, a television, a telescope. The hair can be used to make a mattress or a sofa for the living room.

The nocturnal consumption of one's elders gives direct access to, and is quite literally an incorporation and ingestion of, modernity's spaces of consumption. In this sense, the street is the space for the creation of an alternative modernity in which the established model of colonialist modernity is captured, appropriated, transformed and redefined to fit the terms of these children's own experience. According to some, the word *chégué* originated when Kabila's *kadogos* walked into Kinshasa, resembling small rebels or Che Guevaras. The word, however, existed before Kabila's march to Kinshasa. A more frequently heard explanation is that *shege* derives from Shengen, the town in Luxembourg where European Union member states signed a treaty to abolish their internal frontiers and create a single European zone for the circulation of goods and individuals. Pertinent here is the single visa for travel to all *Shengen* countries. For Kinshasa's *bashege*, for whom travelling to Europe is not an option, the street is an alternative *Shengen* territory. It is the space where food, freedom, sex and money can be had. The world of the *cité*, referred to as *Belesi* (derived from Belgium), is a backward world of constraints. In contrast, the street is seen as modern and exciting.

In popular urban culture, too, children and young adolescents now appear in the limelight. In recent songs of Congolese superstar Papa Wemba the same *shege* who are stigmatized as witches, have been given a prominent place. Papa Wemba and his orchestra Viva La Musica invite them to sing together on stage in acts of public provocation. In a 1999 record entitled *Fula Ngenge*, Papa Wemba picked up on the phenomenon of the *bafioti-fioti* (kiKongo) or *bakamoke* (Lingala), literally 'the little little ones', which celebrates little girls who love to dance (*bafioti-fioti balingi babina*).[1] On stage 12-year-old girls have replaced female dancers in their late teens and twenties to warm up the audiences of Kinshasa's major orchestras with dance and sexual radiation. In the process, the sexual attractions and dangers of little girls, the female counterparts of male child-soldiers, have developed into a widespread urban mythology in which the figure of the *kamoke sukali* (the sweet little one) appears as the ultimate femme fatale and man-eater. In weekly issues of locally produced comic strips, which are in many respects the printed equivalent of pavement radio, the figure of the *kamoke sukali* has become central. She is also related to the *mami wata* siren, another femme fatale who promises access to material wealth in return for human lives. Both these female figures illustrate the linkages that exist between sexuality, gender, age, death, access to modernity's materiality, and the second world.

Children have similarly become central actors in the media. Not only do private television stations in Kinshasa stage regular shows during which individual children are presented and publicly denounced, but the new constellation of meaning being shaped around children and witchcraft is modelled by more global media. Video films produced in Nigeria and Ghana are influential in this respect. These films often relate narratives about the adventures of spirit-children. Audio cassettes are on sale in Kinshasa and are frequently broadcast on popular religious radio and television stations such as the Radio et Télévision Message de Vie, which is owned by one of Kinshasa's most successful preachers, Fernando Kutino, founder of a Church named the Army of Victory.

Children are nowhere more centrally present on the public scene than in churches, particularly during the crucial moments of public confession and *témoignage*. In these instances children can demonstrate the real power they possess because they may implicate in their testimony the adult who allegedly initiated them into the world of witchcraft. Examples include the market woman who offered food to a child to link her to the nocturnal forces of evil, and the father, mother or relative who offered a glass of water to the little friends of their son or daughter, expecting a nocturnal counter-gift of human meat in return. These public accusations can have severe consequences for the adults identified because relatives or neighbours of the children react violently, beating up, lynching or burning the accused adults. Children may also use their narratives and status as witch to settle scores with adults or create the conditions that will allow them to leave home and find freedom in the street. As Barry (1998–99: 143) points out with respect to street children in Ouagadougou, 'a longing for freedom' is a prominent motive for children to take to the streets. Street children in Kinshasa express this by saying:

> It is cold at home. The street, however, is where one is free: if you feel like stealing you can steal, if you feel like fighting you can fight, if you feel like lying, you can lie, if you feel like smoking you can smoke. To stay at home is wrong. At home, eating is a struggle.

While the street is experienced as a space where life is indeed hard and filthy and where one has to sign a contract with death, it is also perceived as a dream-like space of diversion, opportunity and promise. Children say that on the street 'your body belongs to yourself' and you can 'dedouble yourself', by dancing, drinking, dreaming and having fun. These children are not on the street because they have no family, home or relatives or because they are no longer taken care of. Many of them have wilfully decided to extricate themselves from their family. In Kinshasa, becoming a witch is a way to attain independence and to challenge parents, public authority and other forms of established order. Many children perceive the street as the space where they can escape the poverty of their family's home and quench their consumerist dreams by buying clothes, shoes and other things with the money earned and stolen there.

A crisis of kinship models and gift transactions?

These phenomena are only possible in a context of complex social change and community turmoil. The common models of kinship are being restructured due to this turmoil. Geschiere (1997) argues that witchcraft is the shadow side of kinship. Hence, the shifts occurring within the discourses and practices of witchcraft, and the partial disconnection of witchcraft and kinship indicate profound transformations of kinship, and gift relations. In long-standing traditions of witchcraft the danger of bewitchment always emanated from within the family. In Kinshasa today, however, the witch can be a total stranger. The market, for example, is a microcosm of the urban environment. It is a place where the logic of the gift is transformed into a logic of commodification. It is experienced as a potentially dangerous and contaminating place where strangers skilfully intrude into one's life. The drastic changes affecting long-standing and widely shared cultural viewpoints may also explain what Lambek calls 'the sometimes violent rejection of ancestral and parental figures in response to what is understood as their absence, their impotence, or their withdrawal of protection' (Lambek 2000: 12).

At the micro-levels of household, family and lineage, the pressures of social change are most tangibly present in newly emerging relations of authority and respect between the sexes and generations. These new attitudes can be seen in the emerging new division of labour. Where some youngsters have gained financial power and social status by revenues from the diamond trade, most family heads are still men, although frequently unemployed. Only a tiny fraction of Kinshasa's active adult males are employed in the formal sector with a salaried job. Nor do they easily find work in the informal economy, because youngsters, who are often more street-wise and better equipped in terms of social skills, are more competitive. Kinois men are also, as elsewhere in Africa, caught up in processes of migratory labour, travelling, for example, to engage in the diamond traffic. Others have mistresses and children in different areas of the vast city. While men are absent, solidarity networks and strategies invented for daily survival, like rotating credit associations (*mozikis* and *likelembas*), neighbourhood units of cooperation, church support groups, and small-scale production of goods for sale, are largely the work of women.

While it may be commonplace to assert that this goes hand in hand with the erosion of male authority, it helps explain why witch-children tend to accuse women and maternal figures more frequently than male authority figures. Where socio-economic shifts are mediated by gender, the discourse of witchcraft tends to focus on new female figures of authority, rather than on the male elder who had previously embodied the ultimate personification of the witch. When this occurs in a social landscape of kin-based relations under strain, such shifts form an ideal ground for further tensions, like witchcraft accusations among adults or between the adults and the children under their care. The realities of urban polygamy, for example, have introduced a category of rival co-wives (*mbanda*). Unlike rural polygamous households, these urban rivals usually do not live in the same house or neighbourhood. Frequently they do not even know of each other's existence.

Where they do, relations between these women are often very tense. When a rival dies, or when she is absent for a long period searching for a better life elsewhere, her children regularly end up in the Cinderella care of one of her husband's co-wives. Kinois say that 'to take care of the child of one's rival is to take care of a dangerous monster' (*kobokola mwana ya mbanda obokoli elima*). If such a child's father dies, it is particularly vulnerable. Within the family these children end up seriously marginalized, viewed as a burden and an extra mouth to feed. In many Kinshasa households people eat only once every two days: one day a meal is prepared for the children and the next day for the adults (see De Herdt and Tollens in this volume). In such a context, children who occupy a structurally weak position in their kin-group are more likely to be singled out as witches. This applies even more specifically to children who may stand out, for example, due to mental or physical handicaps or idiosyncratic behaviour.

The same socio-economic changes have contributed to a growing intergenerational rift. Children in rural areas certainly no longer wish to live in a small house with a grass roof and till the fields like their parents. Despite its miserable living conditions, Kinshasa continues to be viewed by rural youth as a space of independence and freedom that offers escape from social control exerted by village elders. In Kinshasa and other Congolese urban settings, youngsters create spaces of independence for themselves, like a prayer group or a stable. Boys within the same age group (who frequently, although not necessarily, share the same regional or ethnic background and live in the same neighbourhood) may set up some kind of small-scale moneymaking activity. While the organization of a stable is generally characterized by a strict hierarchy between *grands* and *petits* (fathers and sons), prayer groups, comprising both boys and girls, are more often structured around invented horizontal kinship ties within a single generation. These latter are not, in other words, organized around vertical or intergenerational relations. These Kinshasa prayer groups are often splinters of more established adult churches. Members call each other 'brother and sister in Christ'. They meet several times a week, often during nocturnal prayer events that begin at sunset and end early the next morning. They provide the ideal site for children to escape parental control and other forms of hierarchical relations.

Despite significant transformations, the principles of age and seniority are still important social markers. These principles seem to have become the ground for generational conflict, mediated by gender. Through this conflict, urban youth are transforming themselves into authoritative elders and adopting the syntax of gerontocracy before their time. The current modes of adolescent self-realization in Kinshasa differ only slightly from the old gerontocratic models. These modes include a monopolization of the public space and becoming a maker of a social network that distributes power within one's kin or peer group. Girls and young women are also trying to become more independent vis-à-vis prevailing authority relations. Like their young male counterparts, however, they also replicate these structures while reversing gendered power relations between generations (De Boeck 1999b). Existing patterns of authority remain indelible in this gender and generational conflict, but they are now being appropriated and accessed in new and flexible ways by different categories of social actors who were formerly excluded from positions of power. The fact that this generational conflict erupts today is highlighted by the new discursive fields and practices of witchcraft that focus essentially on children and women.

Changes in the fields of gift, reciprocity and exchange have resulted from the newly emerging links between women and witchcraft. These fields have always underpinned social transactions, especially with respect to marriage and alliance. In today's Kinshasa, however, many young men and their families simply do not have the wherewithal to carry out the gift obligations that make a marriage possible. As one vendor on Kinshasa's central market succinctly put it: *Tosalaka te, tobalaka te* (we don't work so we don't marry). Kinshasa's youth has turned to the short-cut marriage: they start living together, have a child and present both their families with a *fait accompli*, thereby short-circuiting the gift cycle of marriage and bride-wealth trans- actions. This in turn adds to the causes for conflict and witchcraft accusations occurring in urban families.

The transformed nature of women's social positions changes gift and reciprocity patterns that underpin the total social field. It also alters the cultural status of the maternal figure. This may ex- plain why witch-children accuse women and mothers more often than men. Witch-children's stories exemplify a recurring pattern in which children become witches through a poisoned gift offered by a man but more frequently by a woman. In all these stories something is being communicated about the status of the gift, and about the fact that gifts are being redefined in terms of money and commodities.

The emergence of the new notion that one can be bound by a debt that one did not even know one had contracted is crucial in this phenomenon. It can be noted here that it is through similar mechanisms of bewitching debt creation that many children are forced to remain on the street. A common practice among street children is creating fictive debts through which a child is forced to enter into a debt (*kokotisa na nyongo*) and cannot leave the street until the debt is repaid to the group. The group, for example, sends one of its members to the market to sell some goods. Even if the child is unable to sell the commodity in question within a day, the group will consider it sold and will consequently demand payment from the child. Both the market and the second world create relations of dependency in which children are bound against their will.

There is nothing surprising in the linkage of witchcraft and gift, because both are ambivalent and dangerous 'total social facts' (Latouche 1998: 154ff). Bewitchment has always been defined in a context of inverted and perverted social relations and has always been transmitted by means of a gift, mainly food or sex. The witch is therefore a fundamental figure of exchange. The witch is a figure of crisis who sets in motion a destructive internal mechanism of redistribution and eating, defining in a negative way what social reciprocity and eating together (sharing) means in a positive way. In its traditional role of nocturnal shadow or double, the witch had a direct relationship with its diurnal subject. Day and night, life and death, the subject and its shadow were inextricably linked in an intimate relationship.

Within that relationship, the gift operated as fulcrum. It thereby enabled the nocturnal double to contribute to the institutionalization of its other half, the social order of everyday life. The fact, however, that women start to appear as the social actors who manipulate the gift, especially in relation to children, may indicate a growing alienation of the double. This also reveals the changing nature of the *dédoublement*, of the junction and disjunction between first and second worlds, diurnal and nocturnal, or life and death. The image of mother as witch goes radically against the deeply engrained cultural model which views women as genetrix, cultivator and cook, the ultimate figures of physical and social reproduction. They are thus seen as the generative force behind the social fabric.

The cracks appearing in the urban gift logic may have also led to the conceptualization and collective experience of children in terms of witchcraft. In alliance transactions, children represent, even more so than women, the supreme gift or the ultimate binding agents in the cycles of reciprocity and redistribution that underpin social life. It is especially the circulation of children between wife-givers and wife-takers and various other kinship units that create the social architecture of kinship, alliance and residence (Lallemand 1993). Children thus appear both as medium and as actors in the creation and extension of kinship and alliance: without children, there are no gifts. Without gifts, there are no kin, no allies or social body. The demonization of children by adults reveals the incapacity of the people of Kinshasa to deal with current social transformations. The demonization phenomenon may thus be understood as a dark allegory through which the Kinois translate a deep-rooted anxiety about their own future.

Note

1. At the time of writing, Papa Wemba is in prison in France on charges of child trafficking.

The Elusive *Lupemba*:
Rumours about Fame and
(Mis)fortune in Kinshasa

Bob W. White

People in Kinshasa generally assume that popular musicians make use of witchcraft. Publicly, however, the practice is categorically denied. Some musicians break that silence when they join one of the city's increasingly common evangelical Christian churches. Surprisingly, their testimonies focus less on a denial of the power of witchcraft than on their conversion against its use. *Fétiche*, as witchcraft is most commonly referred to throughout central Africa, clearly remains part of a moral universe. It is not guaranteed to work, but if it is performed properly and if its conditions are adhered to, it can lead to success in politics, love, money and music. Of course there is often a price for such success. If *fétiche* is to be effective, one must sacrifice something of close personal value such as a friend or family member.[1]

This chapter examines the connections between sacrificial witchcraft rumours and the success of popular musicians in Kinshasa. In Faustian deals with invisible agents of evil, individuals are said to ensure their success on credit by promising to offer a human sacrifice at some later date. The assumption that musicians who become rich and powerful must have used *fétiche* is relevant in the context of Mobutu's Zaire, where political careers were allegedly made, and by the arbitrary manipulation of money and power. Arbitrariness is explained by tales of fortune-granting mermaids, shape-shifting boa constrictors and jet-setting mystics. If musicians in Kinshasa deny involvement with *fétiche* it is not so much that they are embarrassed by their belief in it, although this may also be the case, but that its practice is considered anti-social, selfish and unpredictable.

The study of these issues illuminates the experience of being Kinois during the Mobutu–Kabila transition period because they are deeply embedded in Congolese cultural beliefs and practices. Significant scholarship on African witchcraft and its ancillary practices (sorcery, divination, spirit possession, secret societies and witch-hunting) reveals much about cultural diversity in Africa. The English term 'witchcraft' is used in this article loosely for a variety of supernatural phenomena and practices. Where possible, however, it is replaced by local terms to temper the perils of translation.[2] Evans-Pritchard's distinction between sorcery and witchcraft is operational in Kinshasa, although in some sense it is inverted. *Sorcellerie* (sorcery) is a mostly nocturnal activity that cannot necessarily be controlled. It is the bulimia of evil and a way of life. *Fétichisme*, by contrast, is action that is premeditated, voluntary and usually limited in space and time. The French terms *sorcellerie* and *fétichisme* are often used in Lingala, but this does not mean that they are used in exactly the same way. Both terms are part of a larger cluster of words having to do with the occult.[3] Like the term 'witchcraft' in English, the word *fétiche* is used with a wide range of meanings in Kinshasa. This chapter examines rumours about sacrificial witchcraft, as opposed to other kinds of witchcraft, because they are more pertinent to the Kinshasa music scene (White, forthcoming). Although it is difficult to prove that sacrifice rumours are the most common ones, they are common enough to help understand the nuances of Kinshasa's particular political culture and cultural politics.

Recent research on popular music in Kinshasa (and Brazzaville) has raised important questions about Kinshasa's particular place in Congolese and African history (Gondola 1997c; Stewart 2000; Tchebwa 1996). Congolese popular dance music, usually referred to as *la musique moderne*, dates back to the late 1930s when the first radio stations were set up in colonial Leopoldville. Today, Congolese popular music, or *soukous* as it is most commonly known outside of the Congo, has become a *musica franca* of sub-Saharan Africa, competing actively with local musical styles in a number of important regional markets outside Kinshasa. Rumours about the mystical work of local celebrities in Kinshasa are a rich source of information about how this unique urban culture is organized and imagined.

After an overview of recent literature on rumours and a more detailed discussion of the particular form they take in Kinshasa's colourful music scene, the case of one musician who was accused of using sacrificial witchcraft to advance his career will be described. The local notion of *lupemba* (roughly translated as 'success') will then be addressed to explain how it is linked to political and moral agency. The concluding section analyses the uniqueness of witchcraft accusations in Kinshasa and how they are related to the political culture of Mobutu's Zaire. The central argument of this chapter is that Kinois use rumours to indicate both closeness to Kinshasa's most visible public figures, the stars of the modern music scene, and to distance themselves from what they consider morally dubious political and cultural practice.

Rumours and rumouring

Despite the importance of *radio trottoir* (pavement radio) in many parts of the world, relatively little attention has been paid to socially and culturally constructed forms of hearsay. *Radio trottoir*, and the rumours that result from it, have been discussed as a means of understanding social networks (Epstein 1969), as a modern form of African oral tradition (Ellis 1989), as a source of information about political events (Ellis 1993) and as a social levelling mechanism (Geschiere 1997). Although rumour can be seen as one of the many faces of popular culture, it is not the exclusive domain of the masses. Artists, writers and politicians draw from and contribute to rumoured knowledge in various ways.

The analysis of rumours should be less concerned with their credibility than with the social dialogue in which they are embedded (White 1993). Building upon this idea, this chapter argues that a more systematic analysis of rumours needs to look at how they are produced, legitimated, versioned and spread. Stephen Ellis (1993) has shown how people from all walks of life participate in the production and transmission of rumours, although rumours told by those with proximity to the rumours' subjects are often accorded special status. He explains how people who tell rumours about political figures in Togo almost never cite their sources and rarely offer empirical evidence for their claims. These observations can be applied to the rumouring situation in Kinshasa. If it is true that rumours are seen as legitimate if they are widely spoken and known (B.W. White 2000: 31), then rumours that circulate between media and everyday conversations may be considered as means of explaining why some people are rich and famous and others are not.

The intimate public

Life in Kinshasa is filled with rumour. There are rumours about important public figures from the worlds of politics, commerce and entertainment, and around particular themes such as Tutsi seductresses, subversive urban tricksters and buffoon government officials (Mudaba 1984; Nlandu-Tsasa 1997; Onyumbe 1994). The figures with whom musicians share the public sphere in Kinshasa are also the subject of stories about mystical wrongdoings. Unlike politicians, however, musicians' power over the public is not based on the threat of violence or the promise of protection. According to many Kinois, it is the musicians' ability to speak on behalf of the ordinary people that most distinguishes them from politicians. Important figures in the world of business and organized sports are also talked about (Schatzberg 2000), but unlike musicians and politicians they are not judged on their mastery of language or on the style of their self-presentation. The local celebrities who bear the most resemblance to musicians are the self-styled evangelical preachers who have become increasingly common in Kinshasa. Indeed, over the past few years, numerous famous musicians have abandoned popular dance music for the music of Jesus. Their new-found commitment to combat witchcraft helps explain their increasing popularity across a wide variety of audiences in this music-loving city.

Spraying money, taking pictures and name-dropping are aspects of a live concert that permit members of the audience to become active participants in the spectacle. Similarly, when people tell rumours about popular musicians, they effectively write themselves into a world outside of themselves by circulating information and contributing to public knowledge about these celebrities. Public knowledge must seem like private knowledge to be convincing, which explains why stories about popular music stars are often told from a personal point of view. They purposefully hint at intimacy between fan and artist. With the help of rumours, ordinary people become active participants in the musicians' world of relative fame, glamour and fortune.

In this context, Kinois would often begin conversations with me by saying: 'Oh, Monsieur Bob, we just came back from Pépé Kallé's place. He's doing really well', or 'I was just hanging out with Werrason. They have a big show tomorrow night.' When asked for more information it became clear they had just walked by Pépé Kallé's house and seen him sitting on the balcony, or had seen Werrason's car in the parking lot during band practice. In reality, they had no contact with the musicians they portrayed as being close personal friends.[4] Proximity stories create an illusion of intimacy with the stars, because information of this kind could presumably only result from first-hand knowledge. Telling stories about absent others is accordingly a source of great pleasure. Music fans talk about their favourite artists in terms such as these:

> Defao's a good kid, very responsible. We grew up together in Kisantu.

> That's just the way Manwaku is, he's lived in Switzerland for a long time. He even has a Swiss wife.

> After Blaise got beat up by those goons, he was never the same. It took him a long time before he could start singing again.

> Koffi likes women too much. The other day he almost kicked Dieudonné out of the band because he caught him running around with one of his new girlfriends.

> Ben would do anything to have Lidjo in his band. He's already offered him a car and all the clothes he wants.

The raw material of rumour

Rumours circulate through both unofficial channels such as word of mouth and through more established media such as fan club news-letters, local newspapers, radio and television programmes, and music and fashion entertainment magazines. Local television is an important source of information about musicians, and live interviews with musicians can have a tremendous impact on public thinking about particular artists and the relationships between them.[5] Distinctions between these rumour channels are blurred. Rumours circulate freely between them, and oral and written sources tend to be mutually constitutive (B.W. White 2000). Reading in most parts of Africa is not constrained by low literacy rates, at least in relation to news-papers. People who are literate often read and translate out loud for the benefit of those who are not, making newspaper reading public and social. Because of their relative permanence and rapid circulation, newspapers and magazines help form a body of public knowledge about what is happening in the world of music and beyond.[6]

The most commonly circulated information about musicians concerns their regular professional activities. *Salongo*, a culture and

news daily, often gives a weekly or bi-weekly roundup of music
events. One issue included a full-page spread with four articles. The
headlines were: 'After his stay in Europe, Madilu Multi-Système is
Back'; 'Despite the departure of two key players, Temple di-Roma
maintains a steady course'; 'Barring unforeseen circumstances, Zaiko
Langa-Langa in Kinshasa at the end of this month' and 'Big Stars:
on the right path as they tour in Zambia' (October 1996). As some
of these headlines suggest, articles on musicians are intended to
promote important events such as splintering, tours or new albums.
These events are also an important source of information upon
which rumours are often based: 'Will Bimi come back to Zaiko?',
'After his return to Paris, Papa Wemba soon to Japan', 'Mbilia Bel
and Rigo Star in the US for a new album'.

Word-of-mouth stories often have a spectacular nature. During
the peak of its success in the late 1980s, Boketchu's Swede Swede
quickly became known as the new darling of Kinshasa political
and business elites. As if to confirm his privileged status, rumours
circulated that the group used to be interrupted mid-show to be
whisked away to Gbadolite for a private performance before Mobutu.
Upon arriving, they were reportedly showered with gifts and given
unlimited access to the president's fleet of fancy cars. Franco's close
association with the Mobutu regime meant that every new album
he issued was accompanied by a series of rumours attempting to
explain particular lyrics in terms of his volatile relationship with the
national political elite (Ewens 1994).

Newspaper stories about band competitiveness and various forms
of intra-band conflict, especially splintering, are also common. Headlines from Kinshasa newspapers reveal the sagas: 'Adamo, Baroza
and Malage spit in the face of N'yoka Longo' (*Ndule*, 1995). 'Defao
Matumona: "I'll stop moonlighting the day that Ben Nyamabo starts
paying me my copyrights in cash"' (*Disco Hit*, 1985); 'Likinga ap-
pointed president of Zaiko Familia Dei, and unhappy Bimi tries to
sell his Mercedes and go into hiding in Europe' (*Disco Hit*, 1985).
Magazine articles concentrate on recently departed (or sacked) band
members and the never-ending conflicts that result from personnel changes: 'Nyoka: "I don't know how Bimi was able to buy a
Mercedes"' (*L'As des As*, 1988); 'The conflict continues between Ilo
Pablo and Nyoka Longo' (*L'As des As*, 1988); 'Nono Atalaku at war
with Ditutala' (*L'As des As*, 1988). In some cases magazines publish
sensational accounts of musicians' lives and later offer the musician an

open forum to refute claims or deny accusations: 'Debaba: "I never asked to join Familia Dei"' (*Disco Hit* 147) or 'Fafa of Molokai says he was never arrested for selling drugs' (*Disco Hit* 60).

Achille Ngoy, a Congolese journalist active in the 1970s Kinshasa music scene, explained that as a young journalist he would encourage musicians to make up stories about conflicts between them. 'Telling artists to fight', he said, 'was a good way to sell papers' (interview, 28 June 1995). Scenes of reconciliation between rival or even feuding artists, often staged during concert time, are often reported: 'Playing on the same stage: Zaiko Langa Langa and L'Empire Bakuba' (*Ndule*, 1995), 'Wemba and Koffi are pals once again: A new record to seal their friendship' (*Le Soir*, 1996). The story of Nyoka Longo's conspicuous presence at Koffi Olomide's tenth anniversary party circulated widely after the event. People speculated whether this was a self-promoting gesture on the part of Nyoka Longo or if it represented a genuine reconciliation between the two rivals.

Music journalists are unable to resist the topic of *fétiche* because it is certain to arouse readers' interest. Musicians have come to expect this topic in most interviews and generally give predictable answers:

> *Music Journalist*: You have been accused of using *nkisi* (charms) to harm your rivals to stay on top of the Kinshasa music scene. Is this true?
>
> *Musician*: Let me declare once and for all that I have never made use of magic or any such thing in order to get where I am today as a musician. Other people may use *fétiche* but I have never done so. If I am popular it is because people like my music, know that I work hard and that I am a Christian. If other people have bad things to say, I don't know why, maybe they are just jealous.

Exchanges like this are frequent. Musicians know journalists will ask the question, and journalists know musicians will deny any involvement. Musicians are evaluated on their ability to answer the question without losing their composure. Fans know that even if the accusations were true, the musician would never confess. Nonetheless, rumours concerning musicians and *fétiche* persist. Public statements by musicians only add to the excitement that surrounds them. A number of classics in this category are still told. One artist was thought to be trafficking in human skulls to finance his lucrative production business in the 1970s. Another was the victim of a spell that made him unable to sing when he stepped before the microphone. Another artist's success resulted from a mystical contract that prevented him from owning a home or investing the money he was earning. That money made from *fétiche* be spent and not saved or invested is a common element in rumours. People believe the ostentatious display characteristic of successful musicians in Kinshasa results from this kind of *fétiche*.

Fame and (mis)fortune

The study of witchcraft has made a dramatic comeback in African Studies in recent years. After the influential work of Evans-Pritchard, anthropological research in the 1970s leaned heavily on the insights of psychology and sociology to explain witchcraft and accusations of witchcraft in mostly functionalist terms. In the 1990s scholars began to look at witchcraft as a means of understanding Africa's particular experience with modernity and the post-colonial state. Witchcraft was 'called on to counter the magic of modernity' (Comaroff and Comaroff 1993: xxv), mediating the encounter with the market (Austen 1993) and various types of political and mystical authority (Geschiere 1997). While much of the recent research on witchcraft and modernity has made progress in delinking witchcraft from African tradition, it nonetheless tends to conflate arguments about modernity with arguments that take place within modernity (Englund 1996). In the context of contemporary Kinshasa, it is therefore more interesting to focus on recent scholarship which views popular culture and mass media as resources for understanding the debates that occur about witchcraft in Africa today (Bastian 1993; Meyer 2000).

Reddy Amisi, a star who made a name for himself as leader of Wemba's Viva La Musica, began to enjoy widespread success after a series of tours and the release of his second solo album in 1995. After a Reddy concert just outside Kinshasa, a car accident resulted in the death of several fans driving home from the show. Concerned about rumours that blamed the accident on his use of *fétiche*, Reddy called a press conference to clarify his position and clear himself of any association with the unfortunate occurrence:

> What the media had to say on this subject caused me a great deal of pain and at some point I stopped being myself. I was asking myself, 'What should I do? Why was I being accused? What proof did they have that I was responsible for this accident?' (Kanyinda 1996: 6)

This was the rumour: people died after Reddy's concert because he had commissioned *fétiche* to ensure that his return to Kinshasa (from his base in Paris) would be a success. In exchange, however, he had to sacrifice several lives, so he designated his fans. The incident is interesting because Reddy took the rumours seriously enough to organize a press conference to clear the air. In explaining the unfortunate occurrence, he recalled that accidents of this type happen frequently on Kinshasa's dilapidated roads and if anyone was to blame it had to be municipal authorities for not repairing broken streetlamps along the road. He also blamed the concert organizers for failing to secure the approval of local authorities and spiritual leaders.

A passage from another Reddy interview stresses the human psychology of those who would rumour witchcraft:

> I'm a *mwana Kin* (a son of Kinshasa), I mean a real Kinois. I grew up in this city and know what people are like. Kinois always have to talk about each other and most of the time all they do is speculate.... As far as I'm concerned, when people start talking about *fétiche* it's nothing new. Even in your family, if you become someone important because of your own efforts, people accuse you of being a witch. It's really sad! I am not responsible for the accident that happened ... it's always people with ill will that are the first to accuse others. (N'zanga 1996: 4)

This incident shows how in the popular imagination the success of musical artists is linked to sacrifice. Other rumours reiterate the theme. One artist is said to mystically eat young women (a metaphor for sacrificial witchcraft) at the request of his mother, who is suspected of being not only a witch but also her son's lover. Rumours about another artist often revolve around a youthful story in which he refused to marry a girl he made pregnant. The girl's father was outraged and commissioned an act of *fétiche* that terminated his daughter's pregnancy and made the singer sterile or gay. Another artist is rumoured to have signed a fourteen-year contract with the Devil to ensure his success as a singer. In exchange for the life of a close friend or family member, the artist was guaranteed a never-ending string of hit songs and the adoration of countless female fans. As the end of his contract drew near, however, he opted out and became a born-again Christian. Today he sings for the glory of God and has remained at the top of the religious charts ever since.

Most rumoured sacrifice occurs through a ritual specialist or *féticheur* (*nganga* in Lingala), who is said to act on behalf of a spirit or supernatural being. The sacrifice is not made to God or to ancestors but directly to the spirit in question. It may be a *mami wata* (a mermaid water spirit), a troubled soul, or the Devil himself. The *féticheur* can play the role of go-between, simply transmitting information from the person requesting his services, or can be more actively involved in the negotiation between spirit and client. The *féticheur* is the object of a great deal of scrutiny, and *féticheurs* are often suspected of exaggerating their importance, even of inventing information to extract more money from potential clients.

Stories about individuals who mutilate themselves as a sacrifice are also common. There are stories, for example, about diamond miners who cut off fingers or toes to ensure success in their quest for gems (see De Boeck 1998). Stories along these lines have been told about the female singer Mpongo Love and about Pepe Kalle (of the musical group Empire Bakuba), both of whom lived as celebrities with visible physical handicaps. People who are unable to have children are said to have sacrificed their fertility for wealth and happiness. People in this category are thought to be unable to sacrifice someone else because they either refuse to do so or because the designated victim is equipped with mystical protection against such attacks.

Rumours of witchcraft explain both misfortune and good fortune, especially of others. Successful musicians in Kinshasa are highly visible public figures and their social and financial success is the subject of much public discussion and scrutiny. Success often leads to jealousy and accusations of witchcraft. This puts musicians in the strangely modern position of having to explain that they earned their status not with the help of witchcraft but through their own personal efforts: *eza nkisi te* (it's not witchcraft).[7] In response to these accusations, or perhaps as a form of anticipatory defence, musicians use song lyrics to deflect potential attacks on their character by embedding their success in a complex set of discourses about family, hard work and faith in God. Lyrics from a recent song by Koffi Olomide illustrate the point:

> My mother told me that in life you shouldn't worry.
> When people talk about you it is only to distract you.
> It's nothing, just like the wind that comes before the rain.
> There is more to life than that.
> It's important to be fair and to respect other people.
> This world belongs to God and death escapes no one.
> It is for us all.

In the meantime, the most important thing is hard work.
We are God's children.
Child, kneel down and heaven will lift you up.
Child, humility is a good thing.
Child, vanity is a bad thing.
Child, don't go too fast in life.
The last judgement is in heaven.

('Kamutshima', from *Attentat*)

When asked to comment on having won two of the prestigious Kora
All Africa Music awards in November 2001, Wenge Musica leader
Werrason explained his success in the following terms:

The secret of my success is prayer, guidance, good strategies, hard work
and taking people's advice. I swear that God has answered my prayer.
Because I just realized one of my dreams: to be chosen as the Best
Artist of Central Africa *and* the Best Artist of Africa. God has proven
once again that he has never been corrupted and that he never will be.
(Mpaka 2000: 2)

These examples raise two questions. First, should rumours about
witchcraft that are published in the local press but that remain
completely anonymous be seen as accusations? While most cases of
witchcraft accusation involve two or more parties who know each
other, there are examples where the accuser remains anonymous. As
language is a form of social action and can have real consequences,
the musician responded to the accusations as if they were real. In
some sense they were, since they threatened his image and his ar-
tistic livelihood.

Second, if rumours without authors are doing the work of accusations, then what does this reveal about the nature of social proximity
and distance in urban African settings? In an article about witchcraft
and the state in Kenya, Diane Ciekawy argues that witchcraft accusations are 'increasingly conducted in a one-way direction, and
that dialogical accusation now is extremely rare' (1998: 133). While
there is evidence of this in Kinshasa, it does not mean that audiences have ceased to debate the moral and political significance of
such accusations.

The elusive *lupemba*

You know that you have *lupemba* when you see that something has changed
in your life: the way that fans adore you, you're in the headlines of all

the papers, you're on the radio and on television, people are talking about you. Everything comes easily. And there are messengers of *féticheurs* that try to persuade you to protect yourself by using amulets or mysticism. (Serge Makobo, personal communication, 30 July 2001)

The concept of *lupemba*, a Lingala term encompassing the notions of success, blessing, good fortune, whiteness, destiny, popularity, natural talent or natural gift, is common in the realm of popular music. It can also be heard in the discussions about prominent religious figures, business people and politicians. *Lupemba* can be acquired through hard work, luck or the practice of *fétiche*. People can also be born with it, in which case it resembles something close to charisma or a gift from God. To get *lupemba* on their own merits, artists must possess qualities like perseverance, charisma and talent. Musicians with remarkable talent or virtuosity are often referred to as sorcerers of their instrument. Franco Luambo Makiadi, for example, was known as *le sorcier de la guitare*. An additional condition of success in the Kinshasa music scene is that the artist must be perceived as being Kinois. With or without these traits, artists help *lupemba* along by prompting rumours about their (usually polemical) relations with other musicians or about their recourse to supernatural intervention.

Acquiring *lupemba* is difficult. Maintaining it is even more of a challenge. Having *lupemba* is similar to finding salaried work: friends and family expect to derive some kind of benefit. Musicians consequently do what they can to enjoy their success while it lasts. *Lupemba* requires an abundance of patience and care. Musicians talk about managing success and the importance of self-control when faced with the pressures of popularity. If an artist is not careful, *lupemba* may go to his head and he will lose touch with fellow musicians and fans. To remain successful, musicians have to renew their musical repertoire constantly. They also have to prove themselves trendsetters in fashion, choreography and popular ways of speaking. They have to strike a delicate balance between cruelty and indifference towards their rivals, and they have to uphold a public image of magnanimity towards fans, especially their most visible and difficult ones, the street children described by De Boeck in the last chapter.

One musician who has proved particularly adept at maintaining *lupemba* is the Wenge Musica dissident Werrason, self-proclaimed *roi de la forêt* (king of the forest). Since the band's most recent series of

fragmentations, Wenge Musica BCBG has splintered into two principal camps. One is headed by singer and co-founder J.B. Mpiana,
and the other by Werrason himself, also a founding member of the
group. This rivalry is probably the one most discussed in the history of modern Congolese music, showing how closely audiences
in Kinshasa follow the movements of musicians and how divisions
within the music scene can lead to divisions within audiences.
Competition between the two stars is fuelled by the fact that they
come from different regions of the country. Observers comment
that Werrason's larger following is not only due to his active use
of *fétiche* but also to the large number of people from his region
(Bandundu) living in Kinshasa. Some degree of his success is also
attributable to the way he emerged from a highly publicized conflict
with another musician as the clear underdog. This status appeals
to the large and growing number of disenfranchised Kinois (Biaya
1997). Where Werrason is seen as a kind of popular hero, his rival
J.B. is criticized as being pretentious and arrogant, which has been
detrimental to his popularity.

Similar criticisms have been made of Werrason's other rival, musical
veteran Koffi Olomide, who adopted the nickname *Nkolo Lupemba*
(the owner of success). Olomide, arguably the most prominent figure
in the Kinshasa music scene of the 1990s, is an artist who has always
been able to emerge from his conflicts with the local press with
his *lupemba* intact. Fans often complain that his music is formulaic,
that he dances poorly and that he has a dubious sense of fashion.
Nonetheless, for nearly ten years he has remained at the top of
Kinshasa's music industry. When Kinois talk about the numerous
Mercedes-Benzes that Koffi purchased for the musicians in his band;
they also note that he retained the titles of ownership. The cars
were loans, not gifts. Werrason, on the other hand, was said to have
given his musicians full possession of the BMWs he purchased for
them, proving his qualities as a fair and generous leader. Werrason's
actions can be seen as creating social capital through the power of
the gift. They can also be perceived as future protection against moral
criticism and mystical aggression. In the context of this rivalry, fans
found Koffi's behaviour to be selfish and manipulative, reinforcing
his image as 'the most stubborn and quarrelsome of all Congolese
musicians' (*L'Avenir*, 10 March 2001).

It was probably with some sense of amusement that Kinois
viewed the cartoon *Force de Frappe*. A Zimbabwean soldier is beating

Koffi up because he refused to submit to a checkpoint search after returning from a concert. The cartoon, based on a real incident, includes an ironic reference to the title of one of Koffi's albums, *Force de Frappe* (Strike force). The caption beneath the title, *système ya fimbo*, refers to the colonial practice of public whippings[8] and satirizes both Koffi and the Zimbabwean armed forces stationed in Kinshasa, who, by the spring of 2001, had earned a reputation for being both unpredictable and brutal. Stories about this incident circulated throughout Kinshasa and even abroad. A reporter from Harare's government-sponsored *Sunday Mail* commented: '[Koffi's] luck ran out one day when ... soldiers exposed him for being just an ordinary musician' (Magwaza 2001).

Kinois, however, do not appreciate ordinary musicians. One reason that Koffi and others have kept the attention of Kinshasa audiences is their shameless self-promotion, excessive charisma and magical use of language (Ossete 1994). These are the things that Kinois expect from famous musicians, and the strategic use of witchcraft is clearly part of this universe of expectation. When fans become disillusioned with musicians it is not because they are rich and famous or because they are suspected of practising witchcraft. Fans lose faith in popular musicians when success causes them to lose touch with their base: both their fan base and their own origins – often just as humble as those of their fans. When musicians are perceived as being conceited, selfish or vain, they are placed in the same category as politicians who consider themselves above the law and beyond moral reproach.

Stories about the success of popular musicians are often linked to morality. The use of *fétiche* may be central to success for many Kinois, but it does not determine the nature of moral claims made about musical celebrities. It does, however, open up a field of saying and doing in which the moral agency of these highly visible public figures is held up for public scrutiny and debate.

Morality in Kinshasa

Narratives of fame in Kinshasa, as elsewhere, provide information that enables audiences to explain the status and special qualities that celebrities enjoy. Rumours cannot, however, be separated from the moral basis of the phenomena they seek to explain. Narratives of celebrity in the United States, for example, are usually stories of eccentricity, persistence and personal triumph. They often include stories of traumatic childhoods, torrid love affairs, bitter divorces and personal struggles with drug addiction. While rumours about American celebrities rarely speak of sacrificial witchcraft, this is not what distinguishes rumours in Los Angeles or New York from rumours in Kinshasa. Rather it is the particular set of moral questions that rumours raise about sociability, leadership and agency. In Kinshasa, audiences are less concerned with how people in the public spotlight obtain wealth than what they do with it and how they behave once they have it. This is consistent with Englund's view that witchcraft discourses are occasions to contest and manage the images of people as moral beings (1996).

The emergence of a modern star system, a phenomenon that has its roots in an earlier period of Congolese music, is a source of wonder and excitement for many Kinois. It represents a model of upward social mobility outside the realm of national politics or other unwhitened forms of post-colonial prestige. For some, however, it is a source of great concern because popular musicians have become role models for an entire generation of young Kinois. Musicians' behaviour is perceived as being symptomatic of a general moral decline in contemporary Congolese society (Devisch 1996). The rumours described in this chapter express the anxiety inherent in this tension. In Kinshasa, rumours are part of a public conversation that produces knowledge about the conditions and costs of becoming rich and famous in an economy of extreme poverty. They are moral barometers that show how the paths of personal advancement are filled with pain and sacrifice – not sacrifice in the Celine Dion or Michael Jackson sense of hard work, no childhood, no privacy, but real sacrifice: human sacrifice!

The content of these rumours is less surprising than the way musicians take them seriously. One possible explanation is that musicians are genuinely concerned about their reputation and the stories that circulate about their actions. The example of Reddy Amisi shows how this can be the case. Another possibility, perhaps more cynical, is that musicians like the attention they receive in the media because any press is good press. To be accused of practising harmful witchcraft could be interpreted as confirmation the musician has achieved a degree of success.[10] In an economy of poverty, accusations of witchcraft are not merely levelling mechanisms. They also represent the accumulation of social and symbolic capital.

Not coincidentally, witchcraft was an important part of the mystique surrounding the Mobutu regime. Rumours that circulated about politicians tended to normalize beliefs about witchcraft in Kinshasa's streets. During this period the number of songs that made reference to witchcraft increased (Onyumbe 1982; Kouvouama 1994; Ossete 1994). In his account of the Mobutu regime's political culture, Ndaywel è Nziem (1993) analyses the confessions of Sakombi Inongo and Bofossa W'Amb'ea Nkoso, formerly important political figures and supporters of Mobutu, but now reformed. They publicly denounced the use of *fétiche* and described the occult practices of Mobutu's inner circle in detail. Both testimonies begin with a suggestion from a friend or colleague to make use of protective magic against potential rivals and for special occasions. The need for continued protection leads to increasingly complex and time-consuming ritual practices and causes both men to seek out an impressive list of ritual specialists from places as far away as Senegal, the United States and India.

What is conspicuously absent from these testimonies, however, is any mention of personal involvement in harmful witchcraft or human sacrifice. When faced with the prospect of sacrificing a family member to ensure continued success, Sakombi immediately decided to renounce witchcraft altogether: 'My children and I were destined to die, but God saved us all' (Ndaywel 1993: 47). That Sakombi and Bofossa conveniently omit human sacrifice from their narrative of conversion supports the argument that there are several forms of witchcraft, and those intended to harm or eliminate others are best left unspoken.

These narratives of conversion circulated widely via videocassette and local newspapers. They confirmed for many Kinois that Mobutu and his inner circle made regular use of *fétiche*. They also confirmed that witchcraft was an effective means of ensuring personal gain and profit in Mobutu's Zaire. While published versions of these histories are rare, there is strong reason to believe that such practices were extremely common among Zaire's political elite (Ndaywel 1993: 39). Mobutu's *recours à l'authenticité*, the state ideology that remained visible well into the 1980s, relied heavily on traditional symbols of power. The efficacy of many of these symbols was based on links to ancestors and other beings from the world beyond. There is also evidence to suggest that officials in the president's cabinet encouraged and even propagated certain types of rumours to add to the mystique surrounding the regime (Nkanga 1997).[9] If witchcraft rumours are common in Kinshasa, however, it cannot be attributed to the Mobutu regime alone. The atrocious history of violence, from King Leopold II to Belgian colonialism, has made it clear to Congolese that evil exists in the hearts of men.

Scholarship on witchcraft in Africa has succeeded in showing the complexity and diversity of its functioning. It has been less convincing, however, in explaining why witchcraft is important and what people do with it (Rutherford 1999). Most models used to explain witchcraft have certain similarities: witchcraft as social release, witchcraft as individual catharsis, witchcraft as a way to make sense of contradiction, witchcraft as a levelling mechanism, and so on. In Kinshasa, as elsewhere in Africa, witchcraft and other spiritual matters are embedded in a matter-of-fact everydayness that is predictable, unglamorous and often insecure.

When witchcraft is a 'permanent suspicion' (Lienhardt in Ciekawy 1998) and the possibility of being accused of it is a constant threat, people use rumours to position themselves in dangerous but potentially rewarding moral worlds. This can be a matter of creating either intimacy or distance or both. Commentary such as 'I don't like the music of so and so because he is a witch' suggests that aesthetic judgements on particular artists are not easily separated from the public perception of the artist as a moral agent. With comments of this sort, Kinois not only mark distance between themselves and a particular type of (im)moral behaviour, they also position themselves in the very serious space of social and moral discourse.

Notes

1. This chapter is based on fourteen months of fieldwork in Brazzaville and Kinshasa in 1995–96 where I studied the local music industry, played with a local band and gathered data about the history and politics of music. Among those who have sacrificed themselves for my benefit, I would like to thank John Grinling for the initial inspiration to write this essay, Vinh-Kim Nguyen for his stimulating conversation about the anthropology of witchcraft in Africa, and Serge Makobo, who was tremendously helpful in gathering some of the background information for this chapter. Luise

White, Eric Gable, Zoe Strother and Michael McGovern offered comments on earlier versions of the essay; Theodore Trefon le editorial eye near the end of the revision process. The following tions generously provided financial support for the research on which this chapter is based: The Zeller Family Foundation, McGill Graduate Faculty, Center for Society, Technology and Development (McGill), and the McGill Associates.

2. On the dangers of translation, see Pels 1998 and Ciekawy and Geschiere 1998.

3. The Kikongo word *nkisi* is used to describe charms and other supernatural accessories that can be harmful or protective, but the variation *kisi* is used to refer to medicines or other objects that are used in the treatment of illness, supernatural or otherwise. The Kikongo word *ndoki* (also *kindoki*) refers to supernatural beings such as witches, spirits or ghosts, but it can also apply to people who, by association, are considered to be sorciers (witches). The term *occultisme* is less common and, though it is closely related to *fétichisme*, it has a more restricted meaning than *fétichisme*, which can be used in the name of evil or in the name of good.

4. Singer J.P. Busé tells stories of fans who 'just want to get close to you to see what you're like so that they can go and talk about you to their friends' (personal communication).

5. Manda Tchebwa's weekly *Karibu Variétés* and a television show called *Le Club des Stars* were particularly popular during the period of research.

6. Of the nearly twenty regular daily or weekly newspapers in circulation in Kinshasa in 1995–96, about half published articles on music, and of that number about five publish music-related articles (rumours or otherwise) in every issue. Music and entertainment magazines number anywhere from three to five in Kinshasa at any given time, with titles such as *Disco Hit*, *L'As des As*, and *Ndule*. They are published less frequently than newspapers, but usually devote approximately 75–80 per cent of their content to music-related stories, the rest being about sports and fashion.

7. 'Personal effort' is an idea that is clearly influenced by Christian ideas about the religious value of hard work, but it implicitly refers back to the threat of witchcraft accusations. J.P. Busé, a Congolese singer based in Toronto, named his first production company EPERS XYZ (Efforts Personnels XYZ). De Boeck (1998) discusses the Kikwit popular painter Paepm, whose assumed name underlines this same personal effort: Peintre Artiste Effort Personnel Midgi.

8. For an interesting analysis of the policy of public whippings, see Dembour 1992.

9. Compare this with Eric Gable's analysis of wealth and secrecy in the Manjaco region of Guinea-Buissau, where 'the last thing men wanted to admit was the possibility that they possessed nothing worth envying' (Gable 1997).

10. A situation which is decidedly different from other parts of Africa, where politicians have been documented as trying to combat witchcraft's spread. See Fisiy 1998; Ciekawy 1998.

Bibliography

André, C. and L. Luzolele Lola (2001) *Politique d'aide de l'Union européenne vis-à-vis des pays impliqués dans la guerre en RD Congo: Levier pour la paix ou encouragement à la guerre?*, Brussels: Réseau Europe–Congo.

Arbyn, M., H. Bruneel, S. Molisho and F. Ekwanzala (1995) 'Human trypanosomiasis in Zaire: A return to the beginning of the century?', *Archives of Public Health*, vol. 53: 365–71.

Augé, M. (1997) *La guerre des rêves: exercices d'ethno-fiction*, Paris: Seuil.

Austen, R.A. (1993) 'The moral economy of witchcraft: An essay in comparative history', in J. Comaroff and J. Comaroff (eds) *Modernity and its Malcontents: Ritual and Power in Postcolonial Africa*, Chicago: University of Chicago Press.

Bakajika Banjikil, T. (1997) *Epuration ethnique en Afrique: Les 'Kasaïens'*, Paris: L'Harmattan.

Banea-Mayambu, J. P. (2001) 'Consommation alimentaire, pratiques de survie et sécurité alimentaire des ménages à Kinshasa', in Mukadi Kankonde and E. Tollens (eds) *Sécurité Alimentaire au Congo-Kinshasa – production, consommation et survie*, Leuven: KUL/Paris: L'Harmattan.

Barber, K. (1997) *Readings in African Popular Culture*, Bloomington: Indiana University Press.

Barry, A. (1998–99) 'Marginalité et errance juvéniles en milieu urbain. La place de l'aide psychologique dans les dispositifs de prise en charge des enfants de la rue', *Psychopathologie africaine*, vol. 29, no. 2: 139–90.

Bastian, M. (1993) 'Bloodhounds who have no friends: witchcraft and locality in the Nigerian popular press', in J. Comaroff and J. Comaroff (eds) *Modernity and its Malcontents: Ritual and Power in Postcolonial Africa*, Chicago: University of Chicago Press.

Bayart, J.-F. (1992) *L'État en Afrique. La politique du ventre*, Paris: Fayard.

BERCI (1997) 'Enquête sur les perceptions individuelles de la pauvreté effectuée sur la population de Kinshasa en septembre 1997', unpublished report, Kinshasa: BERCI/UNDP.

BESCOPLAN/GRET (2000) 'Analyse des effets de l'état des routes de desserte agricole sur l'économie alimentaire à Kinshasa', unpublished report, Kinshasa: Programme d'Appui à la Réhabilitation/Fonds Européen de Développement.

Biaya, T. K. (2001) 'La *kinoiserie*: aux sources de la culture politique congolaise contemporaine', unpublished manuscript.

Biaya, T. K. (2000) 'Jeunes et culture de la rue en Afrique urbaine (Addis-Abeba, Dakar et Kinshasa)', *Politique Africain* 80: 5–31.

Biaya, T. K. (1997) 'Kinshasa: anomie, ambiance and violence', in G. Hérault and P. Adesanmi (eds) *Youth, Street Culture and Urban Violence in Africa*, Ibadan: IFRA.

Biaya, T. K (1994) 'Mundele, Ndumba et ambiance. Le vrai bal blanc et noir(e)', in G. de Villers (ed.) *Belgique/Zaïre: une histoire en quête d'avenir*, Brussels/Paris: CEDAF/L'Harmattan.

Bibeau, G. et al. (1979) 'La médecine traditionnelle au Zaïre: Fonctionnement et contribution potentielle aux services de santé', Ottawa: CRDI.

Bierschenk, T. and J.-P. Olivier de Sardan (1997) 'Local powers and a distant state in rural Central African Republic', *Journal of Modern African Studies*, vol. 35, no. 3: 441–68.

Bruneau, J.-C. (1995) 'Crise et déclin de la croissance des villes au Zaïre: une image actualisée', *Revue belge de géographie*, vol. 58, no. 1–2: 103–14.

Bumba Monga Ngoy (1999) *L'Université de Kinshasa en l'an 2004*, Kinshasa: Editions universitaires africaines.

CRISP (1959) 'Eléments pour une sociologie d'une émeute, Léopoldville, janvier 1959', *Courrier hebdomadaire*, Brussels, 16 January.

Callaghy, T. (1984) *The State–Society Struggle: Zaire in Comparative Perspective*, New York: Columbia University Press.

Canetti, E. (1998) *Crowds and Power*, New York: Noonday Press.

Caputo, V. (1995) 'Anthropology's silent others: A consideration of some conceptual and methodological issues for the study of youth and children's cultures', in V. Amit-Talai and H. Wulff (eds) *Youth Cultures: A Cross-Cultural Perspective*, London: Routledge.

CEPLANUT (2000), 'Enquête nutritionnelle et de consommation alimentaire dans la ville de Kinshasa', unpublished report.

Chabal, P. and J.-P. Daloz (1999) *Africa Works: Disorder as a Political Instrument*, London: James Currey.

Cheuzeville, H. (2003) *Kadogo. Enfants des guerres d'Afrique centrale. Soudan, Ouganda, Rwanda, R.D. Congo*, Paris: L'Harmattan.

Ciekawy, D. (1998) 'Witchcraft in Statecraft: Five Technologies of Power in Colonial and Postcolonial Coastal Kenya', *African Studies Review*, vol. 41, no. 3: 119–41.

Ciekawy, D. and P. Geschiere (1998) 'Containing witchcraft: conflicting scenarios in postcolonial Africa', *African Studies Review*, vol. 41, no. 3: 1–14.

Colenbunders, R., H. Taelman and P. Piot (1984) 'AIDS: an old disease from Africa?', letter, *British Medical Journal*, vol. 289: 765.

Comaroff, J. and J. Comaroff (1993) *Modernity and its Malcontents: Ritual and Power in Postcolonial Africa*, Chicago: University of Chicago Press.

Comaroff, J. and J. Comaroff (1999) 'Occult economies and the violence of abstraction: Notes from the South African postcolony', *American Ethnologist*, vol. 26, no. 2: 279–303.

Comhaire-Sylvain, S. (1950) *Food and Leisure among the African Youth of Leopoldville (Belgian Congo)*, mimeograph, University of Cape Town.

Comhaire-Syvain, S. (1968) *Femmes de Kinshasa: Hier et aujourd'hui*, Paris: Mouton.

Crewe, E. and E. Harrison (1998) *Whose Development? An Ethnology of Aid*, London: Zed Books.

Crossman, P. (1999) *Endogénisation et universités africaines*, Leuven: Katholieke Universiteit Leuven.

Cruise O'Brien, D. B. (1996) 'A lost generation? Youth identity and state decay in West Africa', in R. Werbner and T. Ranger (eds) *Postcolonial Identities in Africa*, London: Zed Books.

Dasgupta, P. (1993) *An Inquiry into Well-being and Destitution*, Oxford: Clarendon Press.

DDK (Département de Démographie de la Faculté des Sciences Economiques de l'Université de Kinshasa) (1998) *La Question Démographique en République Démocratique du Congo*, Kinshasa: DDK/United Nations Population Fund.

De Boeck, F. (2001a) 'Dancing the Apocalypse in Congo: Time, Death and Double in the Realm of the Apocalyptic Interlude', *Bulletin des Séances*, Royal Academy of Overseas Sciences, no. 47: 55–76.

De Boeck, F. (2001b) '*Garimpeiro* Worlds: Digging, Dying and Hunting for Diamonds in Angola', *Review of African Political Economy*, vol. 28, no. 90: 549–62.

De Boeck, F. (2000a) 'Le "deuxième monde" et les "enfants-sorciers" en République Démocratique du Congo', *Politique Africaine*, no. 80: 32–57.

De Boeck, F. (2000b) 'Borderland Breccia: The Mutant Hero and the Historical Imagination of a Central-African Diamond Frontier', in *Journal of Colonialism and Colonial History*, vol. 1, no. 2; http://muse.jhu.edu/journals/journal_of_colonialism_and_colonial_history/toc/cch1.2.html.

De Boeck, F. (1999a) 'Domesticating diamonds and dollars: identity, expenditure and sharing in Southwestern Zaire (1984–1997)', in B. Meyer and P. Geschiere (eds) *Globalization and Identity: Dialectics of Flow and Closure*, Oxford: Blackwell.

De Boeck, F. (1999b) '"Dogs breaking their leash": Globalization and shifting gender categories in the diamond traffic between Angola and DR Congo (1984–1997)', in D. De Lame and C. Zabus (eds) *Changements au féminin en Afrique noire. Anthropologie et littérature*, vol. I, Tervuren/Paris: Musée Royal de l'Afrique Central/L'Harmattan.

De Boeck, F. (1998) 'Beyond the grave: History, memory and death in post-colonial Congo/Zaire', in R. Werbner (ed.) *Memory in the Postcolony: African Anthropology and the Critique of Power*, London: Zed Books.

De Boeck, F. (1996) 'Postcolonialism, power and identity: Local and global perspectives from Zaire', in R. Werbner and T. Ranger (eds) *Postcolonial Identities in Africa*, London: Zed Books.

De Boeck, F. and A. Honwana (eds) (2000) 'Enfants, jeunes et politique', *Politique Africaine*, no. 80.

De Craemer, W. and R. C. Fox (1968) *The Emerging Physician: A Sociological*

Approach to the Development of a Congolese Medical Profession, Stanford: Hoover Institution/Stanford University Press.

de Dorlodot, P. (1994) *'Marche d'espoir'. Kinshasa 16 février 1992. Non-violence pour la démocratie au Zaïre*, Paris: L'Harmattan.

De Herdt, T. (2002) 'Economic action and social structure; the case of "cambisme" in Kinshasa', *Development and Change*, vol. 33, no. 4, September: 683–708.

De Herdt, T. (2001) 'Nourrir Kinshasa en période de guerre', in F. Reyntjens and S. Marysse (eds) *L'Afrique des grands lacs annuaire 2000–2001*, Paris: L'Harmattan.

De Herdt, T. (2000) 'Surviving the transition; institutional aspects of economic regress in Congo–Zaïre', unpublished Ph.D. thesis, University of Antwerp.

De Herdt, T. (1997) 'Dansen met Ntalumanga', *Streven*, vol. 64, no. 1: 64–7.

De Herdt, T. and S. Marysse (1999) 'The reinvention of the market from below: The end of the women's money changing monopoly in Kinshasa', *Review of African Political Economy*, vol. 26, no. 80: 239–53.

De Herdt, T. and S. Marysse (1996) *Comment survivent les Kinois? Quand l'état dépérit*, Antwerp: Centre for Development Studies.

de Maximy, R. (1984) *Kinshasa, Ville en suspens: Dynamique de la croissance et problèmes d'urbanisme, approche socio-politique*, Paris: ORSTOM.

Dembour, M.-B. (1992) 'La chicotte comme symbole du colonialisme belge?', *Canadian Journal of Administrative Sciences*, vol. 26, no. 2: 205–25.

de St.-Moulin, L. (1996) 'Kinshasa, trente ans après, une enquête sur la perception sociale de la justice', *Zaïre–Afrique*, no. 305: 197–220.

de Villers, G. (2002) 'Introduction', in G. de Villers, B. Jewsiewicki and Laurent Monnier (eds) *Manières de Vivre: Economie de la 'débrouille' dans les villes du Congo/Zaïre*, Tervuren/Paris: Institut Africain–CEDAF/L'Harmattan.

de Villers, G. (1992) *Zaïre 1990–1991. Faits et dits de la société d'après le regard de la presse*, Brussels: CEDAF.

de Villers, G. and J. Omasombo (2002) 'An Intransitive Transition', *Review of African Political Economy*, vol. 29, nos 93–94: 399–410.

de Villers, G. and J. Omasombo (1997) *Zaïre, La transition manquée, 1990–1997*, Brussels/Paris: Institut Africain–CEDAF/L'Harmattan.

de Villers, G., with J. Omasombo and E. Kennes (2001) *Chronique politique d'un pays en guerre et des trente derniers mois de Laurent Désiré Kabila (août 1998–janvier 2001)*, Tervuren/Paris: Institut Africain–CEDAF/L'Harmattan.

Desmyter, J., I. Surmont, P. Goubau and J. Vandepitte (1986) 'Origin of AIDS', *British Medical Journal*, vol. 293, no. 6557: 1308.

Devisch, R. (1996) '"Pillaging Jesus": Healing churches and the villagisation of Kinshasa', *Africa*, vol. 64, no. 4: 555–86.

Devisch, R. (1995a) 'Frenzy, violence and ethical renewal in Kinshasa', *Public Culture*, vol. 7, no. 3: 593–629.

Devisch, R. (1995b) 'La "villagisation" de Kinshasa', *Revue Belge de Géographie*, vol. 58, no. 1–2: 115–21.

Devisch, R. (1993) *Weaving the Threads of Life: The Khita Gyn-Eco-Logical Healing Cult among the Yaka*, Chicago: University of Chicago Press.

Douglas, M. (1999) 'Sorcery accusations unleashed: The Lele revisited, 1987', *Africa* vol. 66, no. 2: 177–93.

Drèze, Jean and Victor Srinivasan (1997) 'Widowhood and poverty in rural India: Some inferences from household survey data', *Journal of Development Economics* 54, pp. 217–34.

D'Souza, S., Mboko Mbenza and Muhindo Konya (1995) 'Evaluation du niveau de pauvreté à Kinshasa: Cas de la zone de Matete', *Zaïre-Afrique* 298: 219–36.

Dunn, K. (2001) 'Madlib#32: The (blank) African state: Rethinking the sovereign state in international relations theory', in K. Dunn and T. Shaw (eds) *Africa's Challenge to International Relations Theory*, New York: Palgrave.

Durkheim, E. (1991) *De la division du travail social*, Paris: Presses Universitaires de France.

Elengesa, P. (1997) 'Loisirs et changements sociaux à Kinshasa (1881–1991)', unpublished doctoral dissertation, University of Lubumbashi.

Ellis, S. (1993) 'Rumour and power in Togo', *Africa* vol. 63, no. 4: 462–76.

Ellis, S. (1989) 'Tuning in to pavement radio', *African Affairs*, no. 88: 321–30.

Elster, J. (1992) *Local Justice: How Institutions Allocate Scarce Goods and Necessary Burdens*, New York: Cambridge University Press.

Englund, H. (1996) 'Witchcraft, modernity and the person: The morality of accumulation in central Malawi', *Critique of Anthropology*, vol. 16, no. 3: 257–79.

Epstein, A. L. (1969) 'Gossip, norms and social network', in J.C. Mitchell (ed.) *Social Networks in Urban Situations*, University of Zambia: Manchester University Press.

European Union Delegation/Kinshasa (2000) *Coopération entre l'Union Européenne et la République Démocratique du Congo: Rapport Annuel, 1999*, Kinshasa.

Ewens, G. (1994) *Congo Colossus: the Life and Legacy of Franco & OK Jazz*, North Walsham: Buku Press.

FAO (UN Food and Agriculture Organization) (2000) 'Informations sur la sécurité alimentaire', no. 20, Kinshasa.

FAO (UN Food and Agriculture Organization) (2001) 'Informations sur la sécurité alimentaire', no. 21, Kinshasa.

Fisiy, C. (1998) 'Containing occult practices: Witchcraft trials in Cameroon', *African Studies Review*, vol. 41, no. 3: 143–163.

Fisiy, C. and P. Geschiere (1990) 'Judges and witches, or how is the state to deal with witchcraft? Examples from southeastern Cameroon', *Cahiers D'études Africaines* 118: 135–56.

Gable, E. (1997) 'A secret shared: Fieldwork and the sinister in a West African village', *Cultural Anthropology*, vol. 12, no. 2: 213–33.

Gambetta, D. (1993) *The Sicilian Mafia, the Business of Protection*, Cambridge, MA: Harvard University Press.

Geschiere, P. (1997) *The Modernity of Witchcraft: Politics and the Occult in Postcolonial Africa*, Charlottesville and London: University Press of Virginia.

Geschiere, P. (1980) 'Child-witches against the authority of their elders: Anthropology and history in the analysis of witchcraft beliefs of the Maka (southeast Cameroon)', in R. Schefold, J.W. Schoorl and J. Tennekes (eds) *Man, Meaning and Society: Essays in Honour of H.G. Schulte Nordholt. Verhandelingen van het koninklijk Instituut voor Taal- Land- en Volkenkunde* 89: 268–99.

Gillon, L. (1998) *Servir en actes et en vérité*, Gembloux: Duculot.

Gondola, C.D. (1997a) *Villes miroirs. Migrations et identités urbaines à Brazzaville et Kinshasa, 1930–1970*, Paris: L'Harmattan.

Gondola, C.D. (1997b) 'Jeux d'argent, jeux de vilains: rien ne va plus au Zaïre', *Politique Africaine* 65: 96–111.

Gondola, C.D. (1997c) 'Popular music, urban society, and changing gender relations in Kinshasa, Zaire (1950–1990)', in M. Grosz-Ngaté and O. H. Kokole (eds) *Gendered Encounters: Challenging Cultural Boundaries and Social Hierarchies in Africa*, New York: Routledge.

Goossens, F., B. Minten and E. Tollens (1994) *Nourrir Kinshasa. L'approvisionnement local d'une métropole africaine*, Leuven/Paris: KUL/L'Harmattan.

Granovetter, M. (1993) 'The nature of economic relationships', in R. Swedberg, (ed.) *Explorations in Economic Sociology*, New York: Russell Sage Foundation.

Grodos, D. and X. de Béthune (1988) 'Selective health programs: A trap for third world health policies', *Soc. Sc. Med.* vol. 26, no. 9: 879–89.

Grootaers, J.L. (1998a), '"Reposer en désordre": enterrements et cimetières à Kinshasa à la lumière de la presse zaïroise (1993–1996)', in J.L. Grootaers (ed.) *Mort et maladie au Zaïre*, Brussels/Paris: CEDAF/L'Harmattan.

Grootaers, J.L. (ed.) (1998b) *Mort et maladie au Zaïre*, Brussels/Paris: CEDAF/ L'Harmattan.

Hackett, R. (1998) 'Charismatic/Pentecostal appropriation of media technologies in Nigeria and Ghana', *Journal of Religion in Africa*, vol. 28, no. 3: 258–77.

Hannerz, Ulf (1980), *Exploring the City: Inquiries Toward an Urban Anthropology*, New York: Columbia University Press.

Herbst, J. (2000) *States and Power in Africa: Comparative Lessons in Authority and Control*, Princeton: Princeton University Press.

Hirschfeld, L. A. (1999) '*L'enfant terrible*: Anthropology and its aversion to children', *Etnofoor*, vol. 12, no. 1: 5–26.

Houyoux, J. (1973) *Budgets ménagers, nutrition et mode de vie à Kinshasa*, Kinshasa and Louvain: Presse Universitaire du Zaïre.

Houyoux, J. and Kinavwuidi Niwembo (1975) *Kinshasa 1975*, Kinshasa/Brussels: BEAU/ICHEC.

Houyoux, J., Kinavwuidi Niwembo and Okito Onya (1986) *Budgets des ménages: Kinshasa 1986*, Kinshasa/Brussels: BEAU/ICHEC.

Hunt, N. R., 1999. *A Colonial Lexicon of Birth, Medicalization, and Mobility in the Congo*, Durham, NC: Duke University Press.

Ilunga Kabongo (1984) 'Déroutante Afrique ou la syncope d'un discours', *Revue Canadienne des Études Africaines*, vol. 18, no. 1: 12–22.

IRC (International Rescue Committee) (2001) *Mortality in Eastern Democratic Republic of Congo*, Brussels: International Rescue Committee.

Jackson, S. (2001) '"Nos richesses sont en train d'être pillees!" Economies de guerre et rumeurs de crime dans les Kivus, Republique Democratique du Congo', *Politique Africaine* 84: 117–135.

Janssens, P.G., M. Kivits and J. Vuylsteke (1992) *Médecine et hygiène en Afrique centrale de 1885 à nos jours*, Brussels: Fondation Roi Baudouin.

Kabuya Kalala, F. and Matata Ponyo Mapon (1999) *L'espace monétaire kasaïen. Crise de légitimité et de souveraineté monétaire en période d'hyperinflation au Congo (1993–1997)*, Brussels/Paris: Institut Africain–CEDAF/L'Harmattan.

Kalulambi Pongo, M. (1999) 'Mémoire de la violence: du Congo des rébellions au Zaïre des pillages', *Revue canadienne des études africaines*, vol. 33, nos 2 and 3: 549–70.

Kamenga, M.R., W. Ryder, M. Jingu et al. (1991) 'Evidence of a marked sexual behavior change associated with low HIV-1 seroconversion in 148 married couples with discordant HIV-1 status: experience at an HIV counseling center in Zaire', *AIDS*, vol. 5: 61–7.

Kanyinda, M. (1996) 'La musique au service du mal?' *Salongo*.

Karp, I. (1980) 'Beer drinking and social experience in an African society: An essay in formal sociology', in I. Karp and C. Bird (eds) *Explorations in African Systems of Thought*, Bloomington: Indiana University Press.

Kisukula Abeli Meitho (colonel) (2001) *La désintégration de l'armée congolaise de Mobutu à Kabila*, Paris: L'Harmattan.

Kobia, R. (2002) 'European Union Commission Policy in the DRC', *Review of African Political Economy*, vol. 29, nos 93–94: 431–43.

Kouvouama, A. (1994) 'La magie dans la chanson Congolaise', in J.-M. Devésa (ed.) *Magie et écriture au Congo*, Paris: L'Harmattan.

Kupay, F. (2001) 'Approvisionnement de Kinshasa par le fleuve: Étude des manifestes de navigation entre 1996 et 2001', unpublished report, Kinshasa: GRET.

Kyunga M. (1993) 'Marketing social du préservatif, médias et utilisation du préservatif au Zaire', unpublished document, Kinshasa: World Health Organization.

Lallemand, S. (1993) *La circulation des enfants en société traditionnelle. Prêt, don, échange*, Paris: L'Harmattan.

Lambek, M. (2000) 'Nuriaty, the saint and the sultan: Virtuous subject and subjective virtuoso of the post-modern colony', *Anthropology Today*, vol. 16, no. 2: 7–12.

Lapika Dimomfu, (1989) 'Informal therapy choice: Utilization and satisfaction in Kinshasa', unpublished report, Kinshasa.

Latouche, S. (1998) *L'autre Afrique: entre don et marché*, Paris: Bibliothèque Albin Michel Economie.

L'Avenir (Kinshasa) (2001) 'Koffi Olomide fouetté par les patrouilleurs', 10 March.

Lemarchand, R. (2001) 'The Democratic Republic of Congo: From collapse to potential reconstruction', occasional paper, Centre of African Studies, University of Copenhagen.

Lemarchand, R. (2002) 'The tunnel at the end of the light', *Review of African Political Economy*, vol. 29, nos 93–94: 389–98.

Lumenganeso Kiobe (1995) *Kinshasa: genèse et sites historiques*, Arnaza-Bief: Kinshasa.

Lututala, M. and B. Mukeni (1996) 'Dynamique des structures familiales et acces des femmes à l'éducation au Zaïre; cas de la ville de Kinshasa', unpublished document, Kinshasa.

Luzolele, L., T. De Herdt and S. Marysse (1999) 'La pauvreté urbaine en Afrique subsaharienne. Le cas de Kinshasa', unpublished report, Universitaire Faculteiten St.-Ignatius (UFSIA), Antwerp.

Luzolele, Laurent and Tom De Herdt (1999a) *La pauvreté urbaine en Afrique Subsaharienne: Le cas de Kinshasa*, Kinshasa: CEPAS.

Luzolele, L. and T. De Herdt (1999b) *La pauvreté urbaine en Afrique Subsaharienne: Le cas de Kinshasa; annexes du Rapport Final,* Antwerp: Centrum Derde Wereld.

M'bokolo, E. (2002) Preface in B. Hamuli Kabarhuza, *Donner sa chance au peuple congolais: Expériences de développement participatif (1985–2001),* Brussels/Paris: SOS FAIM/Karthala.

MacGaffey, J. (1991a) 'Historical, cultural and structural dimensions of Zaire's unrecorded trade', in J. MacGaffey (ed.) *The Real Economy of Zaire: The Contribution of Smuggling and Other Unofficial Activities to National Wealth,* Philadelphia, PA: University of Pennsylvania Press.

MacGaffey, J. (ed.) (1991b) *The Real Economy of Zaire: The Contribution of Smuggling and Other Unofficial Activities to National Wealth,* London: James Currey.

MacGaffey, J. (1986) 'Fending-for-yourself: The organization of the second economy in Zaire', in *The Crisis in Zaire: Myths and Realities,* Nzongola-Ntalaja (ed.) Trenton, NJ: Africa World Press.

MacGaffey, J. and R. Bazenguissa-Ganga (2000) *Congo–Paris: Transnational Traders on the Margins of the Law,* Oxford/Bloomington: James Currey/Indiana University Press.

MacGaffey, J. and R. Bazenguissa-Ganga (1999) 'Personal networks and transfrontier trade: Zairian and Congolese migrants', in D. Bach (ed.) *Regionalisation in Africa: Integration and Disintegration,* Oxford/Bloomington: James Currey/Indiana University Press.

MacGaffey, W. (1983a) *Modern Kongo Prophets,* Bloomington: Indiana University Press.

MacGaffey, W. (1983b) 'Lineage structure, marriage and the family amongst the central Bantu', *Journal of African History,* vol. 24, no. 2: 173–87.

Magwaza, P. (June 2001) 'Koffi beaten up', *Sunday Mail* (Harare).

Manwana Mungongo (1972) *Le général Mobutu Sese Seko parle du nationalisme zaïrois authentique,* Kinshasa: Editions Okapi.

Marysse, S. and T. De Herdt (1996) *Comment survivent les kinois quant l'état dépérit?* Antwerp: Centre for Development Studies.

Marrès, J. and P. Devos (1959) *L'équinoxe de janvier. Les émeutes de Léopoldville,* Brussels: Editions Euraforient.

Mata Bafwidinsoni (1992) 'La marche des chrétiens de Kinshasa, dimanche 16 février 1992, vue à travers la presse locale et les récits des témoins', unpublished report, Kinshasa, Centre d'Études et de Documentation sur la Vie Nationale–Bibliothèque Nationale du Zaïre.

Mayimunene, K.H. (1999) 'Les caractéristiques physico-chimiques et bactériologiques de l'eau de la REGIDESO consommée à Kindele, quartier Kimbondo', unpublished thesis, Institut Supérieur des Techniques Médicales, Kinshasa.

Mbembe, A. (1997) 'The "thing" and its doubles in Cameroonian cartoons', in K. Barber (ed.) *Readings in African Popular Culture,* Bloomington: Indiana University Press.

Médecins sans Frontières and R. Job (2000) *Congo 2000: The Poor Health of the Health System,* Brussels: Médecins sans Frontières.

Meyer, B. (2000) 'Ghanaian popular cinema and the magic in and of film', in B. Meyer and P. Pels (eds) *Magic and Modernity: Interfaces of Revelation and Concealment,* Stanford: Stanford University Press.

Meyer, B. (1999) *Translating the Devil: Religion and Modernity among the Ewe in Ghana*, Edinburgh: Edinburgh University Press.

Meyer, B. (1998) 'The power of money: Politics, occult forces and Pentecostalism in Ghana', *African Studies Review*, vol. 41, no. 3: 15–37.

Miakala, N. (2000) 'Rapport annuel d'activités sanitaires de la Province de Kinshasa 1999', unpublished report, Inspection Médicale Urbaine, Kinshasa.

Mianda, G. (1997) *Femmes africaines et pouvoir: les maraîchères de Kinshasa*, Paris: L'Harmattan.

Migdal, J. (1988) *Strong Societies and Weak States: State–Society Relations and State Capabilities in the Third World*, Princeton: Princeton University Press.

Ministère de la Santé Publique, RDC (1999) 'État des lieux du secteur de la santé: profil sanitaire du niveau central, des provinces des zones de santé et des ménages', unpublished report, Kinshasa.

Moser, C. (1996) *Le comportement des ménages face à la crise. Synthèse des réactions contre la pauvreté et la vulnérabilité dans quatre communautés urbaines pauvres*, Washington: BIRD.

Mpaka, J. (2000) 'Werrason: Je dédie mon premier trophée à tous les musiciens de Wenge Musica et le deuxième au Chef de l'État Congolais', *Visa 2000*, November.

Mukadi Kankonde and E. Tollens (eds) (2001) *Sécurité alimentaire au Congo– Kinshasa. Production, consommation et survie*, Leuven/Paris: KUL/L'Harmattan.

Mutamba Makombo Kitatshima, J.-M. (1998) *Du Congo belge au Congo indépendant 1940–1960. Emergence des 'évolués' et genèse du nationalisme*, Kinshasa: Publications de l'Institut de Formation et d'Études Politiques.

Muteba Luboya Kasongo (1999) 'Rivières à Kinshasa: Poubelles publiques et égouts à ciel ouvert : Une étude de la pollution des cours d'eau superficiels à Kinshasa', in 'Actes du 1er Colloque sur la Problèmatique des Déchets à Kinshasa (Congo)', *Med. Fac. Landbouww.*, University of Ghent, vol. 64, no. 1.

Nackers, F. and M. Malengreau (1999) 'La sécurité alimentaire dans les ménages de Kinshasa', unpublished report, Université Catholique de Louvain/École de Santé Publique, Unité d'Epidémiologie.

Ndaywel è Nziem, I. (2002) 'Le territoire médical à l'épreuve de l'informel', in G. de Villers, B. Jewsiewicki and L. Monnier (eds) *Manières de Vivre: Economies de la 'débrouille' dans les villes du Congo/Zaïre*, Tervuren/Paris: Institut Africain–CEDAF/L'Harmattan.

Ndaywel è Nziem, I. (1998a) *Histoire générale du Congo. De l'héritage ancien à la République Démocratique*. Paris/Brussels: Larcier/De Boeck.

Ndaywel è Nziem, I. (1998b) 'Du Congo des rébellions au Zaïre des pillages', *Cahiers d'Études Africaines*, vol. 38, nos 150–52: 417–39.

Ndaywel è Nziem, I. (1993) *La société zaïroise dans le miroir de son discours religieux (1990–1993)*, Brussels: Institut Africain–CEDAF.

Ndundu Nkayamene Dada (2001) 'Le professeur d'université dans l'opinion publique. Cas des étudiants finalistes de l'Université de Kinshasa, 1999–2000', unpublished *mémoire de licence*, Faculté de Psychologie et des Sciences de l'Education, Université de Kinshasa.

Nkanga, D.-C. (1997) '"My twelve children": A father's desperate cry for social justice', Working Paper Series (CAAS, University of Michigan), no. 18.

Nlandu-Tsasa, C. (1997) *La rumeur au Zaïre de Mobutu. Radio-trottoir à Kinshasa*, Paris: L'Harmattan.

Ntambwe Katshay Tshilunga (1983) 'Le *likelemba* et le *muziki*: nature et problèmes socio-juridiques en droit privé zaïrois', *Zaïre–Afrique* 177: 431–40.

Ntoto M'vubu (2001) 'Budget de consommation des ménages: structure et déterminants – cas de quelques quartiers pauvres de la ville de Kinshasa: Kisenso, Kindele et Makala', in Mukadi Kankonde and E.Tollens (eds) *Sécurité alimentaire au Congo-Kinshasa: Production, consommation et survie*, Leuven/Paris: KUL/L'Harmattan.

N'zanga Nguz (1996) 'Reddy Amisi Accusé', *Salongo* (Kinshasa), 16 November.

OCHA (2001) 'Chronicles of a humanitarian crisis, year 2000, Democratic Republic of the Congo', Office for the Coordination of Humanitarian Affairs: Kinshasa.

O'deye, M. (1985) *Les associations en villes africaines. Dakar et Brazzaville*, Paris: L'Harmattan.

Offenstadt, G., Pinta, P., Hericard, P. et al., (1983) 'Multiple opportunistic infection due to AIDS in a previously healthy black woman from Zaire', *New England Journal of Medicine*, vol. 308: 775.

Onyumbe Tshonga (1994) 'Urban music and public rumor: Popular expression against authority in Zaire', paper presented at Northwestern University, Institute for the Advanced Study and Research in the African Humanities, 27 April.

Onyumbe Tshonga (1982) 'Nkisi, nganga et ngangankisi dans la musique zaïroise moderne de 1960 à 1981', *Zaïre–Afrique* 169: 555–68.

Ossete, E.-A. (1994) 'Magie et écriture dans la chanson de Koffi Olomide', in J.-M. Devésa (ed.) *Magie et écriture au Congo*, Paris: L'Harmattan.

Oxfam/Great Britain (2001) 'Aucune perspective en vue: La tragedie humaine du conflit en République Démocratique du Congo', unpublished report, Kinshasa.

Pain, M. (1984) *Kinshasa: la ville et la cité*, Paris: ORSTOM.

Pels, P. (1998) 'The magic of Africa: Reflections on a Western commonplace' *African Studies Review*, vol. 41, no. 3: 193–209.

Persyn, P. and R. Devisch (1992) 'Health cultures in Zaire', in 'Methodology and Relevance of Health Systems Research', unpublished report, Paris.

Pétillon, L.A.M. (1967) *Témoignage et réflexions*, Brussels: La Renaissance du Livre.

Piot, P. et al. (1992) *AIDS in Africa: A Manual for Physicians*, Geneva: World Health Organization.

Pourtier, R. (1997) 'Du Zaïre au Congo: un territoire en quête d'État', *Afrique Contemporaine* 183: 7–30.

REGIDESO (1989) *REGIDESO 1939–1989: 50 ans de développement au service du pays*, Kinshasa.

REGIDESO (1997) *Bilan social*, Kinshasa.

République Démocratique du Congo (1999) 'Mémorandum d'entente sur le PEV entre le Ministère de la Santé Publique et les partenaires', Ministère de la Santé Publique, Kinshasa.

République Démocratique du Congo/UNDP (1998) 'Plan d'actions triennal (1998–2000) Ville de Kinshasa', Kinshasa.

République du Zaïre (1996) 'Asises des états généraux: Rapport des états généraux de l'education', unpublished report, Kinshasa.

Rubbers, B. (2003) Devenir médecin en République Démocratique du Congo: La trajectoire socioprofessionnelle des diplômés en médecine de l'Université de Lubumbashi, Tervuren/Paris: Institut Africain–CEDAF/L'Harmattan.

Rubbers, B. (2002) 'L'Insertion professionnelle des diplômés de l'université de Lubumbashi', unpublished report, Commission Universitaire de Coopération au Développement, Brussels.

Rutherford, B. (1999) 'To find an African witch: Anthropology, modernity and witch-finding in North-West Zimbabwe', *Critique of Anthropology*, vol. 19, no. 1: 89–109.

Sabakinu Kivilu (2001) 'A la recherche du paradis terrestre: Les bana Luunda entre le diamant et le dollar', in L. Monnier, B. Jewsiewicki and G. de Villers (eds) *Chasse au diamant au Congo/Zaïre*, Tervuren/Paris: Institut Africain–CEDAF/L'Harmattan.

Sakombi Inongo, D. (1999) *Kabila, les C.P.P. et le retour du pouvoir au peuple*, Kinshasa: Les Editions la Voie de Dieu.

Samset, I. (2002) 'Conflict of interests or interests in conflict? Diamonds and war in the DRC', *Review of African Political Economy*, vol. 29, nos 93–94: 463–80.

Samuelson, P. (1956) 'Social indifference curves', *Quarterly Journal of Economics*, vol. 70, no. 1: 1–22.

Save the Children/Oxfam/Christian Aid (2001) 'No end in sight: The human tragedy of the conflict in the Democratic Republic of Congo', unpublished report, Kinshasa.

Schatzberg, M. (2000) 'La sorcellerie comme mode de causalité politique', *Politique Africaine* 79: 33–47.

Schoepf, B. (2002) '"Mobutu's disease": A social history of AIDS in Kinshasa', *Review of African Political Economy*, vol. 29, nos 93–4: 561–73.

Senda Lusamba, J. and J. Emina Be-Ofuriya (1999) 'La gestion de l'eau, des ordures et déchets ménagers et les problèmes de santé à Kinshasa', in Actes du 1er Colloque sur la Problèmatique des Déchets à Kinshasa (Congo), *Med. Fac. Landbouww.*, University of Ghent, vol. 64, no. 1.

Shapiro, D. and E. Tollens (1992) *The Agricultural Development of Zaire*, Aldershot and Brookfield: Avebury and Ashgate Publishing.

Shapiro, D. and O. Tambashe (1997) 'Education, employment, and fertility in Kinshasa and prospects for changes in reproductive behavior', *Population Research and Policy Review*, vol. 16, no. 3: 259–87.

SICAI (1976) 'République du Zaïre; enquêtes démographiques et budgétaires des villes de l'ouest du Zaïre', unpublished report, Kinshasa: SICAI.

Simon, B. (1996) 'Les données générales et sanitaires sur la région de Kinshasa', unpublished report, PATS, Delegation of the European Union, Kinshasa.

Stewart, G. (2000) *Rumba on the River: A History of the Popular Music of the Two Congos*, London: Verso.

Sumata, C. (2002) 'Migration and poverty alleviation strategy issues in Congo', *Review of African Political Economy*, vol. 29, nos 93–4: 619–28.

Sumata, C., T. Trefon and S. Cogels (2004) 'Images et usages de l'argent de la diaspora congolaise: les transferts comme vecteur d'entretien du quotidien à

Kinshasa', in T. Trefon (ed.) *Ordre et désordre à Kinshasa. Réponses populaires à la faillite de état,* Tervuren/Paris: Institut Africain–CEDAF/L'Harmattan.

Tchebwa Manda (1996) *Terre de la chanson: La musique zaïroise hier et aujourd'hui,* Brussels: Duculot.

Thines, G. and A. Lempereur (1975) *Dictionnaire général des sciences humaines,* Paris: Éditions Universitaires.

Trefon, T. (2002a) 'Changing patterns of solidarity in Kinshasa', *Cadernos de Estudos Africanos* 3: 91–107.

Trefon, T. (2002b) 'The political economy of sacrifice: Kinois and the state', *Review of African Political Economy,* vol. 29, nos 93–4: 481–98.

Trefon, T. (2000) 'Population et pauvreté à Kinshasa', *Afrique Contemporaine* 194: 82–89.

Trefon, T. (1989) *French Policy toward Zaire during the Giscard d'Estaing Presidency,* Brussels: CEDAF.

Tshibangu Tshishiku, T. (1998) *L'Université congolaise,* Kinshasa: Editions Universitaires Africaines-ACCT.

Tuhiwai Smith, L. (1999) *Decolonising Methodologies: Research and Indigenous Peoples,* London and New York: Zed Books.

UNDP/UNOPS (1998) 'Monographie de la ville de Kinshasa', Ministères de l'Agriculture et de l'Élevage, du Plan, de l'Education Nationale et de l'Environnement, Conservation de la Nature, Forêts et Pêche, Kinshasa.

UNICEF (1996) 'Enquête nationale sur la situation des enfants et des femmes au Zaïre en 1995', unpublished report, Kinshasa.

United Nations (1997) *World Urbanisation Prospects: The 1996 Revision,* New York: United Nations.

Van Balen, H. (1989) 'Les soins de santé au Zaïre', *Pile ou Face, bilan de la co-opération belgo–zaïroise/La revue nouvelle,* Brussels: 203–14.

Van Dijk, R. (2000) 'Christian fundamentalism in sub-Saharan Africa: The case of Pentecostalism, Occasional Paper, University of Copenhagen.

Van Dormael, M. (1997) 'La médecine coloniale, ou la tradition exogène de la médecine moderne dans le tiers monde', *Studies in Health Services Organisation Policy,* no. 1, Antwerp.

Van Nieuwenove, S., B.V. Kande, D.P. Mansina, J. Declercq and C.M.B. Miaka (2001) 'Sleeping sickness resurgence in the DRC: the past decade', *Journal of Tropical Medicine and International Health* 6: 335–41.

Vangu Ngimbi, I. (1997) *Jeunesse, funérailles et contestation socio-politique en Afrique,* Paris: L'Harmattan.

Vata Diambanza (1997) 'Mobutu: la fin d'un mythe', *Congo–Afrique* 318: 491–4.

Vellut, J.-L. (1987) 'Résistances et espaces de liberté dans l'histoire coloniale du Zaïre: avant la marche à l'indépendance (ca. 1876–1945)', in C. Coquery-Vidrovitch et al., *Rébellions–Révolution au Zaïre, 1963–1965,* vol. I, Paris: L'Harmattan.

Verhaegen, B. (1971) 'Contribution à l'histoire politique de Kinshasa', *Cahiers zaïrois de la recherche et du développement,* special issue, vol. 17: 11–44.

Verhaegen, B. (1970) 'Les associations Congolaises à Léopoldville et dans le Bas-Congo avant 1960', *Cahiers Economiques et Sociaux,* vol. 8, no. 3.

White, B. W. (2000) 'Modernity's trickster: "dipping" and "throwing" in Congolese popular dance music', *Research in African Literatures*. vol. 30, no. 4: 156–75.

White, B. W. (forthcoming) *Ndule: Popular Culture and the Politics of Dance Music in Mobutu's Zaire*, Durham, NC: Duke University Press.

White, L. (1993) 'Cars out of place: Vampires, technology and labor in East and Central Africa', *Representations* 43, Summer: 27–50.

White, L. (2000) *Speaking with Vampires: Rumor and History in Colonial Africa*, Berkeley: University of California Press.

Whyms, (1956), *Léopoldville: Son histoire 1881–1956*. Brussels: Office de Publicité.

Willame, J. C. (1991) *De la démocratie 'octroyée' à la démocratie enrayée (24 avril 1990–22 septembre 1991)*, Brussels: CEDAF.

Willame, J. C. (1986) *Zaïre, l'épopée d'Inga: chronique d'une prédation industrielle*, Paris: L'Harmattan.

World Health Organization (1948) *Constitution of the World Health Organization*, Geneva: WHO.

Wrong, M. (2000) *In the Footsteps of Mr Kurtz*, London: HarperCollins.

Yoka Lye Mudaba (1999), *Kinshasa, signes de vie*, Tervuren/Paris: Institut Africain–CEDAF/L'Harmattan.

Yoka Lye Mudaba (1995) *Lettres d'un Kinois à l'oncle du village*, Brussels/Paris: Institut Africain–CEDAF/L'Harmattan.

Yoka Lye Mudaba (1984) 'Radio-Trottoir: le discours camouflé', *Le Mois en Afrique*, November: 225–6.

Young, C. and T. Turner (1985) *The Rise and Decline of the Zairian State*, Wisconsin: University of Wisconsin Press.

Young, C. (1968) *Introduction à la politique congolaise*, Brussels: CRISP.

Zartman, W. (1995) *Collapsed States: The Disintegration and Restoration of Legitimate Authority*, Boulder, CO: Lynne Rienner.

Chapter Abstracts in French

Chapitre 1

En dépit des problèmes majeurs que connaît Kinshasa actuellement, on trouve des exemples étonnants de stabilité, d'organisation et de recherche de bien-être. L'introduction tend à montrer qu'il faut repenser la façon de représenter Kinshasa comme étant au 'cœur des ténèbres' par l'analyse de ces nouvelles formes dynamiques d'organisation sociale qui se recomposent sans cesse afin de compenser la faillite de l'État–nation post colonial. L'introduction décrit les relations entre les individus et l'état, justifie l'idée d'un ouvrage centré sur une ville africaine, met en lumière les fils conducteurs thématiques qui lient l'ensemble des chapitres et, enfin, évoque la question de ce que représente l'identité kinoise depuis le début des années 1990.

Chapitre 2

Ce chapitre décrit un nouveau type d'organisation sociale à Kinshasa: 'la coop'. Ce système de négociation constitue l'élément de base de l'économie politique populaire et permet à deux ou plusieurs parties de gagner 'un petit quelque chose'. Dans ce type de marché, on peut se retrouver tant bénéficiaire que victime. La 'coop' s'est créé afin de répondre au déclin du secteur public, aux attentes sociales et politiques déçues, ainsi qu'à la débâcle économique généralisée. Étant donné la précarité de la vie à Kinshasa, la 'coop' devient une nouvelle forme de réciprocité. Quatre récits illustrent les dynamiques tragi-comiques qui régissent le comment et pourquoi de ce système, son invasion dans la vie quotidienne des Kinois et ses implications sociales.

Chapitre 3

'Le robinet est en grève.' Cette expression est sur les lèvres de tous les Kinois. L'expansion de la ville a provoqué un besoin d'eau évident, que les services publics n'assurent pas. En commençant par une description des problèmes politiques et techniques liés au secteur de la distribution d'eau, ce chapitre examine le contexte social de l'approvisionnement en eau et les stratégies multiples que les ménages ont inventé afin de s'assurer cette ressource vitale. Il démontre que ces stratégies contrastent avec les dispositions de l'état dans ce secteur. Ce chapitre est avant tout une étude sur l'innovation sociale.

Chapitre 4

On peut s'imaginer que la situation relative à la sécurité alimentaire est catastrophique à Kinshasa. Depuis plus de quatre ans, les axes d'approvisionnement ont été rompus par la guerre et la rébellion et les conditions de transport sont très mauvaises. Néanmoins, la ville n'a jamais connu de famine. La situation est-elle dès lors aussi catastrophique que les rapports des experts tendent à le montrer? Quels sont les attitudes et les comportements des gens par rapport à la nourriture? Comment font-ils pour se nourrir? Le chapitre 4 répond à ces questions et conclut que d'importants changements sont survenus dans ce secteur. Les mécanismes de survie, les adaptations et innovations sociales assurent, tant bien que mal, l'alimentation de la ville, remplissant ainsi le vide laissé par le secteur privé formel et compensant les défaillances des politiques récentes qui influencent ce domaine.

Chapitre 5

Le secteur de la santé publique à Kinshasa reflète le destin tragique de la grande majorité des Congolais. Il est miraculeux que la population kinoise n'ait pas encore été décimée. Les problèmes de santé publique sont des problèmes sociaux et indiquent les années de crise politique et économique. Les maladies font partie de la vie quotidienne des Kinois. Leur quête en matière de guérison est le sujet de ce chapitre, organisé en trois parties: le contexte historique du secteur; une discussion sur l'aspect hybride du marché, qui mêle à la fois traitements privés et publics biomédicaux avec ceux des tradipraticiens, ainsi que les nouvelles églises de guérison charismatiques; une analyse des relations entre le corps médical kinois et la communauté internationale.

Chapitre 6

L'enseignement supérieur est, lui aussi, l'un des services publics caractérisé par le paradoxe ordre/désordre. Depuis le début des années 1980, les institutions sont devenues physiquement délabrées et intellectuellement minées. La capacité de l'enseignement et de la recherche va de paire avec la réduction des salaires du corps enseignant. Bien que le système soit aujourd'hui moribond, la faillite totale a été évitée. Les étudiants, les professeurs et les autorités de l'état ont relevé le défi de réinventer l'Université de Kinshasa. Les mobiles des uns et des autres font l'objet de ce chapitre.

Chapitre 7

Les associations de la société civile, les ONG et les réseaux de solidarité communautaires se sont multipliés de manière spectaculaire au début des années 1990. Depuis lors, ils font partie intégrante des stratégies de survie inventées par les Kinois afin de remplacer l'état dans beaucoup de domaines de la vie publique. Le chapitre 7 analyse comment et pourquoi ces associations et ONG se sont constituées, en soulignant leur évolution, typologie et mode de fonctionnement. Leur relation paradoxale et compliquée avec l'état d'une part et la communauté internationale d'autre part, est également abordée. Sans cette nouvelle forme d'organisation sociale, la lutte pour la survie à Kinshasa serait une gageure plus forte encore.

Chapitre 8

Quel est le sens des mots *ménage* et *famille* à Kinshasa? Combien de personnes constituent ces unités, et comment s'adaptent-elles à la crise économique et aux changements politiques et sociaux? Comment l'augmentation du nombre d'individus par ménage influence-t-elle les stratégies de survie, et inversement, comment les stratégies de survie influencent-elles la taille des ménages? Telles sont les questions essentielles de ce chapitre. Les conclusions indiquent que, en dépit de ce que l'augmentation de la taille des ménages est le résultat de la stratégie des personnes pour faire face à la crise et fait donc partie du 'miracle Kinois', elle peut aussi constituer un cauchemar pour d'autres personnes, en particulier les jeunes filles, 'Cendrillon version kinoise'.

Chapitre 9

A plusieurs reprises, les Kinois ont envahi les rues pendant la période de transition démocratique du Président Mobutu et, par la suite, pendant la présidence de L.D. Kabila. Les rues sont devenues, durant ces événements, le principal théâtre de la vie politique. Les manifestations sont toujours associées à un contexte politique ou social spécifique et influencent l'évolution politique du pays tout entier. Ce chapitre montre qu'en dépit de ces nombreuses manifestations, les Kinois restent incapables de faire aboutir cette mobilisation en changements politiques réels.

Chapitre 10

Des milliers d'enfants sont victimes d'accusations de sorcellerie à Kinshasa aujourd'hui et se trouvent, par conséquent, à la rue. Ils sont devenus les protagonistes d'une transformation sociale dramatique, caractérisée par de nouvelles juxtapositions entre le monde visible et le monde invisible, la vie et la mort et la réalité diurne et son dédoublement nocturne. Ce chapitre analyse les nouvelles formes de l'imaginaire collectif kinois à travers une étude ethnographique très pointue.

Chapitre 11

La réputation de Kinshasa comme capitale musicale de l'Afrique sub-saharienne découle du mythe qui entoure ses musiciens. Ceux-ci font sensation à Kinshasa grâce à leur appropriation de la modernité et des symboles occidentaux du pouvoir et leur manière ostentatoire de se comporter. Néanmoins, dans l'imaginaire des Kinois, le prix de cette réussite découle d'un lien avec l'occulte. De même, un réseau complexe de liens entre le monde politique et financier explique aussi ce succès. Ce chapitre offre une analyse des discours contemporains tenus à propos de la célébrité et de la fortune, en s'appuyant sur les rumeurs qui circulent à propos des musiciens et de leurs manœuvres pour se maintenir au cœur des fantasmes des Kinois.

Contributors

Theodore Trefon is an independent consultant and researcher currently based at the Brussels Centre of African Studies (VUB/ULB). His work in the Democratic Republic of Congo, where he travels often, focuses on state–society relations, urban anthropology and environmental governance. After taking degrees at New York University and the Institut d'Études Politiques in Paris, he completed a Ph.D. at Boston University in 1988 on Zairian politics. Dr Trefon has worked on European Union-funded projects for natural resource management in the Congo Basin and has served since 1995 as an adviser to USAID's Central African Program for the Environment. He has also worked as a consultant for CARE, CIFOR (Centre for International Forestry Research), UNESCO and the World Bank. He is visiting professor at the University of Kinshasa's post-graduate school for tropical forest management (ERAIFT). In addition to publishing numerous journal articles and book chapters, he co-edited 'State Failure in the Congo: Perceptions and Realities', *Review of African Political Economy* 93/94 (2002), edited *Ordre et désordre à Kinshasa: Réponses populaires à la faillite de État* (Tervuren/Paris: Institut Africain-CEDAF/L'Harmattan, 2004), and authored *French Policy toward Zaire during the Giscard d'Estaing Presidency* (Brussels: CEDAF, 1989).

Willy Bongo-Pasi Moke Sangol teaches epistemology and philosophy of anthropology in the Philosophy Department at University of Kinshasa, where he received his Ph.D. in 1996. He has been involved in the university's administration for twenty years, serving as Director for Academic Services, Advisor to the Rector for Academic Affairs and Cabinet Director of the Rector since 1990. Since 1997 he has been Director of the University of Kinshasa Press.

Filip De Boeck is Associate Professor of Anthropology at the Catholic University of Leuven–KUL, Belgium. He has carried out extensive field research in the Congo since 1987. His research focuses on changing rural and urban realities, perceptions of modernity and witchcraft. His publications appear regularly in edited books and major journals such as *American Ethnologist, Politique Africaine, Cahiers Africains, Journal of the Royal Anthropological Institute, Development and Change* and *Review of African Political Economy*. His forthcoming volume on children in Africa will be published by James Currey.

Tom De Herdt is based at the Institute for Development Policy and Management of the University of Antwerp, where he researches and teaches in the area of poverty and institutional development. He completed his Ph.D. on economic regress and institutional restructuring in Congo (2000) and continues to work on urban poverty in Kinshasa. His numerous publications include: 'Democracy and the money machine in Zaire', *Review of African Political Economy*, vol. 29, nos 93–4 (2002); 'Economic action and social structure: The case of "cambisme" in Kinshasa', *Development and Change* vol. 33, no. 4 (2002); 'Nourrir Kinshasa en période de guerre', in Filip Reyntjens and Stefaan Marysse (eds), *L'Afrique des grands lacs annuaire 2000–2001* (Paris: L'Harmattan 2001); 'The reinvention of the market from below: The end of the women's money changing monopoly in Kinshasa', Parts 1 and 2 (with S. Marysse), *Review of African Political Economy*, vols 25 and 26, nos 80 and 81 (1999); and (with S. Marysse) *L'Économie informelle au Zaïre: (sur)vie et pauvreté dans la période de transition* (Brussels: CEDAF, 1996).

Gauthier de Villers is Director of the Belgian African Institute–CEDAF. His major publications on Congo include: (with Jean Omasombo and Erik Kennes) *Guerre et politique. Les trente derniers mois de L.D. Kabila (août 1998–janvier 2001)* (Tervuren/Paris: Institut Africain–CEDAF/L'Harmattan, 2001); (with Jean-Claude Willame, Jean Omasombo and Erik Kennes) *République Démocratique du Congo. Chonique politique d'un entre-deux-guerres (Octobre 1996–juillet 1998)* (Tervuren/Paris: Institut Africain–CEDAF/L'Harmattan, 1998); (with Jean Omasombo) *Zaïre. La transition manquée (1990–1997)*

(Tervuren/Paris: Institut Africain–CEDAF/L'Harmattan, 1997) and *De Mobutu à Mobutu. Trente ans de relations Belgique–Zaïre* (Brussels: De Boeck Université, 1995).

Marco Giovannoni is an independent consultant who worked in the Congo from 1995 to 2000, after receiving a degree in Agronomy from the University of Florence. He has worked for Italian NGOs and for the United Nations Food and Agriculture Organization, specializing in agricultural extension and food emergency projects. Much of his work in Kinshasa was devoted to federating local NGOs working in the food and agricultural sectors.

Jérôme Kasongo Banga was awarded a degree in agronomy from the Yangambi College of Agronomy (Congo) in 1976. He has worked for local NGOs and for various food security projects funded by the World Bank and the FAO. He is co-author of the annual *Bulletin d'information sur la sécurité alimentaire en RDC* published by the FAO in Kinshasa.

Fabienne Ladrière is a Belgian MD with a master's degree in International Public Health. She has worked throughout the Congo for over fourteen years in the areas of gynaecology, obstetrics, paediatrics, health awareness, humanitarian aid and HIV/AIDS. In the context of her current position with FOMULAC, a Belgian development NGO, she carries out regular mission to DRC (mainly South Kivu).

Angéline Maractho Mudzo Mwacan teaches social geography at the Institut Pédagogique National (IPN) in Kinshasa. She first studied at IPN and then took an advanced degree from the University of Kinshasa's school for tropical forest management (ERAIFT). Her research focuses on livelihood strategies and environmental issues in Kinshasa.

Charles Mwema was awarded a degree in agronomy from the Yangambi College of Agronomy (Congo) in 1987. Since then, he has carried out research at the Parc National de la Garamba (1989–1991), taught at the Institut Supérieur de Formation des Agents de Développement in Kinshasa (1993–99) and worked as a consultant to Congolese development NGOs. He is currently employed by the FAO.

Anastase Nzeza Bilakila studied at the University of Kinshasa and then at the University of Quebec, where he earned a master's degree in Public Administration. He has worked in journalism and university administration, and served as an economic advisor to President Mobutu. From 1974 to 1986 he was based in Dakar, Senegal, where he was Africa Director for the association of French-speaking Universities (AUF). He now teaches economics at Cardinal Malula University in Kinshasa.

Jean Omasombo Tshonda has been studying Congolese politics for over twenty years and received a Ph.D. from the Free University of Brussels (ULB) in 1987. He is currently a researcher at the African Institute–CEDAF and Director of the Centre of Political Studies at the University of Kinshasa, where he teaches political science. His publications include: (with Gauthier de Villers, Jean-Claude Willame and Erik Kennes) *Guerre et politique. Les trente derniers mois de L.D. Kabila (août 1998–janvier 2001)* (Tervuren/Paris: Institut Africain–CEDAF/L'Harmattan, 2001); (with Benoît Verhaegen) *Patrice Lumumba. Jeunesse et apprentissage politique (1925–1956)* (Tervuren/Paris: Institut Africain–CEDAF/L'Harmattan, 1998); (with Gauthier de Villers and Erik Kennes) *République Démocratique du Congo. Chronique politique d'un entre-deux-guerres (Octobre 1996–juillet 1998)* (Tervuren/ Paris: Institut Africain–CEDAF/L'Harmattan, 1998); (with Gauthier de Villers) *Zaïre. La transition manquée (1990–1997)* (Tervuren/Paris: Institut Africain–CEDAF/L'Harmattan, 1997).

Peter Persyn is an MD who has also studied social and cultural anthropology at the Catholic University of Louvain (KUL). For two years he did field research on traditional medicine and healing churches in Kinshasa (1990–91). In 1999 he returned to Congo to direct the Childrens' Hospital of Kalembe-lembe in Kinshasa for the International Red Cross. In 2000 he was World Health Organization consultant in the polio eradication programme of Congo. He now travels regularly to the Congo in his current position with Fometro, a Belgian medical NGO.

Eric Tollens teaches agricultural economics at the Catholic University of Leuven (KUL) in Belgium. After receiving his Ph.D. from Michigan State University he started his career as a Ford Foundation researcher in Congo in 1971 and became a professor of agricultural economics at the National University of Zaire (UNAZA), first in Kinshasa and later in Yangambi (Haut Congo). He has thirty years of experience in agricultural development, mainly in Central and West Africa, and particularly the Democratic Republic of Congo. He has carried out many missions in the Congo as a consultant for USAID, the FAO and the Belgian government. His publications on the Congo include: (with Mukadi Kankonde) *Securité alimentaire au Congo-Kinshasa. Production, consommation et survie* (Paris: L'Harmattan, 2001); (with Frans Goossens and Bart Minten) *Nourrir Kinshasa* (Paris: L'Harmattan, 1994), and (with David Shapiro) *The Agricultural Development of Zaire* (Aldershot & Brookfield: Ashgate Publishing, 1992).

Télésphore Tsakala Munikengi received his doctorate in Pharmacology from the Catholic University of Louvain in Belgium in 1987. He teaches at the University of Kinshasa and is Visiting Professor at the School of Pharmacy in the Catholic University of Louvain. He is particularly interested to the problems of rational use of drugs in developing countries and in the promotion of natural drugs and biopharmacy. He was Rector of University of Kinshasa 1997–2000 and is currently Assistant Director of the Office Congolais du Contrôle.

Bob White is Assistant Professor in the Department of Anthropology at the University of Montreal, where he teaches courses on visual anthropology, tourism, world music, the public sphere, and popular culture in sub-Saharan Africa. After completing a Ph.D. at McGill University, he taught anthropology for one year at the University of California at Santa Cruz. He has conducted extensive field research on the relationship between popular music and political culture in Kinshasa during the latter years of the Mobutu regime. The result of this research is forthcoming in the form of a monograph that will be published by Duke University Press. Most recently he was the guest editor of a special issue of *Cahiers d'Études Africaines* (2002). Visit www.atalaku.net for more information about his ongoing research.

Index